UNFINISHED WORLDS

Crosscurrents

Exploring the development of European thought through engagements with the arts, humanities, social sciences and sciences

Series Editor
Christopher Watkin, Monash University

Editorial Advisory Board

Andrew Benjamin
Martin Crowley
Simon Critchley
Frederiek Depoortere
Oliver Feltham
Patrick ffrench
Christopher Fynsk
Kevin Hart
Emma Wilson

Titles available in the series:

Difficult Atheism: Post-Theological Thinking in Alain Badiou, Jean-Luc Nancy and Quentin Meillassoux
by Christopher Watkin

Politics of the Gift: Exchanges in Poststructuralism
by Gerald Moore

The Figure of This World: Agamben and the Question of Political Ontology
by Mathew Abbott

Unfinished Worlds: Hermeneutics, Aesthetics and Gadamer
by Nicholas Davey

Forthcoming Titles:

Sublime Art: Towards an Aesthetics of the Future
by Stephen Zepke

Philosophy, Animality and the Life Sciences
by Wahida Khandker

The Becoming of the Body: Contemporary Women's Writing in French
By Amaleena Damlé

Visit the Crosscurrents website at www.euppublishing.com/series/cross

UNFINISHED WORLDS

Hermeneutics, Aesthetics and Gadamer

Nicholas Davey

EDINBURGH
University Press

for Barbara

© Nicholas Davey, 2013

Edinburgh University Press Ltd
22 George Square, Edinburgh EH8 9LF

www.euppublishing.com

Typeset in 10.5/13 Sabon by
Servis Filmsetting Ltd, Stockport, Cheshire,
and printed and bound in Great Britain by
CPI Group (UK) Ltd, Croydon CR0 4YY

A CIP record for this book is available from the British Library

ISBN 978 0 7486 8622 3 (hardback)
ISBN 978 0 7486 8623 0 (webready PDF)

Contents

Acknowledgements

The number of those to whom I owe thanks for extending my knowledge of art and aesthetics is countless but deserving of special mention are Mary Davey, Basil Damer, Professor Paul Crowther, Dr Ian Heywood, Professor Kerstin Mey, Dr Ray Elliot, Professor Leslie Perry, Dr Nick McAdoo and the late Dr Gisella Schmidt. I thank the many students I have had the honour to teach whilst at Cardiff and Dundee. Cecily Davey and Dan Tate made invaluable contributions to the preparation of the final text. Judy Dean kindly supplied the photographic image for Chapter 3. I am also grateful to both the Carnegie Trust and Dundee University for supporting periods of research at the British Library and the University of Freiburg.

I am indebted to the editors of the *Journal of the British Society for Phenomenology*, *The Stanford Encyclopedia of Philosophy* and *Aesthetic Pathways* for granting permission to use extracts from previously published work. Chapter 2 of this volume draws from my essay 'Gadamer's Aesthetics', in *The Stanford Encyclopedia of Philosophy*, 2007. Chapter 5 uses extracts from my article 'Sitting Uncomfortably: A Hermeneutic Reflection on Portraiture', *Journal of the British Society for Phenomenology*, Vol. 34, No. 3, Oct. 2003, pp. 231–46. Much of Chapter 6 appeared as 'Philosophical Hermeneutics, Art and the Language of Art', *Aesthetic Pathways*, Vol. 1, No. 1, Dec. 2010, pp. 4–29.

Series Editor's Preface

Two or more currents flowing into or through each other create a turbulent crosscurrent, more powerful than its contributory flows and irreducible to them. Time and again, modern European thought creates and exploits crosscurrents in thinking, remaking itself as it flows through, across and against discourses as diverse as mathematics and film, sociology and biology, theology, literature and politics. The work of Gilles Deleuze, Jacques Derrida, Slavoj Žižek, Alain Badiou, Bernard Stiegler and Jean-Luc Nancy, among others, participates in this fundamental remaking. In each case disciplines and discursive formations are engaged, not with the aim of performing a pre-determined mode of analysis yielding a 'philosophy of x', but through encounters in which thought itself can be transformed. Furthermore, these fundamental transformations do not merely seek to account for singular events in different sites of discursive or artistic production but rather to engage human existence and society as such, and as a whole. The cross-disciplinarity of this thought is therefore neither a fashion nor a prosthesis; it is simply part of what 'thought' means in this tradition.

Crosscurrents begins from the twin convictions that this re-making is integral to the legacy and potency of European thought, and that the future of thought in this tradition must defend and develop this legacy in the teeth of an academy that separates and controls the currents that flow within and through it. With this in view, the series provides an exceptional site for bold, original and opinion-changing monographs that actively engage European thought in this fundamentally cross-disciplinary manner, riding existing crosscurrents and creating new ones. Each book in the series explores the different ways in which European thought develops through its engagement with disciplines across the arts, humanities, social sciences and sciences, recognising that the community of scholars working with this thought is itself spread across diverse faculties. The object of the series is therefore nothing less than to examine and carry forward the unique legacy of European thought as an inherently and irreducibly cross-disciplinary enterprise.

Christopher Watkin

Everything we see, could be otherwise.

Ludwig Wittgenstein, *Tractatus Logico-Philosophicus*, 5.634

Introduction:
Images of Movement

If art moves, understanding moves. Schleiermacher and Dilthey showed how within hermeneutics, understanding upholds itself by a constant, irresolvable and inconclusive movement between part and whole. The philosophy of Hans-Georg Gadamer uniquely transfers insights relating to the movement of understanding to the question of aesthetic attentiveness. In his thought, aesthetic contemplation no longer attends to changeless forms but participates in the movement of a work's constitutive elements. Aesthetic contemplation is no longer passive but an active participant (*theoros*) in the bringing forth what a work can disclose. Where Dilthey laments the inconclusiveness of understanding, Gadamer celebrates it. The ceaseless movement between part and whole which for Dilthey renders understanding incomplete perpetuates for Gadamer the play of a work's disclosive elements, ensuring endless new reconfigurations of a work's meaning. Such movement is made possible by key communicative elements within a work acting as placeholders in the interplay between the interests of hermeneutic transmission and those of hermeneutic reception. Aesthetic understanding is paradigmatic of this hermeneutic interplay. However, for aesthetic attentiveness to be grasped as a mode of understanding's movement demands a major shift in how the relations between aesthetics and hermeneutics are conceived. This study reflects on how Gadamer's thinking achieves such a transposition and explores its theoretical and practical consequences.

This study is the first full-length monograph in English to offer a sustained philosophical reflection on Gadamer's significant conjunction of hermeneutics and aesthetics, a fusion which has considerable consequences for both disciplines. Tradition has it that hermeneutics is concerned with the apprehension of meaning whilst aesthetics handles the particularities of sensual experience. Gadamer, we argue, reverses the equation: aesthetics comes to dwell on the visual apprehension of meaning whilst hermeneutics starts to reflect on the singularities of experience. Our concern is not just with charting this reversal but also with exploring its consequences. These include an anti-essentialist account of the relational nature of an artwork's constitution, a thorough-going revaluation of the theory–practice relationship within art and the humanities, the development of a remarkable hermeneutics of transformative experience and a major philosophical reworking of the nature of aesthetic attentiveness. Mapping these consequences is of wider philosophical interest. It suggests how the problem of 'excess' meaning which so exercises Derrida and Žižek can indeed expand rather than constrain understanding of the aesthetic.[1] To demonstrate these points, we have to go beyond Gadamer's own formulations in constructive but probing and critical ways. This, we claim, offers an appropriate practical complement to his hermeneutical *modus oper-andi*. Understanding what is entailed in a philosophy is not a matter of reconstructing or re-experiencing its claims: rather, it is learning how to 'think with' a way of reasoning by applying it in new and unanticipated ways. Our concern will be to think through the problems of art and aesthetics in a Gadamerian manner rather than to offer an account of Gadamer's study of art. His arguments are complex and extended. To do justice to them, we shall concentrate on them alone and leave the matter of comparison with other contemporary aestheticians to another volume. However, let us lay out the primary presuppositions of this study.

This volume explores Gadamer's assertion that artworks address us. This entails the supposition that artworks have a meaningful cognitive content. Philosophical hermeneutics contends that meaning is relational. The experience of art addressing us is a transformative one which entails the cognitive relations within a spectator's outlook being transformed by those which constitute the work. This is made possible because of the surplus of meaning attached to visual signs and symbols as well as to the images of literature and poetry. Symbols and poetic ideas can serve as placeholders in a variety of discourses such that the meaning of a central term in one's own framework of understanding can be transformed when that term meets different deployments within a foreign horizon. In a transformative encounter the spectator's horizon is not displaced but achieves a new and significant permutation of its form. The transactional capacity of symbols, poetic ideas and what Gadamer terms subject-matters (*Sachen*) to act as placeholder terms across and between contrasting frameworks of meaning offers not just an insight into how transformative experiences of art are structured but also an understanding of how the transformative capacity of interdisciplinary study depends precisely upon the movement of shared placeholder terms between different practices. Philosophical hermeneutics suggests an account of aesthetic attentiveness as a practice, a practice not concerned with the passive appreciation of art and its aesthetic qualities in any standard sense but with actively facilitating movement between significant semantic placeholders in the horizons of both the artwork and the spectator so as to promote the possibility of transformative experience.

This study primarily concerns the relationship between philosophical hermeneutics and visual art: it is not an examination of Gadamer's analysis of the 'poetic word', which has been ably treated by other scholars.[2] What is attempted here is a Gadamerian 'poetics' of the visual, an exploration of the antecedent cultural and historical conditions which allow an image to communicate effectively. Whilst this poetics must uncover analytically the elements at play with a work, it must also consider how they combine to render the work an effective communication. The notable value of this hermeneutical poetics lies in the answer it offers to a question raised in Heidegger's essay 'The Origin of the Work of Art' – how do artworks 'work' and how is this 'working' to be understood?[3] The answer proposes a response to the riddle at the heart of Gadamer's aesthetics: how do silent images speak? If the response succeeds, the claim at the heart of his *magnum opus* can be vindicated: art does indeed have a demonstrable cognitive content. Two motifs, then, guide our reflections: what does it mean to be addressed by a speechless image; and what are the formal conditions of receiving that address?

In a post-modern climate, Gadamer's hermeneutical aesthetics is instructive. Aesthetic experience confronts the spectator with something ineffable. Such experience challenges philosophy's general ambition of bringing clarity to the objects of its reflection. The complexity of intense experience quickly compromises the adequacy of words. Yet, Gadamer's position refuses despair: profound experience may elude linguistic capture but instead of insisting on silence before what transcends speech, it demands the seeking out of new words that better approximate and do justice to the complexities of experience. This places Gadamer's hermeneutical approach to aesthetics at the interstices of experience, language and reflection. Practitioner and theoretician need no longer confront each other as opponents but as dialogical partners able to draw out, exchange and mutually realise different aspects of their experience of a work. Because an aesthetic object will formally exceed all interpretation, neither practitioner nor theoretician can monopolise its understanding. Taken together, the two approaches enable a greater understanding. As well as offering a make-weight to post-modern scepticism, Gadamer's hermeneutical aesthetics suggests a dialogical rapprochement between theoretician and practitioner, the implications of which have been inexplicably overlooked in contemporary aesthetic education. This study will address this oversight.

In any consideration of aesthetics, confronting the question of subjectivity is unavoidable. Its methodological challenges have shaped the development of modern hermeneutics from Schleiermacher to Ricouer, who famously analysed Heidegger's response to the problem in his ontological turn.[4] Gadamer's hermeneutical aesthetics relies on the specific tension between his defence of the subjective immediacy of our experience of art and his demand that the cognitive claims of such experience be rendered legitimate. Though Gadamer's thought about aesthetics bravely starts with the reality of subjective experience, he is more concerned with the substantialities that underwrite it. As a mode of consciousness, aesthetic awareness is unknowingly shaped by the objective horizons of language and tradition. The latter form subjectivity's cognitive content and shape art's claim to truth. Evidential experience provides the gateway to a phenomenological reflection on the objectivities that sustain it. Though a plausible ploy to rid aesthetics of 'the scandal of subjectivity', it poses too crude a reversal: overtly emphasising the 'objectivities' of transmission underestimates the hermeneutic processes of reception. Michael Kelly implies that in his rush to proclaim the objective element of aesthetic experience, Gadamer's aversion to aestheticism leads him to underestimate the role of subjectivity in the formation of aesthetically communicated meaning.[5]

This book explores how subjectivity plays a constructive role in Gadamer's account of aesthetic experience and the relationality that informs it.[6] Five points are salient. (1) Transformative experience is dependent upon shifts in the objective horizon of a tradition which have no significance in themselves other than in relation to the subjectivities that embrace it. (2) Though Gadamer dismisses Kant's notion of aesthetic disinterestedness, he has to reinvent it in a phenomenological framework in order to defend the constructive role of subjectivity within aesthetic experience. (3) The role of subjectivity within Gadamer's aesthetics is pertinent to current debates about art's alleged displacement of established religion. Aesthetic experience emerges as a way of negotiating what is entailed in being-in-the-world. (4) We shall argue that the spiritual dimension of Gadamer's position involves an intensity of experience occasioned by an artwork intervening in, changing and thereby inducing a sense of expansive movement in understanding. (5)

Aesthetic subjectivity is of enormous importance for what it reveals of its objective ground. The ontological preconditions of aesthetic experience concern Gadamer the most. What must be assumed as being already in place for an experience of art to be possible? What are the preconditions of art's effectiveness? What comes to being within a work and what does it reveal of Being itself?

The principal value of a hermeneutical aesthetics lies in its participatory account of an experience of art. Gadamer's dialogism is acknowledged but its consequences for a relational aesthetics are not understood. Focusing on the cognitive content of an artwork, dialogism deprives the theoretician and practitioner of any privileged interpretative power. This is not just because Gadamer's ontological orientation transfers effective agency from subjective consciousness (the part) to its ground in language and tradition (the whole). Emergence, transformation and transmission demand participation. Aesthetic subjectivity is not dissolved but serves as a catalyst for the reception, mutation and development of the cultural subject-matters that both inform and transcend it. This suggests that intense aesthetic insight does not transcend its informing language but must be interpreted as a transformative variant. Dialogism implies that the content of such insight is expressible in public terms.

Dialogism implies conversation and conversation points to a 'mode of living', 'a form of acquaintance or being familiar with', as in being 'conversant with'. A convert assumes a mode of familiarity. Conversation is, in effect, already under way. Its start presupposes a tacit acquaintance with a set of cultural norms and expectancies. Conversations have a dual character, assertive and expressive. They involve assertions about their central subject-matters and give indirect expression to aspects of the cultural horizon which ground them. Conversational utterances prompt other insights, revealing tacit aspects of the hermeneutical horizons of the interlocutors. The vital point is that without participation in the conversational exchange of assertions or viewpoints, the cognitively expressive aspects of a subject-matter – what Gadamer refers to as its speculative dimension – would not emerge. Participation in cognitive exchange (whether in a conversation or dialogical reflection) focused upon the content of an artwork is a condition of the spontaneous emergence of what is implicitly or tacitly understood about it. The 'said' occasions the emergence of the 'unsaid'; the 'seen' brings forth the 'unseen'. Gadamer's dialogism is shaped by a speculative aesthetic, the central intuition of which is that words, symbols and images all point beyond themselves. All mean more than initial acquaintance suggest. Its hermeneutical logic is easily summarised: $x = x+$. This explains why Gadamer's aesthetic is dominated by figures of movement, especially the passage from first understanding a topic to understanding it better. This also reveals why Gadamer's aesthetics places such emphasis on dwelling with an image, that is, taking the time to allow it to unfold its complexities of meaning.

Dialogism clearly governs the productive aspect of Gadamer's hermeneutic operation: within conversation there is no telling when and where one thought will summon another. Gadamer's procedure is, in effect, to set our understanding at play, inserting words and images into on-going cultural conversations to induce further reflections to come to the fore. Gadamer's work should not be judged on its formal argumentation but on its rhetorical effectiveness, that is, on what it brings about and its effectiveness in altering our understanding of a subject-matter. Such work is not the work of a detached analyst. It demands participation in the conversations between horizons so that further insights can be drawn into the open. For Gadamer, remaining aesthetically neutral achieves nothing: what is key is participation, participating in the movement of experience and reflection, for only through such participation can we become reflectively aware of what is performatively at play within our experience of art. Concerning the experience of art, the task Gadamer suggests is to '*Begreifen, was uns ergreift*' – to grasp what has taken hold of us.[7] This study will debate what is entailed in this claim and consider whether its linguistic analogies are appropriate to the task of understanding the 'speechless image'.

The vitality of a tradition can be judged by the degree to which its 'continuities of conflict' assert themselves.[8] Aesthetics is certainly 'quick', riven by arguments between those who, like Ernst Gombrich, regard its alleged subjectivity as a continuing methodological scandal and those who, like Terry Eagleton, value its subjectivity and expressive spontaneity as an important moderation of reason's singular claim for a universality of method.[9] The analogical value of aesthetics for hermeneutical reflection immediately asserts itself: twentieth-century hermeneutics is almost defined by its epistemological struggle with method. Gadamer's contribution to this debate within aesthetics and hermeneutics has been considerably underestimated. He is universally recognised as a severe critic of methodological reductivism but by no means is he an iconoclast of anti-method. His thinking offers to both contemporary aesthetic and hermeneutic debate a singular capacity to bring the argument for method and the case for spontaneity into mutual dialectical reflection. On the one hand, Gadamer's commitment to a speculative theory of meaning undermines the universal claim of method to capture all aspects of an image's meaning. The majority of commentators on

Gadamer fail to note that how this does not undermine the limited use of the methodical within interpretation. To the contrary, recognising the speculative excess of meaning suggests that methodical devices can be knowingly deployed to probe undisclosed aspects of experienced meaning. Method is not the antithesis of aesthetic spontaneity but a potentially disruptive device for prompting established meanings to disclose more of what they contain. This study will accordingly challenge the view that Gadamer's hermeneutical approach to art is a conservative apologetics for received meaning. On the other hand, his rejection of method does not justify a *laissez-faire* approach to aesthetic interpretation. Whilst rejecting universal method, he nevertheless insists on the validity of art's truth claim. What makes Gadamer's writing on art compelling for hermeneuticians and aestheticians alike is that it offers a post-modern case study of how art's cognitive claims might be made on a non-foundational basis. Without this demonstration, the antithesis of his challenge to the universality of method amounts to a vapid subjectivism.

The dialectical dexterity of Gadamer's philosophy is indicated by the fact that method and spontaneity are not treated as opposites but as reflections of each other. His hermeneutical thought is characteristically speculative. Thesis and antithesis are not regarded as formal opposites but as speculative modes of one another. Hermeneutical engagement allows each position to re-describe itself in the language of its other. The being of a subject is moderated when another reveals how it can effectively reflect on its own being by using the language of the other. This is not a case of a subject assimilating its other but of a subject becoming-other-to-itself as a consequence of learning how, in Peter Duerr's terms, to walk on the wild side, to think of itself in the other's terms.[10] We shall argue that Gadamer's speculative thinking outlines a distinctive doubled hermeneutics for aestheticians, art theoreticians and practitioners alike, in which the self-understanding of each party is moderated by a subtle exchange: the process of becoming different to oneself by learning to think about oneself in the language of one's other.[11] Transformation, not translation, is the issue.[12] The aesthetician or art theorist is not rendered a practitioner but is brought to understand that theory can be as spontaneous and playful in its interventions as art practice. Gadamer's doubled hermeneutics suggests that theory's credibility relies upon what is, in a certain sense, its opposite: the ability to disclose itself in practical instances. Nor is the practitioner translated into the theoretician. Practice is not theory's opposite but displays a reasonableness of its own. Elements in Gadamer's hermeneutics suggest how this reasonableness might be articulated. This asserts the value of

Gadamer's hermeneutics for aesthetic education: it demonstrates the informing and guiding of practice by the theoretical components of its environment. The operational force of this doubled hermeneutics shapes the character of Gadamer's quest: to determine art's cognitive claims on a non-foundational basis.

Wolfgang Iser eloquently describes hermeneutic doubling as a function of recursive looping within hermeneutical reasoning.[13] He emphasises that it is not the multiplication of opposite positions *per se* that is hermeneutically effective but the cognitive and experiential movement of doubling back between them. Active doubling back is a figure of thought in Schleiermacher's and Dilthey's hermeneutics, activated to achieve a movement of understanding within classic part–whole relationships. For Schleiermacher, to understand a particular linguistic expression requires a broader understanding of the linguistic forms within which the expression is made. Similarly, access to linguistic forms is possible only through particular expressions.[14] For Dilthey, the particularities of experience presuppose the generalities of understanding, whilst understanding presupposes experience. For both thinkers it is the movement between part and whole that is crucial. This announces a leading theme of our study: the way aesthetics, in particular, exhibits understanding and its movement. Gadamer's predecessors bring attention to a related recursive figure in his own thought which we will identify as a doubled hermeneutics in an additional sense: to understand what a work is saying is also to understand how it is able to say what it says.

What a work says and how it is able to say what it does are not opposing concerns reflecting a sterile opposition between fine art practice and art criticism. Gadamer's doubled hermeneutics claims that to understand the truth claim of a work is also to understand how the enabling conditions of a work are manifest in its claim. This offers a significant ontological reworking of the part–whole relationship within hermeneutics. Whilst Gadamer offers sensitive 'readings' of the paintings of Paul Klee and the writings of Paul Celan, his thought also offers a 'poetics' of aesthetic communication.[15] This entails the claim that to understand *what* a work is saying is also to understand *how* it works as a work of art. Indeed, Gadamer's discussion of the hermeneutical context of art tables a significant response to an issue raised by Heidegger in his essay 'The Origin of the Work of Art': what work does an artwork do?

The doubling effect within Gadamer's hermeneutics involves the continuous interplay between two levels of hermeneutical operation, grasping what a work asserts or claims and understanding what the assertion indicates or signifies. This is a distinction between what a work expresses (or states) and what comes to expression in it (what it discloses). Grasping the first requires a hermeneutical analytics whilst the second demands participation in a speculative hermeneutics. (1) Understanding what a work asserts demands an analytical or grammatical approach, demonstrating how the meaning of a literary or visual statement arises from the interplay of the components within a constituent discourse. An analytics of artistic assertion endeavours to demonstrate how what a work is 'saying' is configured by different part–whole relationships within a given expressive language, whether verbal or visual. (2) A speculative hermeneutic approach to the same declarative meaning is also required because, despite their singular force, literary or painterly statements lack autonomy: they arise in broader hermeneutical fields upon which their significance depends. These fields operate as the enabling conditions of aesthetic statements, transcending the utterances they enable and enabling them to communicate more than they state. The symbol exemplifies this exchange between the analytical and speculative dimensions of meaning. Though a functioning symbol may be attributed a determinate meaning within a work, its broad meaning remains indeterminate. Nuance, allusion and profundity depend on this excess. It permits artists to subvert or undermine a particular meaning by invoking its other determinations. The *double entendre*, intended or not, exemplifies what is, within philosophical hermeneutics, a crucial interplay between analytical and speculative aspects of meaning.

Though an artist may mean something specific by a word or image, it can, by virtue of belonging to spoken or visual language, come to mean something more. Gadamer's deployment of the speculative depends upon a part–whole structure but not in any fixed sense. As any word or image arises, ontologically speaking, from language as a whole, each reflects differently the (changing) totality of meaning it is inflected with. This gives a word or image its centrifugal force, pushing us towards wider semantic frameworks. Images and words function as placeholders for such pluralities of meanings, setting into play more meanings than an artist might intend. The placeholder function of words and images also has a centripetal capacity, which allows pluralities of meaning beyond what an artist intends to flow back into a work, deconstructing its initially intended meaning. A practised artist will know how to deploy the speculative charge or 'excess' of a given image, allowing it to bring forth nuances of meaning which transcend those initially articulated. Such a work can hold various meanings in creative tension and interplay. A less accomplished practitioner, one who cannot control the hermeneutic interplay which placeholder images allow, will suffer his or her communicative intentions becoming over-whelmed by the force of contrary meanings. The consequence is a work that will appear incoherent, confused or inconsistent. In conclusion, what comes to expression in a work are those speculatively revealed dimensions of historical and cultural meaning which transcend (yet enable) any individual artistic statement.

This study argues that the key contribution philosophical herme-neutics makes to understanding how an artwork *works* concerns its articulation of the interplay between the analytical and the specula-tive dimensions of meaning. Exposing the elements of that interplay offers an intelligible account of what a work expresses and how it does so. The interplay offers a twofold revelation: how an artwork communicates effectively beyond what a writer or visual artist intends; and how dimensions of historical cultural meaning which transcend any individual artistic statement nevertheless come to expression with it.

A 'poetics' of how artworks effectively work may properly identify the analytical and speculative components of an artistic discourse but these should not be considered as opposing but rather as different reflec-tions of the doubled nature of all meaning. The analytical dimension of assertions cannot, as Pannenberg has shown, be understood other than in relation to the wider unstated dimensions of linguistic practice that inform them.[16] His argument reflects a maxim of classical hermeneu-tics: it is not possible to understand the part (the particular expression or idiom) apart from the whole field of expression of which it is a part. Though that whole (what Gadamer calls a totality of meaning) cannot be brought to statement without contradiction, its existence is made discernible in the particular statements it informs. The argument pre-supposes a major ontological assumption, the consequences of which will dominate this study: the existence of the whole is not independent from the totality of its parts. Understanding involves thinking of the enabled part and the enabling whole as the reversed doubles of each other. Were this all to Gadamer's position, it would amount to little more than a reworking of the analogical hermeneutics of William Blake and Johann Goethe: to discern the universal in each particular; and to see in each particular the universal particularised. By contrast, it is the continual doubling back and forth between the analytical and the speculative that is crucial to Gadamer's account of the meaningful within the experience of art. Such experiences subject us to the further effects of such interplay.

Confronting a written or visual statement initiates such interplay but is not its beginning. The formal grounds of an experience of art's effects

lie in the condition of existential thrown-ness, which casts each and every individual adrift on *already* formed currents of meaning. These pre-reflective historical and cultural horizons form an individual's expectancies: they influence what might or might not be perceived as an artwork. Such pre-reflective horizons are far from static. They are acquired and adapted through processes of acculturation, providing individuals with the hodological maps to navigate their experienced environment. The extent of this pre-reflective stock outstrips what we are conscious of. Its signs and symbols, whose significances we are vulnerable to, have a content greater than any moment of reflection can capture. Such 'excess' of meaning establishes the effective onto-logical base for an experience of art's address. The task of Gadamer's doubled hermeneutics is to reveal how the enabling speculative horizon becomes effective within the customary analytic of everyday meanings.

In the pursuit everyday tasks, the operation of signs and symbols is constrained to render the communication of instructions and guid-ance as uncomplicated as possible. The most important thing, as Wittgenstein would say, is knowing how to go on.[17] Though the execu-tion of ordinary tasks demands that the language of a given practice be highly circumscribed, their constituent signs and symbols do not lose their intrinsic hermeneutical excess. The meaning of an instruction depends upon a prior understanding of the figure–ground relationship for key terms in any given practice. Acquaintance with the contextual frame of that practice grounds the appropriate foreground determi-nations of a word's or image's meaning. The risk of any slippage of meaning or contamination from hermeneutic excess is marginalised. A practice's conventions establish an analytics of control over its key signs and symbols. The experience of art, however, occasions a return of the speculative dimensions of meaning to the foreground of awareness.

Gadamer's interest in visual art lies neither in the formalities of aesthetic objects nor with analysing how an artist manipulates a figure–ground relationship in order to bring an image or symbol to the centre of a visual field. He emphasises above all the *experience* of art. The experience of art is when an artwork 'speaks to us' and this, he insists, is the *event* of art, the occasion when *it* makes a claim upon us, irre-spective of our willing and doing. This is effected when an established analytic of meaning is disrupted by its speculative entailments.

The importance of Gadamer's hermeneutical aesthetics lies in the suggestion that the power of an artwork resides not in itself, as an autonomous aesthetic object, but in its dialogical capacity to 'effect' change in a spectator's field of understanding. We might appreciate a work for its painterly confidence and compositional strength but, Gadamer claims, we *value* it not for its aesthetic effects but for what it has to 'say' to us. A novel configuration of hidden or overlooked elements in a symbol's horizon of speculative meaning can impose an unaccustomed penumbra of significance, forcing us to rethink and revalue its customary expressive deployment. Art shocks and illuminates because it draws from a word's or an image's speculative excess, provocative realignments of meaning which disrupt the conventional status of a sign or symbol. Gadamer's aesthetics establishes that his doubled hermeneutics is not a logic of assertion and counter-assertion. The power of art does not reside in its ability to displace one field of meaning with another but in its capacity to effect a transformative engagement, that is, enabling us to grasp a familiar field of meaning in unfamiliar ways. This is not to be grasped as an artwork translating commonplace fields of meaning into its terms but rather as its language transfiguring the ordinary so that we come to see it as extraordinary. Gadamer's aesthetics provides a hermeneutical economy whereby the effective relations that achieve what Danto calls the transfiguration of the commonplace can be understood.[18]

Gadamer's doubled hermeneutics indicates that the key to the effective relationality that constitutes the 'event' of an artwork speaking to us lies in the placeholder status accorded to words and symbols by virtue of their operating in several speculative horizons. This means that the field of meaning in which a placeholder term appears can affect other fields of meaning in which it operates. Clever associations of meaning, amusing juxtaposition of terms, visual puns, literary *double entendres* or surreal alignments of images require that an artwork make a spectator conscious of being positioned between different fields (horizons) of meaning in such a way as to facilitate the doubled reading of one framework in the language of its other. The emergence of such a doubled reading within experience indicates, as we have argued, the return of the speculative dimensions of meaning to the foreground of a spectator's awareness. How is the hermeneutical exchange which drives such doubling to be articulated?

This exchange is not a matter of replacing one's customary way of seeing with another. Such abandonment jettisons the initial motivation, as Nietzsche once put it, to see around one's own corner.[19] Nor does it involve the ubiquity of 'cultural exchanges' which claim to show how other art traditions render common subject-matters in their distinct ways. The English Lake District as depicted by a Chinese watercolourist presents a *curio* to the European eye and as such it is, hermeneutically speaking, ineffective. Hermeneutic doubling is not a logic of substitution. To the contrary, in the experience of art, the mode of relations that constitute an alien artwork come to permeate those that form a customary way of seeing in such a way as not to displace it but rather to achieve a new and significant permutation of it, permanently altering its initial configuration.[20] This exchange or doubling should be understood as the deep inflection of one framework with the terms of another. This study suggests that hermeneutic doubling is a productive engagement, the success of which is marked by the generation of the permutation as a third element. This entails an obversion of form in which, because of its engagement with a set of foreign relations, the home framework becomes a qualitatively different world. The emergence of this third term reveals itself as the transfiguration of what the exchange has left behind (the original framework). Hermeneutic doubling opens a space between 'the once understood' and 'the now understood'. The difference is articulated by what the emergence itself achieves: a distinction between the transformed framework and the prior untransformed framework, from which the transformed framework emerges as a permutation. The emergence of a traversable, conceptually differentiated space between a transfigured and an untransfigured framework of meaning provides the spectator with a means to gauge the extent of a change in understanding.

Gadamer's aesthetics are, indeed, speculative. The discussion of art and aesthetics in Part One of *Truth and Method* points to so much more than is initially stated. Aesthetic experience is presented as a counterfoil to the cognitive claims of science and, yet, though Gadamer carefully identifies in tradition the formal preconditions of aesthetic experience, he does little to articulate how the spectator's horizon is permeated transformatively by the artwork. Thinking with Gadamer rather than against him, this study develops what his hermeneutical aesthetics suggests but does not state. The justification for this lies in the application of his own claim that to understand a thinker or artist is to think with him or her, even when entering unknown territory.[21]

Gadamer's approach to art is known primarily for its rehabilitation of tradition but it merits philosophical attention for so much more. His aesthetics reveals that philosophical hermeneutics offers not only a study of the philosophical preconditions of aesthetic experience but also an acute insight into the educative processes operating within hermeneutic transmission and reception. The transformative nature of these processes relies on what we have described as Gadamer's doubled hermeneutics, which merits serious attention by all in the theory communities of aesthetics, art and hermeneutics. This doubled hermeneutics expands into an account of the following.

1. It suggests that the cognitive value of art depends upon a conception of a work as a body of significant relations which interact with and affect other sets of significant relations in its cultural environment.

2. The role of words and images as placeholders within such frameworks promises a 'poetics' able to address how artworks 'work'.

3. Such a 'poetics' suggests a non-metaphorical account of Gadamer's key claim that art 'speaks' and an explanation of what the 'effectiveness' of art's historical reception resides in. We shall argue that the address of art is its 'effect': it is the experience of one framework being transformatively inflected by another.

4. The deployment of hermeneutical excess within speculative reasoning establishes a principle of incommensurability which explains why the movement of understanding is both never ending and self-perpetuating. Within the constraints of appropriacy, any work or interpretation can legitimately deploy a symbol but neither may claim to exhaust its meaning. There is always incommensurability between what a symbol says and what it is capable of saying (its excess). This differential offers a twofold procedural guarantee of both creative optimism (no matter the power of a given meaning, there is always more to be said) and interpretive modesty (whatever the confidence placed in an interpretation, it is formally subject to being adjusted by alternative readings deriving from the hermeneutical excess of its subject-matter). Either way, the principle of hermeneutic incommensurability upholds the movement of understanding. The more an interpretation seeks to diminish the differential between an image and its speculative horizon, the more it drives other possibilities for understanding into the open.

5. The presence of a speculative totality of meaning attached to a word or image is invoked through the particular expression or utterance. This places artistic and hermeneutic practice at the interstices between what is in play in a speculative horizon and what that horizon facilitates in the way of particular readings or expressions. The originality of Gadamer's position lies in the suggestion that the creation of new artworks is not an end in itself but a means of soliciting from the unspoken horizons that enable and inform them, other as yet unrealised possibilities for meaning. Artistic practice becomes a means of keeping the transformative movement between horizons of meaning in play.

The significant merit of Gadamer's doubled hermeneutics for philosopher and practitioner alike is that by placing the subjective experience of art within the objective horizons and mechanisms of dialogical exchange, it promises an objective, ontologically based account of what takes place within subjectivity, that is, the transmission, reception and transformation of aesthetic meaning. If the vitality of a tradition can be judged by the degree to which its 'continuities of conflict' assert themselves, Gadamer's principles of hermeneutical excess and incommensurability offer a perceptive account of how such continuities of conflict maintain themselves and productively so. It is these principles that justify what this study offers: a rethinking of aesthetic experience in hermeneutic terms.

Much has been made of the enigmatic quality of art, that it always seems to promise more than it discloses. Gadamer, following Heidegger, is acutely aware of what a work 'withholds' from a spectator and how it makes the presence of that absence felt. This gives to a work, in the words of Joanna McGregor, a 'quality of mystery and melancholy, of shadows, pauses and memory'.[22] In formal terms, her statement reiterates the axiom of hermeneutic incommensurability: $x = x+$. That is, how a work is interpreted or self-interprets itself can never be rendered commensurate with what the work might yet mean (the withheld). The statement presages an important ontological claim. On the assumption that the artwork has no predefined essence or meaning but is a specific set of part–whole relationships, what that work can be understood as yet meaning depends upon the spectator achieving or witnessing new and significant movement in the relations that embody the work. We argue that it is the principle of incommensurability that draws a spectator further into a work in search of its 'yet to be disclosed' elements, even if they are hidden in the visible, and that it is this involvement which sets in motion, once again, the part–whole relations upon which the possibility of transformed understanding rests. Developing such reasoning requires thinking well beyond Gadamer's arguments but to them go the credit for opening the way to a hermeneutical aesthetics capable of altering our understanding of the workings not just of art but of the humanities generally. This book seeks to extend the conversation about art that Gadamer started.

Chapter 1 considers the intellectual context informing Gadamer's hermeneutical reformation of aesthetics. It introduces the concepts appearance, presentation and language. We claim that rather than avoiding aesthetic subjectivism, Gadamer needs a reconstructed account of subjectivity as an interactive agency in the event of aesthetic experience, in order to secure the effectiveness of his doubled hermeneutics. Chapter 2 examines Gadamer's broad reflections on the nature of the experience of art and explores the speculative dimension of his thinking

in particular. The broad debate of these early chapters sets the context
for what follows: a detailed examination of the philosophical specifics
of Gadamer's stated and implied arguments with regard to the experience of art.

Chapter 3 addresses the defining paradox of Gadamer's aesthetics:
how to reconcile the alleged disinterestedness of aesthetics with the cognitive interests of a phenomenological analysis of experience. We shall
argue that Gadamer's implied approach to aesthetic attentiveness offers
a persuasive reconciliation of the interested and the disinterested. The
reconciliation is one of Gadamer's greatest unremarked contributions
to contemporary aesthetics. Aesthetic attentiveness is no unthinking
receptiveness but a complex reflective practice capable of transforming
understanding.

Chapter 4 concerns itself with the notions of *theoros*, aesthetic
spectatorship and participation. Gadamer's reconstruction of aesthetic
experience as a participatory act adds a new valence to the part–whole
relationship within hermeneutics. Hermeneutical part–whole structures
cannot be understood from the 'outside', as it were, but only by being
participated in. This implies that an understanding of a given element
within an artwork requires a sense of its whole. A grasp of the latter is
conditional upon where in a field of relationships an observing subject
stands. To understand more of both part and whole requires a shift
of spectorial position within its nexus. This insight contributes to one
of the greatest achievements of philosophical hermeneutics within
aesthetic education: the deconstruction of the theory/practice divide.
The consequences of this realignment of theory and practice we shall
discuss in detail. Once again, the argument depends upon abandoning
the notion of a detached aesthetic observer. To understand the dynamics of aesthetic experience, phenomenalist indifference must be replaced
with phenomenological involvement.

Chapter 5 develops the consequences of Gadamer's critique of aesthetic subjectivity. If, phenomenologically speaking, an involvement
with art's subject-matters demonstrates that the experience of meaning
has primacy over the experience of aesthetic properties, the communication of meaning emanates from the conveyance of significance within
bodies of semantic relations: meaning's mode of being, whether visual
or literary, is *presentational*. With characteristic restraint, this simple
move in Gadamer's aesthetics prompts a major ontological shift in
thinking about the ancient but nonetheless ever contentious question
of art's relation to reality. Establishing 'appearance' as the ontological
mode of a subject-matter grounds Gadamer's argument that temporal
appearances add to rather than detract from the reality of their subject

concerns. This argument prompts a revaluation of the ontological status of both 'likeness' and image as potentially transforming the part–whole relationships from which they spring. Likenesses become visualisations of future possibilities held within a part–whole relationship, whilst images in art assume a cognitive significance by allowing their objects 'to become more what they are' (*Werden zum Sein*). Such arguments rework the classical distinctions between *mimesis* and *imitation*. They culminate in a novel reappraisal of the part–whole relationship in hermeneutics which suggests that what art discloses is not the actual *per se* but analogous patterns of reasoning which intimate different readings of how the actual might be understood.

Chapter 6 attends to the signature claim of Gadamer's aesthetics: art addresses us. What does Gadamer mean by this argument? An answer requires expanding the conventional meaning of language as tied to just the spoken and written. Gadamer's conception of linguisticality extends provocatively the notion of language so as to include any set of communicative relations, whether visual or musical. Our argument develops a hermeneutic conception of the artwork as a body or 'measure' of relations. This broader conception of linguisticality allows art to be considered as language: like all sets of communicative relations, those that constitute art have a speculative capacity to refer beyond themselves. This capacity is central to what Gadamer means by art 'addressing' us. The speculative dimensions central to the experience of art's address clarify how the 'truth' of art's cognitive content can be grasped. The relationship between art and language allows Gadamer's aesthetics to revitalise a hermeneutical conception of truth, based upon plausibility rather than formal demonstration.

Chapter 7 offers a summary of the principal arguments of this study. It suggests that Gadamer's deconstruction of traditional aesthetics culminates in a threefold redemptive revaluation of the discipline. First, the endeavour to redeem aesthetics by absorbing it within hermeneutics depends upon prioritising the question of meaning within the experience of art. This shifts aesthetic experience into a participatory mode and in consequence revitalises the importance of the part–whole relationship in aesthetic reasoning. Second, aesthetic attentiveness returns us not to an original way of seeing but to a way of seeing which facilitates origination within and amongst the aesthetic ideas and subject-matters which shape any experience of art. Third, we suggest that the aesthetic image has a twofold redemptive function in relation to the complexities of human experience. Like the doubled hermeneutics operating within Gadamer's thinking, the image has both summative and projective aspects. The poignant image brings to summative resolution strands of meaning already at play within our environment and suggests, controversially, how our unfinished and incomplete understanding of actuality might be transformed by projective visions of the impossible, that is, meaning made whole. The fiction of completed meaning in art is redeemed not by its vision of a different actuality but because it offers a different way of envisioning *this* actuality. The principal claim of a hermeneutically orientated aesthetics is that we are vulnerable to art's address precisely because our experience of both ourselves and our world is unfinished.

NOTES

1. See Colin Davis, *Critical Excess: Overreading in Derrida, Deleuze, Levinas, Žižek and Cavell* (Stanford: Stanford University Press, 2011), and my review of that work: Nicholas Davey, 'Review of Colin Davis, *Critical Excess: Overreading in Derrida, Deleuze, Levinas, Žižek and Cavell*', *Screen*, Vol. 53, No. 2, summer 2012, pp. 180–2.
2. See in particular John Arthos, *The Inner Word in Gadamer's Hermeneutics* (Notre Dame: University of Indiana Press, 2009), pp. 1–30, pp. 335–62.
3. Martin Heidegger, 'The Origin of the Work of Art', in *Poetry, Language and Thought*, trans. A. Hofstadter (New York: Harper, 1971), p. 39.
4. See Paul Ricouer, *Hermeneutics and the Human Sciences*, trans. John Thompson (London: Cambridge University Press, 1981), pp. 54–9.
5. Michael Kelly, 'A Critique of Gadamer's Aesthetics', in Bruce Krajewski, *Gadamer's Repercussions: Reconsidering Philosophical Hermeneutics* (Berkeley: University of California Press, 2003), p. 103.
6. This theme is discussed at length in Chapter 6.
7. Hans-Georg Gadamer, 'Classical and Philosophical Hermeneutics', in *The Gadamer Reader*, ed. R. E. Palmer (Evanston: Northwestern University Press, 2007), p. 61.
8. Alasdair MacIntyre, *After Virtue* (London: Duckworth, 1993), p. 222.
9. Gombrich speaks of the subjectivity which vitiates the possibility of a plausible aesthetics – see his *The Sense of Order* (Oxford: Phaidon, 1984), p. 117 – whilst Eagleton refers to the political importance of aesthetics in that 'the work of art can gather the unruly materials of everyday life into a shapely whole without losing anything of their vitality. If it is a riposte to political absolutism, it is also an argument against anarchy' – see his *Holy Terror* (Oxford: Oxford University Press, 2005), p. 87.
10. Peter Duerr, *Dreamtime: Concerning the Boundary Between Wilderness and Civilisation* (London: Blackwell, 1985), Chapter 12.
11. Anthony Giddens coined the phrase 'double hermeneutic' to refer to the process where categories which are part of a life-world are appealed to in a description of that life-world. See his *New Rules of Sociological Method* (London: Hutchinson, 1987), p. 162. Gadamer's position implies that a

doubled hermeneutics has a speculative or mirroring element: a subject comes to think of its initial self-understanding differently when it meets that understanding doubling back in the language of an opposing party.

12. Duerr, *Dreamtime*, p. 129.
13. Wolfgang Iser, *The Range of Interpretation* (New York: Columbia University Press, 2000), Chapter 4.
14. Friedrich Schleiermacher argues: 'The understanding of the whole is not only conditioned by that of the particular, but also, vice versa, that of the particular by the whole. For if the particular is to be understood as a member of the sequence, the exponent, the tendency, the manner of the whole must be known; and if (it is to be known as) a product of language, then it must already be known what linguistic usage one is actually dealing with.' See Friedrich Schleiermacher, *Schleiermacher: Hermeneutics and Criticism and Other Writings*, ed. A. Bowie (Cambridge: Cambridge University Press, 1998), pp. 231–2. Wilhelm Dilthey contends that 'the whole must be understood in terms of its individual parts, individual parts in terms of the whole.. . . So understanding of the whole and of the individual parts are interdependent.' See Wilhelm Dilthey, *Selected Writings*, ed. H. P. Rickman (London: Cambridge University Press, 1976), p. 262.
15. See Gadamer, *Literature and Philosophy in Dialogue: Essays in German Literary Theory*, trans. R. H. Paslick (Albany: State University of New York Press, 1994).
16. See Wolfhart Pannenberg, *Theology and the Philosophy of Science* (London: Darton, Longman and Todd, 1976), pp. 178–9.
17. Ludwig Wittgenstein, *Philosophical Investigations* (London: Blackwell, 1953), Sections 151 and 179.
18. Arthur Danto, *The Transfiguration of the Commonplace* (Cambridge, MA: Harvard University Press, 1981).
19. Friedrich Nietzsche, *The Gay Science*, trans. Walter Kaufmann (New York: Vintage, 1974), Section 374.
20. Anyone who knows the British national anthem will have their perception of it quite altered after listening to Charles Ives's variations on the hymn tune 'America'.
21. This is not to be thought of as reconstructing an agent's thoughts so as to understand the motivations of his or her actions, *pace* Collingwood, but of following that agent's thoughts and developing them into forms that surpass the achievement of the original thinker. See R. J. Collingwood, *The Idea of History* (London: Oxford University Press, 1961), pp. 170–6.
22. Joanna McGregor, 'On the Pleasures of Harrison Birtwistle's "Difficult Music"', *Guardian* 22 May 2009.

1. *Hermeneutics and Aesthetics: Contextual Issues*

1.1 INTRODUCTION

Jan Faye's book *After Postmodernism: A Naturalistic Reconstruction of the Humanities* reworks the hermeneutical part–whole relationship within the following conceptual configuration: all expressions of human communication fall into an 'intention–context–dependency, persuasion' nexus.[1] Leaving aside the question of the persuasiveness of aesthetical communications, which will be discussed later, the intellectual context of Gadamer's reformation of aesthetics requires a preliminary mapping. The important claims that Gadamer makes about the cognitive content of art and the transformative character of aesthetic experience are not established by strict deductive reasoning or by a dialectic of assertion and counter-assertion. Gadamer's is a dialogical rather than an analytical method. Its main claims arise and gain their sense from the field of reflection in which they are in play. In this sense, they are context dependent. This chapter establishes the broad conceptual field that will attune us to the particulars of Gadamer's revaluation of aesthetics. The following sections introduce its key elements: experience, appearance and language. These themes will be explicitly dealt with in Chapters 4, 5 and 6. Our present concern is to identify them in the play of Gadamer's arguments and anticipate their formative role in the articulation of a hermeneutical aesthetics. The particulars of his reformation of aesthetics will be discussed in Chapter 2.

1.2 HERMENEUTICS AND THE LIMITATIONS OF AESTHETIC THEORY

What does philosophical hermeneutics have to do with aesthetics and the experience of art? The immediate answer to this is, to make aesthetics more ambitious philosophically, to turn it from a reflection on the nature of pleasurable sensations to a consideration of the horizons of meaning that manifest themselves in the experience of art.

Hermeneutics, conventionally understood, is the discipline of reading and interpreting. Philosophical hermeneutics may be understood as an enquiry into the conditions of meaning and its experience, of which the address of art is presented as the paradigmatic case. Hermeneutics for Gadamer is decidedly not a guide to deciphering an artwork, nor is it a method for divining an artist's intentions. Gadamer describes his aesthetics as hermeneutical in that the focal point of his reflection is the apprehension of 'the immediate truth-claim that proceeds from the [art] work itself'[2] and the comprehension of what makes the experience of aesthetically apprehended meaning possible.[3] What makes Gadamer's contribution to this question notable is his passage from a Kantian reflection on the epistemological preconditions of such experience to a Heideggerian consideration of its ontological preconditions. His hermeneutical aesthetics attempts to reveal what Robert Pippin has called 'the world at work' within our experiences of art and to attest to its continuing presence. In Gadamer's hands, aesthetics is more a Heideggerian testament to appearing rather than to appearance, and to the bringing forth of what is hidden.[4]

A hermeneutical aesthetics is an idiom of theory but Gadamer is acutely aware of the difference between those that impose models of interpretation on art and those that theorise in order to understand an experience of art more completely. Theorising an experience of art is indicative of an attempt to become open to and to enhance what is held within the work, to enter into the play of its elements. For Gadamer, every intense experience of art entails its own ellipsis, that is, something unsaid or not immediately apparent. This relates to the 'speculative' dimension of Gadamer's aesthetic and informs his resistance to any reduction of the object of aesthetic experience to one form of conceptual modelling. The complexities of experience demand a multi-perspective approach. This means that it can be ably approached from the perspective of the philosopher or the art theorist. Gadamer does not offer any *one* theory of art or aesthetics. 'Fundamentally', he writes, 'I am not proposing a method'.[5] He approaches art more as a philosophical critic, seeking to open and be opened by works in a variety of ways. This open-ended approach is entirely appropriate, not just because of its dialogical character but also because it is consistent with his account of experience as *Bildung*: education to and through art is a formative experience, forever open and on-going. This is consistent with the view that the primary aim of theorising an experience of art is to deepen it.

As such, hermeneutical aesthetics offers not a doctrine but a *rationale* for a hermeneutically orientated poetics that seeks to reveal and engage with what is held within our experience of art.

Hermeneutical aesthetics makes a fundamental claim: artworks address us and in addressing us assert a truth claim which demands a response, such that to refuse it would be disingenuous. When an artwork speaks, we experience a 'concretion of meaning'.[6] Its subject-matter addresses us on its terms, directly, irrespective of our willing and doing. Before the artwork, 'subjectivity and self-consciousness' fall away.[7] Standing in front of a van der Goes painting, we stand before the truth that is the stillness of a beautiful image. Looking into the drawings of David Jones we bear witness to the truth of artistic drive and commitment. Such experiences betray a relation of value: recipient response indicates that these works *mean*; they point to something of concern. This is not a matter of understanding a declarative utterance. Though I understand an instruction, it might mean nothing to me of consequence. Gadamer believes that we cannot turn away from art's address: it implicates our self-understanding and places it at risk. The strong claim of hermeneutical aesthetics is that traditional aesthetics, because of its tendency to dwell on the episodic character of the pleasurable and momentary, cannot offer an acceptable account of art's truth claims. Without such an account, the cognitive significance of art within society diminishes. These suspicions drive the claim that the whole scope and character of aesthetics need *rethinking*. How are the limits of traditional aesthetic theory to be overcome? The answer is unequivocal: 'aesthetics has to be absorbed into hermeneutics . . . hermeneutics must be so determined as that it does justice to the experience of art'.[8]

1.3 THE ABSORPTION OF AESTHETICS INTO HERMENEUTICS

Why is a new approach to aesthetics required and why a hermeneutical one? The question of subjectivity confronts traditional aesthetics with three hindrances: the marginalisation of aesthetics; the devaluation of aesthetic appearance; and the forfeiture of any rational status. First, Gadamer senses that Baumgarten's and Kant's elaboration of aesthetics as a *scientia cognitionis sensitivae* results in the blinding of aesthetics. Stuart Hampshire clearly sees the consequences of this approach:

> [it has] detached aesthetics as an autonomous domain (with the result that it is) only contingently connected with other interests. The enjoyment of art and art itself is trivialised as a detached and peculiar pleasure, which

leads to nothing else. Its part in the whole experience of man is then left unexplained.[9]

A hermeneutical aesthetics insists that it is precisely other existential interests that ground, shape and legitimate aesthetics. By excluding them from debate, traditional aesthetics debars itself from reflecting on what an experience of art makes manifest: a demonstrable link between art and an experience of the world. Responding to the scandal of subjectivity in which Kant interred aesthetics and the humanities,[10] Gadamer's *Truth and Method* attempts to free aesthetics from subjectivism, to ground aesthetic claims to truth in the inter-subjective participatory structures of language and tradition, and to legitimise art's claims to 'truth' against those who would have scientific reasoning monopolise the gateway to truth. To avoid banishment to the realms of arbitrary subjective preference and irrational belief, aesthetics requires a new grounding. A hermeneutical aesthetics offers a major revaluation of subjective response and what comes to expression within it.

Second, the grounding of aesthetic appearances in subjective response marginalises them as a reflection of spectorial preference. Once it is re-presented as an ontological mode, appearance can be grasped as a field in which art's subject-matters come to light. It is notable how Heidegger, whose essay 'The Origin of the Work of Art' achieved such a radical reformation of aesthetics, was openly reticent about using the term. He clearly associated it with the very subjectivism his phenomenology endeavoured to escape.[11] Nevertheless, his 'ontological turn' opens the way for Gadamer to think of appearance as a form of cultural emergence, that is, as a shared mode of being.

Third, Gadamer's resistance to the Enlightenment's privileging of reason fuels a key misunderstanding of recent hermeneutics and aesthetics, that they abjure reason and science as the principal arbiters of truth and embrace the irrationalism of subjective prejudice. To the contrary, the value of Gadamer's hermeneutics lies in its ability to show how aesthetic judgements can be inherently *reasonable* without conforming to method. In order to shed its reputation as a 'dismal science', aesthetics needs to reappraise its subjectivist associations not by becoming a demonstrable science but by becoming a persuasive one. Chapter 6 will attend to how a hermeneutical aesthetics can articulate the persuasiveness of aesthetic judgement. A question remains: why is hermeneutics particularly relevant to a reform of aesthetics?

Gadamer's reform of aesthetics suggests that in order for the discipline to achieve a proper effectiveness in exploring how the transmission of visual meaning operates, it must find its middle voice. At one extreme, if aesthetics remains a study of the sensual dimensions of visual meaning without any consideration of its intelligible structures, the discipline dooms itself to inconsequentiality. At the other extreme, if aesthetics becomes a purely philosophical consideration of art, it is reduced to a science of generalities which disregards the defining particularities of the experience of art. Kant's insistence that '*Gedanken ohne Inhalt sind leer, Anschauungen ohne Begriffe sind blind*' is instructive.[12] To argue for an aesthetics that achieves a complementarity between the sensual particular and the theoretically general is not to propose a perfect fit between concept and instance. Hermeneutic theory acknowledges a principle of incommensurability: concepts exceed their particulars in range and scope, and particulars possess individuating features that, as Adorno recognised, elude conceptual capture.[13] Philosophical hermeneutics offers to aesthetics a non-reductive fusion of cognition and sensibility which compels art theory and art practice to continually renegotiate their relationship, keeping the movement between them in play.

Gadamer's hermeneutics maintains a creative tension between sensibility and intellect. The phenomenological foundations of his aesthetic thinking embody a version of the Kantian synthesis of intuition and concept. The visual nature of Kant's terminology is instructive. Intuitions (*Anschauungen*) involve a looking-at or a looking-upon. Without concepts, intuitions are *blind*; that is, we cannot *see* what they relate to. The intervening faculty of the imagination supplies an intuition with the power of insight and significant reference. On the other hand, a concept without intuition is an empty abstraction. We might understand it intellectually but cannot see its relevance. For concepts to be illuminating, they must gain purchase on a set of particulars and achieve critical bite. The relevance of Gadamer's hermeneutics to aesthetics concerns this moment of purchase or application.

Aesthetics' middle voice resides in the moment of hermeneutic application. It does not remove the differentiation between intuition and concept but, on the contrary, requires it. Understanding requires that transmission within a part–whole relationship has taken place, that a sensual particular has become infused with general significance and that a certain form of meaning has achieved an exemplification. The argument is reminiscent of Goethe's claim that 'alles Faktische schon Theorie ist'.[14] '*Das Allgemeine und Besondere fallen zusammen: das Besondere ist das Allgemeine, unterverschiedenen Bedingungen erscheinend.*'[15] The equation is unstable.

Though an aesthetic particular cannot be captured by a concept in all its detail, it must intend one in order to be seen as something.

Equally, concepts which lack any perceptual reference remain formal and without obvious application. Aesthetics, then, can be culturally effective only if it regains a middle voice, upholding the constant transmission between thought and sense. Art's ability to excite these transmissions opens the way to Gadamer's response to the question of how artworks work. If aesthetic and hermeneutical judgements do not reduce their objects to concepts, how do they prevent *Anschauungen* from becoming blind? Gadamer's response is intriguing.

His phenomenological inheritance is sceptical of any rigid distinction between thought and perception. Gadamer's defence of the Aristotelean claim that 'all perception tends towards a universal' does not commit him to the view that all perception leads to a universal.[16] He is inclined to Wittgenstein's stance that it is difficult to separate thought from seeing and concept-use from sensing. Mary Warnock observes, 'not separating these things entails that we must think of perception as containing a thought-element, and, perhaps, that we must think of thinking as containing a perception-element'.[17] Note how the non-reductive interplay between sense and thought accords with Kant's description of an 'aesthetic idea'.[18] As an *Anschauung*, an aesthetic idea involves a sensual element but an intelligible component also that, in Kant's words, *strains* towards a rational idea (concept) but never becomes *pure idea*.[19] Continuing in the same vein, Gadamer remarks, 'aesthetic vision is certainly characterised by *not* hurrying to relate what one sees to a universal, the known significance, the intended purpose, etc. but by dwelling on it as something aesthetic'.[20]

Philosophical hermeneutics insists that art's cognitive import cannot be grasped if aesthetics retains a Kantian account of aesthetic consciousness. Two opposed accounts of subjective consciousness are at issue. For Kant, subjective consciousness is naturally endowed with *a priori* categories of aesthetic judgement. Because these categories govern what is represented within consciousness, consciousness cannot *know* whether what it experiences is indeed what another consciousness experiences. Questions of aesthetic taste and preference are *internalised* if not isolated from external mediation. Aesthetic judgement has a 'determining ground [that] cannot be other than subjective'.[21] Aesthetic pleasure 'denotes nothing in the object, but is a feeling which the subject has of itself and of the manner in which it is affected by the representation'.[22] Aesthetics in the Kantian mode is enclosed within the subjective and loses its cognitive legitimacy. For Gadamer, however, subjective consciousness has a communal ground.

> The anticipation of meaning that governs our understanding of a text is not an act of subjectivity, but proceeds from the commonality that binds us to the tradition.[23]

'The aesthetic attitude is [then] more than it knows of itself':[24] it is not circumscribed by categories internal to subjective consciousness alone but is shaped by what transcends it, that is, its communal grounding in language and tradition. Hermeneutics suggests how aesthetics can redeem its cognitive status. By placing it between thought and perception, aesthetics can partake in the same centripetal and centrifugal movements between part and whole that characterise hermeneutic meaning and thereby establish a cognitive status for itself. If it remains within the confines of subjectivity, aesthetics loses its ability to address and reflect the communal world in which it is grounded. Though what is pleasing is an important element in how an artwork gains attention, pleasure is not the primary issue. The cognitive power of a work lies in its ability to probe the substantive meanings and values inherent in the cultural and linguistic horizons which shape our being. If aesthetics is to overcome the constraints of subjectivity, it must be absorbed within hermeneutics.

1.4 AESTHETICS, HERMENEUTICS AND THE EXPERIENCE OF ART

If aesthetics remains marginalised as mode of subjective pleasure, Gadamer fears that the experience of art will lose its critical and educative potential. Questioning is an important element within the relationship between hermeneutics and art. The Socratic maxim that 'a life unquestioned is a life not worth living' is true of art, for several reasons. (1) Artworks which neither question nor provoke questioning about their subject-matter are not worthy of the name 'art', in that they fail to turn our heads and make us look again. Nothing is more damaging for an artwork than to be passed by. What is overlooked cannot address us and 'work' as art. (2) The questioning intrinsic to art aims not at definitive answers to the questions life may pose but at achieving new ways of being attentive to them. The understanding such questioning promotes has less to do with endorsing a way of seeing but more with achieving new if not transformative perspectives. (3) Questioning is profoundly educative: the addressee comes to think differently about the subject-matters addressed and to realise the limitations of how he or she had initially grasped them. (4) Art that aspires to excellence will be inherently controversial. It will not only question the adequacy of its conventions but also invite the question of whether it has surpassed them. For an artwork to be controversial, it must question previous conceptions of its subject-matter. It may demand new forms of audience response. Modernist art is paradigmatic though by no means exhaustive of such a view. It questions what has been understood as art and demands that it be understood differently.[25] Questioning ties modernist art to the philosophical hermeneutics of Hans-Georg Gadamer in particular.[26]

Understanding a work or a thinker entails participating in an appropriate pattern of thought. The art of asking a question is to do with 'breaking open the being of an object'. This does not concern grasping a fixed 'essence' but knowing how to question further, partaking in the field of cognitive movement that the question invokes. This movement permits an expansive conception of questioning and answer. Discerning the right question to ask is itself an art. It requires empathy or a 'feel' for the *epistémè* in which an artist lives and a knowledge of what concepts within a given life-world could plausibly be embraced in an interpretation of his or her work.[27]

Contemporary hermeneutics requires the skills of philological clarification as a means, not an end. It seeks, in Eberhard Scheiffele's phrase, the 'questioning of one's own from the perspective of the foreign'.[28] Philological clarification is a necessary prelude to enhancing the role of texts, canvasses and scores as hermeneutical 'raiders' able to challenge a contemporary audience's assumptions about given subject-matters. Contemporary hermeneutics seeks dialogical exposure to works of foreign provenance precisely to probe and test its own perspectives. Like much modernist art, it is suspicious of the complacency of everyday consciousness which neither questions nor seeks to extend its outlook. Contemporary hermeneutics and modernist art celebrate difficulty. Modernist art questions the norms of sensual and intellectual expectancy by confronting the latter with radically different perspectives. Contemporary hermeneutics uses the past to estrange us from our immediate horizons. Like modernist aesthetics, it acts as a provocation to the adequacy of established horizons. Neither contemporary hermeneutics nor modernist aesthetics seeks controversy and difficulty for their own sake. They share the conviction that learning, understanding and insight are possible so long as movement in and between mental perspectives can be sustained. Both have the pedagogic aspiration of making us look and think again, of rendering us strange and difficult to ourselves, of encouraging a mode of being in which to be is, controversially, always to be in question or, in Rilke's phrase, to 'live in question'.[29]

1.5 AESTHETICS, HERMENEUTICS AND THE CONCEPT OF APPEARANCE

It is a measure of Hans-Georg Gadamer's intellectual achievement that under his tutelage philosophical hermeneutics has ceased to be a handmaiden to textual commentary and become a first order reflection on the conditions appertaining to the *appearance* of meaning in the humanities. The notoriously misunderstood claim to universality made by philosophical hermeneutics has little to do with the proclamation of a common mode of understanding or with the pursuit of a sameness of understanding.[30] It has to do with the efforts of philosophical hermeneutics to uncover the general conditions (time, tradition, language and cultural horizon) which facilitate the appearance of the meaningful. The nature of aesthetic appearance is central to philosophical hermeneutics, for two reasons: first, its concern with the epiphanic nature of the meaningful locks it into mainstream aesthetic debate; and second, philosophical hermeneutics extends the meaning of aesthetic appearance, especially with regard to the question of the relationship between aesthetic appearance and the real.

For philosophical hermeneutics, appearance is an effective mode of being. Aesthetics is never characterised as a poor relation of the sciences. Gadamer articulates his philosophical purpose in a manner characteristic of much modern hermeneutic theory: objectivist methodologies of the *Naturwissenschaften* are judged inappropriate for the *Geisteswissenschaften*. Whereas the former requires its observers to assume a methodological distance from their objects of study, hermeneutics and other humanist disciplines require the direct phenomenological involvement of interpreters with their subject-matters. Appearance matters: it is in and through appearance that the subject-matters of art and their reality reveal themselves.

In Gadamer's judgement, neither truth nor meaning shows itself in a singular way. It would be philosophically ludicrous if not barbarous to insist that claims to truth which are not or cannot be objectified in the language of demonstrable propositions are without significance. To restrict such truth claims ignores the speculative workings of language and its ability to bring things to the mind. Such workings depend upon unspoken reservoirs of culturally embedded meanings. These hermeneutical aquifers do not defy speech but, like tradition and social imaginaries, they antedate and can never be rendered fully explicable in propositional terms.[31] Yet what appears to us within aesthetic experience matters. What comes into appearance through either the word or the image can challenge ordinary expectancies long taken for granted.

Such experiences are 'aesthetic' in that a realm of meaning is made to appear and 'hermeneutical' in that a life-world or social imaginary is brought to the mind's eye.

Gadamer's hermeneutical aesthetics brings much traditional philosophical discourse about appearance to a close. Appearance no longer diminishes the real but actualises it. A key aspect of hermeneutical aesthetics is that the world that art brings forth becomes all the more real for being disclosed. This demarcates hermeneutical aesthetics from the classical aesthetics of Plato and Kant. Hermeneutical aesthetics ends the Platonic denigration of art as a distorter of reality and proclaims art to be precisely that which 'raises reality to its truth'.[32] This accords art practice an ontological dimension of Promethean proportion.

Underlying the notorious critique of art offered by Plato in Book Ten of the *Republic* is the assumption that art is at two removes from the proper subject-matter of knowledge, that is, those ideas (*eidos*) which, like concepts, transcend their exemplification in nature and art. In presenting us with alluring images of what is purportedly real, the artist endeavours to convince us that a perceived representation is either real in itself or is as real as the reality it depicts. Art proffers a base coinage, passing off counterfeit appearances as the real thing and in so doing removing us further from the original. Gadamer does not speak much of the *eidos*. The key term for him is subject-matter (*Sache*), the intended content. The subject-matter of an artwork is its content, what is addressed or what the work intends (leans to or points to). Whereas, for Plato, art distances and distracts us from the *eidos*, Gadamer conceives of art as taking us closer to a *Sache* and of being able to realise other aspects of its being. The clash of underlying assumptions is dramatic: against the classical Greek view that Being is complete and appearance a falsifying distraction stands the modern conception of Being as a process of self-formation with appearance as a mode of its display. These remarks set in context the crucial differences between the two ontological readings of aesthetics. Gadamer inverts the representationalist aesthetics of Plato's *Republic*: far from corrupting reality, art allows what is held within actuality to realise itself. Hermeneutical aesthetics sets out to renegotiate the relationship between art and reality. Gadamer's distinction between representation (*Vorstellung*) and presentation (*Darstellung*) is strategic.

Representation implies that an artwork re-presents something independent of the work. The distinction between the object re-presented and the represented object is vital to Kant's argument that the existence or non-existence of the object re-presented has no bearing upon the aesthetic pleasure associated with the artistically represented object. Presentation has an altogether different set of conceptual associations. *Darstellen* (to present) suggests a placing (*Stellung*) there (*da*). It hints at what an artwork *presents* or *offers* up. It concerns that which comes to picture. Gadamer remarks, 'The ideality of the work does not consist in its imitating and reproducing an idea, but as with Hegel, in the appearing of the idea itself.'[33] Appearing is not secondary to the subject-matter (as it would be for Plato) but is a presentation of something that is essential to that subject-matter.

> *A work of art belongs so closely to what is related to it that it enriches the being of that as if through a new event of being.* To be fixed in a picture, addressed in a poem . . . are not incidental and remote from what the thing essentially is; they are presentations of the essence itself.[34]

Darstellung is associated with the idea that a work increases the being of its subject-matter. That art should occasion an increase in the being of an *eidos* would have been anathema to Plato. Considered within the aesthetics of presentation, the question is not whether a portrayal of Hamlet is true to an original but how it adds to and extends the cultural reality and historical efficacy of the dramatically original figure that is Hamlet.

Gadamer insists that it is by means of appearance that art raises untransformed reality to its truth.[35] This claim supports the 'transformation into structure' argument which develops a case for the efficacy of artistic fiction. The finitude of being dictates that no meaning can ever be complete. Art's quest for completeness appears a lie. However, the Latin root of fiction relates to the verb *fingere*, meaning to mould or to fashion. The question becomes what does art make of or 'fashion' from the undecided potentialities for meaning within actuality? This suggests that when understood as a creative bringing to fruition, art does not recover hidden or forgotten truths but perceives in an indeterminate set of meanings as yet unrealised fulfilments of truth. Of course, what is then realised is not the whole truth. No work can exhaust its subject-matter. However, insofar as the work allows a hitherto unseen aspect of a *Sache* to become true, art brings to completeness that which could not of itself occur without art's mediation. Hermeneutic aesthetics defines 'reality . . . as what is untransformed and art as the raising up [*Aufhebung*] of this reality into its truth'.[36] The notion of *Darstellung* inverts the negative relations between art, appearance and reality in the Platonic heritage.

The contrast between Plato and Gadamer becomes the more stark if the latter's positive ontology of art is compared to that of Kant. In *The Critique of Judgement*, Kant remarks:

As far as aesthetics is concerned, all one wants to know is whether the mere representation of the object is to my liking, no matter how indifferent I may be to the real existence of the object of this representation. . . .

One must not be in the least pre-possessed in favour of the real existence of the thing.[37]

Kant argues that the question of whether a portrait is successful is internal to the aesthetic properties of the painting and does not depend on its relation to the sitter. The existence or non-existence of the subject has no bearing upon the success of the work. Clearly, the reality of the sitter is not diminished by any destruction of the portrait. For Gadamer, the reverse is the case: the destruction of an artwork diminishes the actuality of its subject-matter. If philosophical hermeneutics is right, an aesthetics of presentation enables art to be proclaimed for what it is, a midwife to the actual.

1.6 AESTHETICS, HERMENEUTICS AND LANGUAGE[38]

The contentious relationship between word and image constitutes a critical tradition in its own right. Though Gadamer resists the supposition that the linguistic capture of art and aesthetic experience is possible, he claims that the speculative workings of language offer a crucial insight into how artworks work.[39] The ability of the said to bring forward something clear against a background of implicitly understood but indistinct assumptions suggests a paradigm for grasping the workings of aesthetic experience. If art 'speaks', it is because art is language-like. It is language-like in that it, too, functions speculatively. Both art and language attest to the worlds at work within them.

If language consisted solely in the exchange and analysis of propositions, we would be limited to talking only of those sets of assertions which are logically connected or deductively derivable from their primary subject. Gadamer's speculative account of language rightly insists that language also operates synchronistically. Metaphor, simile and other modes of imaginative association demonstrate how topics which are not logically or causally connected can nevertheless be bound by nuance and suggestion. Conversational turns disclose subtleties of connection which, though strikingly reasonable, are not foreseen by any logical analysis. What is said is often not as important as what the poetic and rhetorical charge of the said brings to mind as unspoken. Were converse merely an exchange of subjective preferences, no conversation would take place. It occurs when its participants undergo an intimate and unexpected change of outlook, resulting in all who entered the exchange leaving it transformed. Gadamer's claim that aesthetic experience is intrinsically *dialogical* assumes a phenomenological equivalence between experiencing conversation's alethic powers and experiencing what art discloses to us. Both occasion events (hermeneutic insights) which, though they require participation in linguistic and cultural horizons, happen independent of our willing and doing. These events not only disrupt self-possession but can alter understanding of the horizons we participate in.

Gadamer defends the self-presencing of language. Self-presencing is not unique to language. Being is self-presentation and all understanding is an event of being.[40] The self-presencing of language is an instance of the self-presencing of Being: 'Being that can be understood is language'.[41] Whereas for Heidegger it is solely the self-presentation of language that recalls us to an awareness of the self-presentation of Being, for Gadamer all Being is language-like insofar as all Being is self-presencing. The unsaid summoned by the said and the invisible called forth by the visible are both aspects of Being. He suggests that 'we speak not only of a language of art but also of a language of nature – in short, of any language that things have'.[42] Things, silent gestures, the touch of another have a language insofar as they can 'speak'. If they address us, they 'mean' something and if they mean something they reach out to us. Things, looks, artworks and gestures are *readable* not in the sense that they are translatable into spoken or written form but because they have a *language of their own* in the sense that, like spoken language, their different patterns bring something into being. This does not mean that a non-verbal gesture means something in its own right. If it means anything it will be because it points beyond itself. Non-verbal gestures can be enigmatic because they are part of communicative structures which reveal and disclose and have speculative resonances of their own. In this they are like any other language and, indeed, reflect the unceasing disclosure which is Being. The articulateness of careful utterance resides not in what is declared but in how the declared comes to resonate in the mind of the listener the nexus of meaning that the utterance it belongs to. Hermeneutics invokes linguisticality to demonstrate that aesthetic experience is not solipsistic but an integral part of a shared discourse concerning epiphanies of meaning. Far from subordinating image to word, hermeneutical aesthetics is concerned with the sensitive use of words to bring forth what is held in an image. Though the totality of what is held within a painting can never be seen in a single glance, it is the word that can direct us to what has not yet been seen. The appeal to linguisticality as the collective foundation for aesthetic experience is instrumental to Gadamer's campaign to release aesthetics from the strictures of subjectivism.

1.7 THE CASE FOR HERMENEUTICAL AESTHETICS

Why should hermeneutical thought be seen as a possible basis for an aesthetic theory? What exactly is it that allows hermeneutical thought to reflect on art's workings? Hermeneutical thought is well suited to reflect on aesthetic experience: both are occasioned by a productive friction between the sensual and the intellectual and it is this unstable relationship which offers an explanation or, rather, poetics of how artworks *work*.

Let us assume that artworks do indeed *work*. That they do is in part because of their ability to intimate new paradigms of sensibility. They not only reveal something of the world outlooks which animate them but they can also challenge and 'unfound' some of the assumptions underwriting our interpretive horizons. If aesthetic experience involves not just the transformation of one's understanding but a challenge to it, aesthetic experience is underwritten by a dialogical conception of mutual engagement. It is this that enables hermeneutics to offer a most pleasing account of what happens in our experience of art.

Hermeneutics and aesthetics are similarly structured by an unstable synthesis of idea and sense which is distinctly 'eventual' in character.[43] There is, on the one hand, a hermeneutical (interpretive) element in aesthetic experience that brings meaning and content to what is seen and, on the other, there is also an aesthetic element in hermeneutical experience which gives 'weight' to interpretation by lending it sensually concrete instances (applications) of its thematic concerns. However it is characterised, hermeneutics, like aesthetics, achieves understanding through the particular case.[44]

Any theorisation of the hermeneutical element within aesthetic experience raises a fundamental question about the relation of aesthetic experience to language. If the hermeneutical or ideational element of aesthetic experience suffuses the sensational element with meaning, and if meaning is linguistically mediated, as it clearly is, aesthetics can no longer be conceived as a solitary monologue on private pleasure but, rather, as an integral part of a shared historical discourse concerning the realisation of meaning. A hermeneutical aesthetics would not be an instance of subordinating our experience of art to the interests of theory. It would be indicative of an attempt to bring into language that which is held within an image, not to the end of surpassing the visual but with the aim of enabling us to see more of what has yet to be seen within the particular. It would be a mistake to assume that this fusion of the aesthetic and the hermeneutical is a stable one. Because the fields of meaning associated with words are relatively unstable, perceptions of meaning which reach out to *Sachen* will be subject to more rapid change than those tied to the realms of concept definition. The very instability of linguistic meaning facilitates shifts of nuance and association that initiate further changes of insight and outlook. The unstable nature of the image–word relationship promotes shifts in the horizons that inform art's cognitive content. The ability of this relationship to force change in modes of understanding drives the cognitive movement which is fundamental to aesthetic experience. It brings the clear awareness of having come to see and to feel differently about a significant subject-matter and, hence, to think differently about ourselves.[45] Gadamer's hermeneutical appeal to language horizons resolves the question of how he can simultaneously insist that aesthetic experience has a cognitive content and hold that aesthetics should not be reduced to concepts.

If it is understood that perceptions tend towards *Sachen* – fields of linguistically housed meaning and association – rather than to determinate concepts, Gadamer can indeed claim that aesthetic experience has a cognitive content that is not based on concepts. The instability of the image–word relationship establishes the strategic importance of aesthetics in his dispute with concept-based models of philosophical reasoning. Philosophical orientations based on language rather than reason give rise to at least two types of cognitive 'truth'. Artworks can expose and probe what we understand to be true of our world and in so doing reveal truths relating to the finitude of our understanding. To insist that philosophy should recognise only truths derived from reason or method limits (if not devalues) vital areas of cognition within human experience. Gadamer's hermeneutical revision of aesthetics clearly forms part of a much broader critique of Western philosophy.

What makes hermeneutics relevant to aesthetics is the observation that if the aesthetic object is meaningful, it is also an unstable site articulated by the oscillation between the sensual and the ideational. David Carroll writes:

> The 'aesthetic' as a critical sense is never a field or state [which opens] on to itself, for the question of the aesthetic is rooted deeply in a split or rift that is never mended or overcome. Art is thus always in a fundamental tension with non art, with what the rift opens art onto, perhaps in spite of itself. And because the 'aesthetic' is never in itself, 'theory' can never capture or encom-

pass the aesthetic as such, and this institutes a rift at the heart of theory that it can also never overcome.[46]

We suggest that aesthetics and its relevance to hermeneutics are constituted by the tensions which characterise the very *in-between* nature of the aesthetic idea, which Kant describes as follows:

> By an *aesthetic idea* I mean that representation of the imagination which induces much thought, yet, without the possibility of any definite thought whatever, i.e. a concept, being adequate to it, and which, language, consequently, can never get quite on level terms with or render completely intelligible. It can easily be seen that an aesthetic idea is the counter-part (pendant) of a *rational idea* which conversely, is a concept, to which no intuition (representation of the imagination) can be adequate.[47]

The case for a hermeneutical approach to aesthetics becomes clear. If the aesthetic image is a meaningful image, it becomes the object of hermeneutical study. As meaningful, the image will embody a fusion or application of the ideational and the sensual. As an aesthetic image, its meaning will be unstable: it cannot be reduced to a rational idea or concept. Yet the instability of incommensurability guarantees that any attempt to elaborate the meaning of the image will extend or change its meaning and, in turn, facilitate movement in the understanding of the spectator. The case for a hermeneutic approach to aesthetics entails a subtle but important shift of approach to the aesthetic image.

Gadamer is not alone in his concern to re-articulate aesthetics as a philosophy of experience able to emphasise, through the perceived particular, a movement of cognitive transformation. Hans von Balthasar observes that in 'hermeneutics and aesthetics and their relationship to the "beautiful" or "splendid" object', we tend to succumb 'to a static view which cannot do justice to the phenomenon' of art. 'Aesthetics must abandon itself and go in search of new categories. . . .'[48] Balthasar's comment points to a distinction crucial to our argument that a hermeneutical aesthetics opens the way to a participatory form of aesthetic attentiveness. The aesthetic image should no longer be hypostasised as something in and for its own sake. To do so is to treat it as an object of importance for the viewing subject only because of its pleasurable qualities. A hermeneutical approach to the art image demands that it be treated as a contemplative object important not because of its intrinsic aesthetic properties but because of what it brings into play. The play of horizons initiated by transmission and reception is discursive and participatory by nature. It demands a spectator's involvement. The art image is valued not as an object in itself but for what it facilitates, for its status as a mover of understanding.

1.8 SUMMARY

Philosophical hermeneutics takes the fact of art's address as given. In so doing, it places the experience of art as prior to the experience of an aesthetic object. The latter requires the abstraction (extraction) of an 'object' from its perceptual field and then subsequent reflection on its (rarefied) aesthetic properties. To adopt Plato's language, such properties are two removes from the initial address. Art's address is, then, directly hermeneutical: it involves the vivid if not forceful experience of being in the presence of something meaningful. Such enquiry is also philosophical, in that it asks after the conditions of such experience. This leads to an analysis of the elements of meaningful experience, that is, the bodily or the sensual and the ideational, with its linguistic and historical horizons. All artistically communicated meaning involves the material particularisation of something more general or universal. It would, however, be a mistake to assume that such analysis confirms the prior existence of the separate elements of such experience. To the contrary, the analysis attempts to simplify and render thinkable the complex nature of art's address, that is, its simultaneously sensual and ideational nature. This is not an attempt to 'fix' or, as Nietzsche would suggest, 'mummify' the experience of art but, rather, to understand its poetics, the nature of its movement. Philosophical hermeneutics is concerned with dynamic nature of that experience (*Erfahrung*) of art. Grasping its elements enables a better appreciation of what comes into play within that experience. Understanding that movement shows how the constant play between the sensual and the ideational creates possibilities for transformation and transcendence through an engagement with an art image. Such possibilities are sustained by the hermeneutical axiom that $x = x +$, that is, by the claim that experience, language and thought always point beyond themselves. This underlies the hermeneutical drive towards a poetics of the art experience: it can demonstrate that responses to art are not just inconsequentially subjective but have intelligible, effective and discursive components. As a subjective event, the experience of art and its occasion are unpredictable. Reaction, however, is explicable: there is always a context to the reception of art. Answering the question 'What does an image address?' actually suffices to demonstrate a relational notion of subjectivity: it reveals the difference between the rationale of a work and that of the response. It also indicates on three levels the potential reasonableness of that response: (1) whether it is appropriate to the context of its own horizon and the horizon surrounding the production of the work; (2) whether it is internally coherent and consistent as a reading; and (3) whether its structure supplements or expands the intelligible content of the work. Philosophical hermeneutics is concerned to demonstrate the cognitive content of the experience of art and to undermine the charge that aesthetic responses are purely subjective. This it attempts to do by insisting that the experience of art is primarily a participatory experience of meaning as opposed to a private response to the aesthetic qualities of an object. Meaning implies shareable and open discursive horizons and the possibilities of reasonable exchange. The defence of art's cognitive content requires the further claim that the subjective experience of art is grounded in ontologically prior horizons of meaning.

The formal case for considering aesthetics from a hermeneutical perspective has, as this chapter has suggested, several advantages. These will be discussed at length throughout this study. In summary form, these leitmotifs are:

1. Hermeneutical aesthetics endeavours to reveal the life-world *already* at work within an artwork (the ontologically prior horizons of cultural meaning) and to discern our presence within it.
2. It promotes the hermeneutical practice of theorising our experiences of art so as to explore, extend and enhance what is held within them rather than seeking to control or fix their content.
3. Philosophical hermeneutics defends the openness of cognition and therefore adopts a multi-perspective approach to our experience of art, the practice of which is to expand our understanding of its content.
4. The ontological priority of discursive meaning over individual aesthetic response permits a consideration of the reasonable persuasiveness of aesthetic judgements.
5. Philosophical hermeneutics develops a practice of attentiveness which displaces Kant's concept of disinterestedness and permits a significant re-articulation of aesthetic attentiveness and aesthetic education.
6. Philosophical hermeneutics brings the traditional philosophical discourse surrounding the term 'appearance' to a new culmination and develops a provocative account of the ontological status of the artistic image.
7. Philosophical hermeneutics and aesthetics are structured by a similar unstable synthesis of idea and sense which is distinctly 'eventual' in character. It is the eventual character of aesthetic experience which allows it to function transformatively.
8. Appreciating the difference between the understanding that is in an artwork and how we understand it is the end of hermeneutical

aesthetics, though this end will always prove another dialogical beginning.

9. Philosophical hermeneutics is committed to aesthetics of movement. Neither it nor modernist aesthetics seek controversy and difficulty for their own sake. They share the conviction that learning, understanding and insight are possible so long as movement in and between mental perspectives can be sustained. Both have the pedagogic aspiration of making us look and think again, of rendering us strange and difficult to ourselves, and of encouraging a mode of being in which 'to be' is, controversially, always to be in question.

We have considered the intellectual context which informs Gadamer's intention to achieve a hermeneutical reform of aesthetics. Now let us turn to Gadamer's own reflections on art and aesthetics.

NOTES

1. Jan Faye, *After Postmodernism: A Naturalistic Reconstruction of the Humanities* (London: Palgrave Macmillan, 2012), p. 4.
2. Hans-Georg Gadamer, 'The Universality of the Hermeneutical Problem', in *The Gadamer Reader*, ed. R. E. Palmer (Evanston: Northwestern University Press, 2007), p. 79.
3. See Hans-Georg Gadamer, *Truth and Method*, trans. and ed. Joel Weinsheimer (London: Sheed and Ward, 1989), p. xviii. This text will be referred to as TM from now on.
4. For this nuanced use of the word 'hermeneutics', see Robert B. Pippin, *The Persistence of Subjectivity: On the Kantian Aftermath* (Cambridge: Cambridge University Press, 2005), p. 68.
5. TM, p. 512.
6. Ibid., p. 397.
7. See Gadamer's foreword to J. Grondin, *Introduction to Philosophical Hermeneutics* (Albany: State University of New York Press, 1994), p. x.
8. TM, pp. 144, 116, 164.
9. Stuart Hampshire, *Thought and Action* (London: Chatto and Windus, 1959), p. 246.
10. Wilhelm Dilthey, *Selected Writings*, ed. H. P. Rickman (London: Cambridge University Press, 1976), pp. 109–21.
11. Heidegger comments, 'Almost from the time when specialized thinking about art and the artist began, this thought was called aesthetic. Aesthetics takes the work of art as an object, the object of *aisthesis*, of sensual apprehension in the wide sense. Today we call this apprehension experience. The way in which man experiences art is supposed to give information about its nature. Experience is the source that is standard not only for art appreciation and enjoyment, but also for artistic creation. Everything is

an experience. Yet perhaps experience is the element in which art dies.' See Heidegger, 'The Origin of the Work of Art', in *Poetry, Language and Thought*, trans. Albert Hofstadter (New York: Harper, 1971), p. 79.

12. 'Thoughts without content are empty, perceptions without concepts are blind.' Immanuel Kant, *Kritik der reinen Vernunft* (Hamburg: Felix Meiner, 1956), p. 95, A 51, B 76.

13. Theodor Adorno, *Negative Dialectics*, trans. E. B. Ashton (London: Routledge and Kegan Paul, 1973), pp. 135–207.

14. 'Everything factual, is already theory.' Johann Goethe, *Maximen und Reflexionen* (Munich: Deutscher Taschenbuch Verlag, 1968), p. 69.

15. 'The universal and the particular occur together. The particular is the universal appearing under different conditions.' Ibid., p. 68.

16. TM, p. 90. This argument is explored in detail in Chapter 3.

17. Mary Warnock, *Imagination* (London: Faber and Faber, 1976), p. 192.

18. The conceptual connection between Kant's notion of the 'aesthetic idea' and Gadamer's appeal to the 'subject-matter', which cannot be reduced to a concept alone, is discussed in Chapter 3.

19. Immanuel Kant, *The Critique of Judgement*, trans. J. C. Meredith (Oxford: Oxford University Press, 1978). He writes that aesthetic ideas may be termed 'ideas . . . because they strain after something lying out beyond the confines of experience, and so to speak to approximate to a presentation of rational concepts (intellectual ideas), thus giving to these concepts the semblance of an objective reality'. See p. 176 (emphasis added).

20. TM, p. 90.

21. Kant, *The Critique of Judgement*, Section 1.203.

22. Ibid.

23. TM, p. 292.

24. Ibid., p. 116.

25. It is a travesty of Gadamer's position to suggest that his defence of tradition identifies him as anti-modernist. His writings on Paul Klee and Paul Celan indicate the opposite. The formal difference between Gadamer and modernists such as Nietzsche is that whereas modernism questions the norms of the past in order to break away from them, philosophical hermeneutics questions them in order to extend if not radicalise our relational understanding of them.

26. The parallels between modernism and aspects of Gadamer's approach to art coalesce as a theme in Gerald Bruns's essay 'The Hermeneutical Anarchist: Phronesis, Rhetoric and the Experience of Art', in *Gadamer's Century, Essays in Honor of Hans-Georg Gadamer*, ed. Jeff Malpas, Ulrich Arnswald and Jens Kertscher (Cambridge, MA: MIT Press, 2002), pp. 44–76.

27. Having an intuitive feel or empathy for a way in which an artist or a poet works does not necessarily invoke the psycho-logistic form of interpretation associated with Dilthey's hermeneutics. It has, arguably, more to do with Wittgenstein's notion of entering a 'form of life', that is,

understanding a pattern of thought so that one knows how to go on with it and anticipate the next move. Understanding the inherent logic (rhetoric) of a writer or a painter is, in other words, not to be associated with possessing 'psychologistic' gifts.

28. Eberhard Scheiffele, 'Questioning One's "Own" from the Perspective of the Foreign', in *Nietzsche and Asian Thought*, ed. Graham Parkes (Chicago: University of Chicago Press, 1991), pp. 31–50.

29. Rainer Maria Rilke, *Letters to a Young Poet*, trans. M. Norton (New York: Norton, 1954), pp. 34–5.

30. The title of Jürgen Habermas's original critique of *Truth and Method* was 'The Hermeneutic Claim to Universality' and appears in Kurt Mueller-Vollmer (ed.), *The Hermeneutics Reader* (London: Blackwell, 1985), pp. 294–319.

31. See Charles Taylor, *Modern Social Imaginaries* (Durham, NC: Duke University Press, 2004).

32. TM, p. 113.

33. Ibid., p. 144.

34. Ibid., p. 147 (emphasis added).

35. Ibid., p. 113.

36. Ibid.

37. Kant, *The Critique of Judgement*, Section 205, p. 43.

38. The themes in this section are developed from my essay 'The Hermeneutics of Seeing', in *Interpreting Visual Culture: Explorations in the Hermeneutics of the Visual*, ed. Ian Heywood and Barry Sandywell (London: Routledge, 1999), pp. 3–30.

39. See Chapter 6.

40. TM, p. 484.

41. Ibid., p. 474.

42. Ibid., p. 475.

43. The term 'eventual' reflects Heidegger's argument that an artwork is more an event (*Ereignis*) than an object. The eventual character of an artwork is something that manifests itself in each of our interpretive encounters with it. See Heidegger's argument concerning 'Art [as] the setting into work of truth' in his essay 'The Origin of the Art Work', in Heidegger, *Poetry, Language and Thought*, p. 77.

44. Wilhelm Dilthey insists that the relationship between part and whole is only ever given in the particular case. See Dilthey, *Selected Writings*, pp. 210–11.

45. There is a parallel between the unstable nature of words and the hermeneutical nature of a journey or pilgrimage: a journey has a prescribed destination but on the way the expectancies of the traveller often collides with the unexpected, forcing a review of what was previously understood as the nature and purpose of the journey.

46. David Carroll, *The States of Theory: History, Art, and Critical Discourse* (Stanford: Stanford University Press, 1990), pp. 16–17.

47. Kant, *The Critique of Judgement*, pp. 175–6.
48. Hans Urs von Balthasar, *Theo-Drama: Theological Dramatic Theory, Vol. 1: Prolegomena,* trans. Graham Harrison (San Francisco: Ignatius Press, 1998), pp. 16–17. For a discussion of von Balthasar's aesthetics see Oliver Davies, 'The Theological Aesthetics', in *The Cambridge Companion to Hans Urs von Balthasar*, ed. Edward T. Oakes and David Moss (Cambridge: Cambridge University Press, 2004), pp. 131–42.

2. Gadamer's Re-Orientation of Aesthetics

2.1 INTRODUCTION

> The inquiry developed here deliberately transforms the systematic problem of *aesthetics* into the question of the experience of *art*.[1]

Gadamer's approach to aesthetic experience stands squarely in the phenomenological tradition: his concern is with the place of art in our *experience* of the world.[2] His reflection on aesthetic theory is a rare intellectual achievement, simultaneously deconstructive and constructive. It dismantles elements of the grand traditions of Platonic and Kantian aesthetics but offers, nevertheless, a phenomenological reconstruction of many of their central insights. This makes for a flexible philosophical approach to artwork which ranges freely over a number of art forms and styles, discussing both the singularity of works and their broader significance. The approach is hermeneutical: it re-acquaints us with those received meanings and preoccupations which underlie our experience of art.

Openly influenced by Heidegger, his later essays on language and poetry in particular, Gadamer's aesthetics are far from traditional. He proposes that:

1. Aesthetics is not the study of specific types of subjective pleasure derived from art. It is a study of what objectively informs our subjective awareness of art.
2. Hermeneutical aesthetics seeks to break through the pleasurable distractions of aesthetic consciousness in order to disclose the cultural and linguistic realities that manifest themselves within it.
3. Hermeneutical aesthetics presupposes intense phenomenological involvement with the subject-matters of art rather than disinterested detachment in the Kantian sense.

4. Hermeneutical aesthetics regards aesthetic objects not as a distraction from the real but as the vehicle through which real subject-matters reveal themselves, overturning the notion that artworks are at one remove from reality.

5. Hermeneutical aesthetics is dialogical in character. It contends that both practitioner and theoretician share in bringing a subject-matter to light and plays down any theory/practice division in the arts. Interpretation is a means to a work's realisation.

6. Hermeneutical aesthetics does not seek a concept of art but a deepening immersion in the experience of art. Theory is to guide and intensify but never to overwhelm the contemplation of artworks.

7. Gadamer's aesthetics is respectful of art's ability to disrupt and challenge customary cultural expectations. It attributes an ethical significance to art for being able to reveal the limitations of fixed cultural expectancy and for opening the spectator towards the other and the different.

The arguments underpinning these proposals concern the following intellectual dispositions.

2.2 AESTHETIC EXPERIENCE AND THE REFIGURING OF SUBJECTIVITY

This study is an exercise in thinking with and beyond Gadamer's remarks on aesthetics. Having explored the context dependence of his reforming intentions, we turn to Gadamer's comments on art as a crucial resource for developing a hermeneutical aesthetics. We will canvass those elements of Gadamer's discussion of art that move towards the articulation of aesthetic attentiveness, the nature of which is crucial to understanding the transformative capacity of art. Though Gadamer seeks to recover the cognitive dimensions of aesthetics by criticising the discipline's subjectivist leanings, he does not negate them entirely. That would render any claim for the transformative power of art nonsense. He endeavours, to the contrary, to transcend, if not transfigure, subjectivity by demonstrating the substantialities of language and tradition that underlie and manifest themselves through it. His thinking expedites the doubled hermeneutics discussed in the Introduction. In the experience of art, the mode of relations that constitute an alien work comes to permeate those of subjectivity in such a way so as not simply to alter its outlook but to achieve a new and significant permutation of how it understands itself. Aesthetic subjectivity achieves reflective articulacy by being folded into the ontic substantialities that inform it. This requires that the subject foster an attentiveness towards the mystery of the given and its unexpected folds of meaningfulness. In order to rediscover its grounding, Gadamer has to start with the intensity of subjective experience itself. Any image worthy of being called a work of art has the power to affect us immediately.[3]

Gadamer announces that 'art addresses us'. The assumption that 'art is able to say something directed to somebody'[4] alludes to the surprise, shock and, sometimes, dismay of being spoken to abruptly. The argument is beguilingly simple but it raises major questions, to be discussed later: in what language does art speak and what is it for that language to speak? Gadamer asserts emphatically that, with regard to the experience of art, meaning is prior to the question of formal aesthetic properties.

> The consciousness of art – the aesthetic consciousness – is always secondary to the immediate truth-claim that proceeds from the work of art itself. To this extent, when we judge a work of art on the basis of its aesthetic quality, something that is really much more intimately familiar to us is alienated. This alienation in aesthetic judgment always takes place when we have withdrawn ourselves, and are no longer open to the immediate claim of that which grasps us.[5]

'The experience of art is an experience of meaning' and, to this extent, 'aesthetics is absorbed into hermeneutics'.[6] This distances Gadamer from conventional justifications of the aesthetic as offering a special kind of pleasure. In *The Relevance of the Beautiful* he suggests that 'the mere on-looker who indulges in aesthetic or cultural enjoyment from a safe distance, whether in the theatre, the concert hall, or the seclusion of solitary reading, simply does not exist'.[7] People who take themselves to be such an onlooker misunderstand themselves. 'Aesthetic self-understanding is indulging in escapism if it regards the encounter with the work of art as nothing but enchantment in the sense of liberation from the pressures of reality, through the enjoyment of a spurious freedom'.[8]

Gadamer observes that this hedonistic personalisation of aesthetic response has two alienating consequences. (1) The judgement that aesthetic experience is purely subjective severs the individual from communal networks of meaning capable of illuminating personal experience. (2) Attempts to render subjective experience academically legitimate by presenting it as a social product estrange the individual from his or her experience by translating it into third-person terms he or she may neither endorse nor recognise.

In contrast to Dilthey, Gadamer defends an *Erfahrungs-Ästhetik* which claims that, as with significant life experiences, our relationships with artworks are deep and on-going: we revisit them and, in doing so, our understanding is continually renegotiated. Gadamer speaks of the 'interminability' of such experience (*die Unabschliessbarkeit aller Erfahrung*), which, as we shall see in later chapters, remains forever open because of its cognitive movement.[9] The cumulative nature of such experience is an instance of *Bildung* (formation and learning through experience) and is, as such, a process of becoming (*Werden*) which marks the living motion of our being.

Gadamer's aesthetics avows an (alleged) anti-Kantianism. It abjures phenomenalist disinterestedness for the sake of phenomenological involvement. However, a major claim of this study is that Gadamer is forced to reinvent a version of Kant's notion of aesthetic disinterestedness. His aesthetics is also anti-idealist: it refuses the notion that in aesthetic experience we perceive 'a pure integration of meaning'. The position is also anti-representationalist; there is something in the artwork which resists integration within a concept.[10] He contends that even Hegel's definition of the beautiful as the 'sensual appearing of the Idea' presumes that aesthetic experience is able to reach beyond the specific type of appearance to its underlying idea; aesthetic experience becomes the expectation of a semantic fulfilment. When the idea behind the appearance is grasped, 'the whole of its meaning would have been understood once and for all and thus brought in to our possession so to speak'. The work of art becomes a carrier of meaning, to be abandoned once 'the lead story' has been grasped. But, he argues, 'Our understanding of art works is manifestly not of this type. Everyone knows this from his or her own encounters with art, from concerts, visits to museums, and from his or her reading.'[11] This denial of idealist aesthetics grounds the claim that an artwork is essentially enigmatic.

Gadamer's opposition to aesthetic idealism is supported by the observation that art 'cannot be satisfactorily translated in terms of conceptual knowledge'.[12] Its meaning is not to be grasped in such a way that it can be simply transferred to another idiom. Indeed, because it invites many meanings, an artwork acquires an ideality of possible meanings which cannot be obviated by any possible realisation.[13] The work has, therefore, an autonomy which cannot be substituted by anything else or, to put it another way, the work is always in excess of its readings. Two important consequences arise from this.

First, Gadamer's conception of art is presentational (*darstellen*) rather than representational (*vorstellen*). As a work does not represent anything other than itself, the meanings it carries can come to the fore only in its self-presentation. Yet, the emergent meaning is never given in its entirety. This is consistent with the *eventual* nature of art. 'When a work of art truly takes hold of us, it is not an object that stands opposite us which we look at in hope of seeing through it to an intended conceptual meaning. . . . The work is an *Ereigniss* – an event that "appropriates us" to itself. It jolts us, knocks us over and sets up a world of its own, into which we are drawn'.[14] What is revealed remains but an aspect of the work which, when it appears, drives others into the background. Disclosure and hiddenness are not contraries in Gadamer's aesthetics but mutual dependencies: the disclosed reveals the presence of the undisclosed in the disclosed. It is in the sheer being there (*Dasein*) of the work of art that our understanding experiences the depths and the unfathomability of its meaning.[15]

Second, the claim that a work's meaning can never be completely fulfilled is supported by a linguistic analogy concerning the speculative: art has a language in that its signs and symbols function like semantic units. Gadamer comments on the living virtuality of meaning contained in each word, an inner dimension of multiplication. Accordingly, language is not the representation (*mimesis*) of a set of pre-given meanings but a 'coming to language' of a constant reserve of meaning.[16] The finitude of linguistic expression is such that no utterance can be complete.[17] 'The only thing that constitutes language . . . is that one word leads to another, each word is, so to speak, summoned, and on its side holds open the further progress of speaking'.[18] No meaning can be completely revealed. Because we can revisit artworks repeatedly, the meaning disclosed initially can be expanded or changed. 'The work of art consists in its being open in a limitless way to ever new integrations of meaning'.[19] The inexhaustibility that distinguishes the language of art from all translation into concepts rests on an excess of meaning.[20]

Gadamer's conversation on aesthetics announces his thematic pre-occupations: art is interrogative by nature, artworks *work* through a disclosure of meaning, disclosures of meaning establish art's cognitive status, the cognitive content of art is partly intelligible and partly enigmatic, and artworks are always open to reinterpretation. These are not free-standing arguments but are informed by a constellation of various positions. To these arguments we now turn.

Gadamer's determination to reveal the cognitive content of aesthetic experience requires exposing the ontological grounding of subjectivity. To approach artworks solely on the basis of subjective responses or to read them only in terms of an artist's intentionality is always to miss the point. Hermeneutically speaking, the philosophical focus should be on what shapes subjectivity and guides its expectations. This initiates a speculative refiguring of aesthetic subjectivity. In *Truth and Method* he writes:

All self-knowledge arises from what is historically pre-given, what with Hegel we call 'substance,' because it underlies all subjective intentions and actions, and hence both prescribes and limits every possibility for understanding any tradition whatsoever in its historical alterity. This almost defines the aim of philosophical hermeneutics: its task is to retrace the path of Hegel's phenomenology of mind until we discover in all that is subjective the substantiality that determines it.[21]

This amounts to the claim, as we later suggest, that subjective responses to art are the epistemological mode of ontological interactions. In *The Relevance of the Beautiful* Gadamer elucidates substance as follows:

'Substance' is understood as something that supports us, although it does not emerge into the light of reflective consciousness, it is something that can never be fully articulated, although it is absolutely necessary for the existence of all clarity, consciousness, expression and communication.[22]

Uncovering the ontological foundations of aesthetic experience does not undermine the primacy Gadamer gives to art's immediate address. He aims to demonstrate the cognitive legitimacy of subjective experience by revealing how aesthetic experience is both involved in something larger than itself and reflects (*speculum*) that larger actuality within itself. The ability of aesthetic experience to express trans-individual phenomenological structures or social imaginaries explains what is meant by substance. Gadamer's aesthetics is properly concerned with *experiencing* what underlies its more abstract concepts. This is not a matter of naming or describing the reality which manifests itself in aesthetic experience but of trying to say something about the experience an individual has of it. Gadamer's reflections commence with the immediacy of art's claim, its contemporaneous nature, and then explore what influences the experience of that claim. The aim is seemingly paradoxical: to understand that which shapes, lies beyond but only 'shows' itself in aesthetic experience. This demands a refiguring of the subjective.

2.3 ART AS EVENT

The notion of art as an event emphasises its participatory nature. Involvement with the experience of art entails an element of *ecstasis*: subjects are drawn out of their sense of singularity and are forced to recognise if not yield to the collective dimensions of their being. These dimensions are made manifest by three participatory structures: play, festival and symbol.

2.3.1 *Play*

Gadamer's discussion of the relation between art and play must not be equated with any suggestion that art is a trivial game or pastime. Schiller's *On the Aesthetic Education of Man* offer the precedent: artworks are dramatic in that *they put something into play*.[23] The analogy is plain: aesthetic consciousness is not self-contained but taken up in the play of something larger than what is made evident to subjective awareness. Spectorial participation (like art research) demands immersion in that which cannot be fully anticipated or controlled by individual consciousness. The game and the artwork are both forms of self-movement which require spectators to play along with what they bring into being.[24] Gadamer asserts the 'primacy of the play' over consciousness: 'the players are merely the way the play comes into presentation'.[25] Participation takes the individual players out of themselves so that they become absorbed in the event of presentation itself. The work of art is also 'the playing of it'; an autonomous event comes into being and 'changes all that stand before it'.[26]

The play/playing analogy undermines approaches to art that are exclusively intentional, material and conventional. The subjectivity of an artist cannot be an appropriate interpretive starting point for interpretation. What transpires in a player's consciousness does not reveal the nature of the game being played. Neither can art, nor the game, be understood by reference to its tools and equipment alone. Art has material requirements but it is not constituted by its equipment. Comprehending a game or an artwork requires an appreciation of the appropriate rules and conventions. What constitutes fair or foul play depends upon a set of pre-understood principles, just as what is esteemed excellent in art requires normative expectancies. Yet art's vitality does not reside in a rule book but, more often than not, in its transgression of expected norms. The argument is not that an artwork cannot be reduced to intention, material or convention but rather that each of these elements only comes into its own when taken up within the play which is the practice of art itself.

The game analogy implies that the act of spectatorship contributes to bringing what is at play within the artwork into fuller being. The spectator just as much as the artist performs a role in realising the subject-matters art brings into play. The aesthetic spectator is swept up by the experience of art, absorbed in its play and potentially transformed by that which spectatorship helps constitute. Though the argument distances itself from traditional subject-object paradigms, it retains certain features of Kant's aesthetics.

Whereas Kant attributes a non-purposive rationality to the aesthetic attitude, Gadamer attributes it to the playful process of art practice itself. Both art and the game share a to-and-fro movement not tied to any specific goal other than to fulfil themselves for their own sake:[27] no one knows how a game will end and no one knows to what end an artwork works.[28] What is clear is that it is what occurs when the artwork or the game is in play that matters, and this can occur contrary to the willing and doing of the aesthetic or sporting spectator.

2.3.2 *Festival*

Conventional accounts of aesthetic experience stress its intense and individuating nature as a heightened form of sensation (*Erlebnis*). Yet, despite its intimacy, Gadamer claims that aesthetic involvement entails a degree of communal activity. The analogy between aesthetic experience and the festive is telling.

> Work is something that separates and divides us. For all the cooperation necessitated by joint enterprise and the division of labour in our productive activity, we are still divided as individuals as far as our day to day purposes are concerned. Festive celebration, on the other hand, is clearly distinguished by the fact that here we are not primarily separated but rather gathered together.[29]

Gadamer's thinking has a certain Kantian inflection. Kant's conception of aesthetic experience requires that the egotistical interests that frame the commerce of everyday life are suspended, allowing for the emergence of a community formed around shared, non-hostile, compatible pleasures. Gadamer's notion of aesthetic experience is not concerned with a putative Kantian kingdom-to-come but with rediscovering and forging the communality that we, historically and linguistically speaking, already are. Despite this difference, aesthetic experience establishes for both thinkers a meditative space in and through which something can be occasioned. The underlying point is that whereas for Kant it is a change in the disposition of subjective consciousness (i.e. its adoption of an aesthetic attitude) which initiates a better disposition towards the community, for Gadamer it is participation in a trans-subjective event which effects a change in subjective disposition towards the community.

When Gadamer argues that 'the mystery of festive celebration lies in this suspension of time', he refers to how festivity suspends work-time. This initiates that 'play-time' in which another order of events emerges. The festive 'represents a genuine creation, [for] something drawn from within ourselves takes shape before our eyes in a form that we recognise and experience as a more profound presentation of our own reality'.[30]

This distances Gadamer from the view that aesthetic experience is solely a subject's personal response to an artwork. In the festive – an analogy for the communal dimensions of aesthetic experience – the individual subject comes to stand differently in his or her relationship to others. Just as the artwork comes to stand in the festival, so too does the artwork bring its spectators to stand as a community: 'in the festive the communal spirit that supports us all and transcends each of us individually represents the real power of the festive and indeed the real power of the art work'.[31] The festival occasions individuals to surpass their everyday view of themselves as potentially hostile competitors and to see themselves as a community formed around a shared interest in what the artwork brings forth. This is an analogy for something more fundamental. Instrumentalist conceptions of language persuade us that the spoken and written word are but communicative tools, but for Gadamer participation in language acknowledges that an individual is located within a substantive horizon of ever-changing constellations of meaning that transcend subjective consciousness. Pragmatic concerns encourage the forgetting of such interconnectedness but when such individualism is suspended by the festival or, indeed, by the adoption of an aesthetic attitude, the rediscovery of oneself as belonging to an extensive community of shared meanings and involvements becomes possible. The artwork's communicative capacity awakens the realisation that, in as much as I understand myself as being addressed, I must acknowledge that I already belong to something larger than myself. If a work means something to me, it is more than likely that it will mean something not just to me. The artwork *festivises*: it reveals our personal indebtedness to past and future communities of meaning. The festive event of art demonstrates that we belong to a hermeneutic collective which serves as the effective underpinning of art's ability to communicate in a language-like manner. This will prove a key element in Gadamer's endeavour to demonstrate the conditions under which artworks come to operate effectively. The limits of subjectivity are once again exposed. Subjectivity is not the *non plus ultra* of aesthetic experience, a claim that is further elaborated in Gadamer's discussion of the symbol.

2.3.3 Symbol

A discussion of the symbol forms the third aspect of Gadamer's case that aesthetic experience involves an *ecstasis* of the aesthetic subject. The word 'symbol' is a Greek term for a token of remembrance (*tessera hospitalis*) that could be broken in two so that should a descendant of a former guest enter that house, the co-joined pieces would kindle an act of recognition in the former host.[32] The symbol connotes explicitly what we recognise implicitly.[33] It is associated with the fragmentary and with a promise of completeness which 'in turn alludes to beauty and the potentially whole and holy order of things'.[34] Its connection with the speculative is best appreciated by reference to the sign.

If the sign's proper function is to refer to its referent, it is self-cancelling. The road-side sign that is so attractive that it distracts from the danger it refers to and causes new accidents by prompting drivers to admire it does not function properly. The symbol, however, does not refer to something outside itself but presents its own meaning. The symbol is, indeed, the place where that meaning becomes present. Yet the symbolically delivered meaning is never given completely. Its meaning is indeterminate. References to the symbol as fragmentary anticipate the possibility of wholeness. The speculative dimension of such reasoning resides in the premise that every stated meaning brings forth more than is actually spoken. The 'speculative' capacity of an image or word concerns its ability to sound out or insinuate the unstated nexus of meanings which sustain a given expression but are not directly given in it. The speculative power of an image or phrase has something in common with the sublime: it illuminates in the spoken or visual image a penumbra of unstated meanings whose presence can be sensed but never fully grasped or conceptualised. Gadamer's aesthetic offers a hermeneutic reworking of the sublime. It does not so much denote what is incomprehensible for a knowing subject but articulates the dependent being of that subject, revealing its grounding in an untheorisable total-ity of relationships that informs and shapes its existence. Gadamer's principal argument is, then, that an artwork can always mean more and insinuate a transcendent dimension of meaning which, though never exhausted by a symbol, is nevertheless present within it. The promise of meaning is always shaded by the threat of the limiting case, that is, its collapse into non-meaning. Gadamer indeed recognises the frustration of expectancy as the basis of human insight. 'Every experience worthy of the name', he argues, 'thwarts an expectation.'[35]

The symbol and its reticence about revealing the withheld aspects of its meaning do not connote something utterly alien to us. The yet-to-be revealed is a dimension of meaning overlooked, forgotten or not perceived within what has already been shown or grasped. It lies hidden in the visible. In other words, the power of the symbol resides in its ability to reveal that, unbeknown to ourselves, we are already in com-munion with something larger than ourselves, namely those horizons of meaning which implicitly sustain reflection. The mystery of the symbol is its promise of transcendence: an effecting and affecting which reveal that we belong to a hermeneutic community larger than we envisage. The analogy of the festival is telling. In the festival, individuated work roles are renounced as we rediscover communal ties. Gadamer's arguments about play, festival and symbol serve, then, as the basis for his claim that aesthetic experience (our experience of art) is a demonstrable instance of how subjectivity is informed by a substantiality that transcends it. As mentioned at the start of the section, involvement with the experience of art as a participatory event entails an element of *ecstasis*, with subjects brought to recognise that they belong to what do not belong to it, that is, the collective dimensions of their being.

2.4 ONTOLOGICAL IMPLICATIONS

The discussion of play, festival and symbol reminds us of the collective dimensions appertaining to any subjective experience of art. Not only do these dimensions transcend individual subjectivity but they indicate a collective phenomenological structure which reflects the ontological dimensions of an artwork and how it is experienced. These involve questions of presentation (how the artwork makes itself manifest), of subject-matter (what the artwork addresses), of language (how art speaks to but of something beyond the spectator) and of tradition (how art transmits and revitalises meaning).

2.4.1 *Presentation*

Gadamer's account of the symbol establishes that artworks are presentational rather than representational; they occasion the meanings they invoke and do not represent a meaning independent of themselves. The argument effects a profound and significant change in the meaning of aesthetic appearance. The representational view of art relegates art to a secondary status: the artwork brings to mind something other than the artwork, an original state of affairs, a specific meaning or reality. Art's objective co-relative is, accordingly, positioned outside the work, so that the work becomes the mere appearance of something else. The presentational account of art insists that what comes to appearance in the artwork is the real itself. Following Heidegger, Gadamer adopts the thesis that the fundamental characteristic of Being is self-presentational. Being is self-presentation, for 'what presents itself in this way is not different from itself in presenting itself'.[36] There is no hidden reality, no thing-in-itself, behind the presentation: *appearing* is of the essence. With this simple assertion, the reality–appearing conjunction becomes synonymous with original creation, with the truth of Being's perpetual self-disclosure. Aesthetic appearance is not secondary to reality or truth (*imitatio*) but is the medium through which the work's truth shows/presents itself (*mimesis*). The claim that each artwork has its own temporality implies that each work never reveals itself completely. Like the symbol, appearance is always partial and yet alludes to something beyond itself as the yet-to-be-revealed.

The truth of an artwork is not its simple manifestation of meaning but rather the unfathomableness and depth of its meaning.[37] Its truth embraces a tension between revelation (what appears) and what is concealed (what has yet to be shown). The artwork does not simply offer 'a recognisable surface contour' but has an inner depth of self-sufficiency which Gadamer calls, after Heidegger, a 'standing-in-itself'. In short, the mark of a substantial work is that it tantalisingly veils possibilities of meaning. Such resistance is a stimulus to further inter-pretation. Substantive works, like significant symbols, have an opaque aspect. They demand interpretation, emphasising the dialogical relation between hermeneutics and aesthetic presentation, that is, the need to bring out the possibilities of meaning within a presentation. As we shall see, it is not the sheer multiplication of meaning *per se* that is at issue but the generation of unanticipated meanings capable of testing our presuppositions in unexpected ways.

2.4.2 *Subject-Matter: The Issue in Question*

Gadamer's aesthetics involves a variety of interlocking arguments, one of the most significant of which concerns the *Sache selbst*. The term refers to a work's subject-matter, to what it addresses. It evokes phe-nomenological notions of intentionality: what a work points to. The *Sache* is not a determinate concept but an area of significant meaning-fulness, a constellation of concerns which orbit affective, conative and cognitive complexities such as grief, love or duty. The *Sache* underpins Gadamer's claim that aesthetic experience has a significant cognitive content. In Jacques Maritain's phrase, the transcendental implication of *Sachen* is that 'they give more than they have'.[38] Subject-matters may transcend an individual work, in that no one work can exhaust their significance, but they are not independent of the works that exemplify them. If they were ontologically distinct, the idealism Gadamer rejects would be forced on him and he would be compelled to argue that art is representational, refers to a concept beyond itself and, indeed, disap-pears into that concept once evoked. If, however, art is presentation, a work's meaning is not independent of it. Art does not copy and thereby re-present a subject-matter in another idiom but configures a visual or literary space from out of which and to which a subject-matter is summoned. With some justification, Gadamer destroys an ancient line of argument that regards art as secondary to the real. The consequences of the argument are explored in detail in Chapter 5. Contrary to the Platonic tradition, his argument insists that art *adds* to the reality of its subject-matters. Gadamer's evaluation of the aesthetic contrasts vividly with Kant's in this respect.

Kant considers aesthetic experience to be indifferent to whether or not its object is real.[39] A work's success does not depend on its relationship to an original or co-relative. Whether what is represented exists or not is inconsequential. What matters is the aesthetic merit of the work, not the strength of its likeness. Should the artwork be harmed, the being of the correlative is unaffected. Gadamer's presentational aesthetics is profoundly anti-Platonic: a work's disappearance does indeed diminish the reality of that which presents itself through it. Any impoverishment of art diminishes the historical effectiveness of a given subject-matter. Were John Donne's love poems all lost, our understanding of the exquisite joys and honing pains of human love would be irreparably diminished.

The *Sache selbst* is a key element in Gadamer's insistence that art has a cognitive content. If a subject recognises the address of a work, it is because he or she is in a certain sense already acquainted with it. Becoming re-acquainted with the subject-matter demonstrates that the response is not merely arbitrary but indicative of the ontological circumstances of that the spectator already participates in unknowingly and that are subsequently re-engaged with knowingly through the experience of the artwork. The doubling nature of Gadamer's hermeneutic is apparent once again. However, horizons of concern invoke the question of whether *Sachen* have a specific language.

2.4.3 *Language*

The strategic centrality of language is a signature motif of Gadamer's aesthetics. His concern is not with how an 'an interpreter can capture pictorial or sculptural works in words' but with 'how it is possible to find a pointing word that ... leads to a better seeing of the work itself'.[40] Furthermore, the ability of artworks to bring things to mind and to hint at unseen meanings suggests that, in its speculative capacities, art functions essentially like a language. Yet Gadamer acknowledges that linguistic means of expression are inadequate to the task of conveying what occurs within an experience of art:

Language often seems ill-suited to express what we feel. In the face of the overwhelming presence of works of art, the task of expressing in words what they say to us seems like an infinite and hopeless undertaking . . . One says this, and then one hesitates.[41]

Two claims underwrite this scepticism: words do not readily capture the complexity of aesthetic experience; and the finitude of language itself prevents it from capturing the fullness of such experience. The experience of art always just eludes theoretical containment. This is not a difficulty with language *per se* but reflects the limited capacity of the mind to grasp the totality of its involvements. Yet these negative aspects incentivise further hermeneutical involvement with aesthetic experience. The incompleteness of any interpretation of an artwork opens the possibility of something more to be said. The temporal nature of experience and its interpretation prevents closure and leaves experience open to further interpretive approaches. The argument reinforces the claim that art and its interpretation extend the being of the subject-matters addressed.

What is meant by the notion that an artwork addresses us with a meaning? Although an agent of the linguistic turn of the twentieth century, Gadamer's reflections on language run counter to many semiotic theories. According to Weinsheimer, 'the dualism of signifier and signified has no phenomenological basis' for Gadamer, 'since in speaking we have no awareness of the world as being distinct from the word'.[42] Gadamer speaks of the perfection of the word as being the disappearance of any gap between sense and utterance. Poetry would be the 'paradigm case' of an artwork with a clear and immediate presentation of meaning. Yet this is seemingly inconsistent with notion of a work that 'stands-in-itself'. If aspects of its meaning are withheld, sense and utterance are once again separated. The word signifies something beyond itself after all. There is, in other words, a tension between Gadamer wanting to hold that the work of art and the world that comes forth within it are indivisible and saying that the world which a work invokes is larger than the work itself. Gadamer's speculative account of meaning seemingly collapses into a referential account of signs. Speculatively charged words refer to other signs or patterns of meaning, suggesting that words are self-negating signs, disappearing into what they refer to. The operation of words as representational signs seems contrary to the account of art functioning in the manner of a symbol. Closer inspection suggests that Gadamer's account of speculative meaning is presentational after all.

Does the excess of meaning which a work speculatively invokes exist apart from that which summons it? The speculative dimensions of art suggest that an artwork is indeed a host for that which lies beyond it and yet, at the same time, the transcendent dimensions of meaning (its excess of meaning) remain immanent within the work that invokes them. The presence of the transcendent only manifests itself through the work that hosts it.[43] The full resonance of a subject-matter which extends beyond any one work is discernible only through the works that host it. But, with regard to the tension between representation and presentation, the speculative charge of artworks does indeed suggest that they function as representational signs always referring beyond the given meaning. Yet this is only another way of saying that, onto-logically, artworks functions as symbols. Considered as a referential sign, what the artwork refers to is not a world independent of the sign but another set of signs. Such configurations of meaning may mean more than the signs that invoke them but that excess is inherent in those signs. The signs which refer speculatively to other dimensions of meaning also function symbolically: the other horizons of meaning invoked are immanent within the work's autonomy. As a hermeneu-tical host, the artwork holds that which refers beyond itself within itself.[44] There is no inconsistency, therefore, between the affirmation of art's autonomy and the insistence that artworks point beyond themselves. Furthermore, the sign/symbol distinction is fundamental to Gadamer's ontological deconstruction of aesthetic consciousness. Signs are associated with the activity of the spectorial subject, whilst symbols are themselves presentational powers. This suggests that signs are assembled according to the will of the subject, whereas the meaning of a symbol asserts itself over and against the subject's intentions and expectations.

Gadamer's appeal to linguisticality as the foundation for aesthetic experience suggests a problem. If aesthetics is to be subsumed within hermeneutics because it concerns meaning, and if language is a vehicle of meaning, is aesthetics to be consumed by language after all? To engage with artworks discursively is to bring generalisations about a work to bear, placing them in a wider context of associations. The movement to the broader horizon of generalisation also returns the spectator to the particular, since generalisation enables an understanding of what is singular about a work, locating it within a broader background. This double hermeneutic movement is highly characteristic of Gadamer's aesthetical hermeneutics. It recognises that the cognitive dimension of aesthetic experience is, like all linguistic experience, both centrifugal and centripetal in nature. Yet the question remains: is not the passage from the immediacy of the given artwork to theoretical contemplations about its subject-matter an instance of moving from the particular given quality of a work to a more abstract level of reflection about its subject-matter? Does not the contemplative movement away from the work betray its particularity and suggest that the sense of a work lies beyond it, that is, in its concept or idea? For Gadamer, it is part of an intense experience that it should seek the right words for its nature. Experience endeavours to bring itself into words. These words will, by virtue of their semantic associations, place the experience in a wider context (the centrifugal) and at the same time these words will, because of their poetic capacity for singularity, make the experience clearer and more distinct (the centripetal). This suggests that Gadamer is not applying a linguistic or hermeneutic method to aesthetic experience but seeking to expose the hermeneutical movement from part to whole *within* aesthetic experience. In other words, the claim that aesthetics should be taken up within hermeneutics is not an attempt to reduce aesthetics to another idiom. It announces an endeavour to articulate the hermeneutic dynamic of aesthetic experience itself. In the essay 'Word and Picture' he expresses sympathy with Schleiermacher: 'I hate all theory that does not grow out of practice'.[45] To conclude, if aesthetic experience is hermeneutical, in that artworks speculatively illuminate meanings beyond what is immediately disclosed, hermeneutical experience should equally be taken up by aesthetics, in that subject-matters manifest their presence only in the singular and particular.

2.4.4 *Tradition*

The reliance of art and language upon communicative conventions ties them to the question of tradition. Gadamer's appeal to tradition is a direct consequence of his critique of aesthetic subjectivism. The experience of art has its ground not in the preferences of subjective consciousness but in the objective consciousness shaping powers of tradition. What binds us to a tradition is not a misplaced conservatism but the questions that a canon of work asks of us and against which we define ourselves.

The question of tradition is one of the most controversial within Gadamer's philosophy. The controversy arises because of the way he establishes individual and collective learning on the acquisition of contingently accrued experiences (*Bildung*) and practices rather than upon any methodological norm. He asserts the ontological priority of acquired pre-understanding and tacit knowledge over methodological consciousness. Contrary to the Kantian version of the *sensus communis* as something to aspire to, being rooted in a common set of practices and evaluations is for Gadamer a condition of spectorial activity. For

Habermas, Gadamer appears to favour inherited and, hence, individuating prejudices in preference to the collectivising tendency of critical method. Kant, too, appears to vilify tradition. If all human beings share the same inherent rational capacities, the question arises as to why human communities have consistently endeavoured to aggressively assert and differentiate themselves. For many *philosophes*, the particularising influence of religious and historical practices nurtures destructive mythologies concerning 'the chosen people'. Such divisiveness can, it is argued, be countered by appeals to reason to displace such regionalism with an appeal to a universal community of rational agents. Gadamer's aesthetics exposes and opposes the Enlightenment prejudice against prejudice.

His argument suggests that the liberating and universalising aspects of reason marginalise and chastise the culturally different and the historically particular as divisive and irrational.[46] The unqualified hypostatisation of reason and its methods has the unfortunate consequence of condemning as methodologically groundless the valuations that ordinary linguistic and experiential practices are based on. The issue is not the exasperation the Socratic insistence upon the justification of practical values can cause (since no practice can be theoretically objectified in full) but the frustration of having to articulate how and why it is that a practitioner comes to 'know' instinctively what to do in a challenging situation or emergency. The 'feel for practice' cannot be brought before the 'tribunal of reason'.

Gadamer is not unsympathetic to Nietzsche, who rejects the claim that humanity is shaped by external necessity. Our existence within the world and our place within it are, metaphysically speaking, utterly contingent. If metaphysical necessity does not govern human practices, why should we even ask for a methodological grounding when language has neither required nor functioned with such a licence? Like Wilhelm Dilthey before him, Gadamer insists that nothing justifies and gives meaning to life other than life itself. This is not the invocation of an action-based nihilism, for life does not occur in a vacuum. Creatures such as humans that have no predetermined essence survive only by remembering what has worked well in a practice, and by constantly testing the remembered against contemporary needs and circumstances. A constant tension exists between acquired experience, the need to stabilise its lessons and the need to question and thereby destabilise the tried and the tested against the demands of the tried and tested. Expressive practices depend upon an inheritance of insight and valuation. They depend on accrued learning and experience. Such observations agitate Gadamer's critics who see in the unreflective acceptance of the given an irresponsibly conservative privileging of the received, and a wilful blindness to possible repressive or exclusionary practices within inherited modes of operation. In response to such scepticism, it must be acknowledged that inherited practices can, logically speaking, have negative entailments but a commitment to tradition is not a commitment to remaining the same.

Traditions incapable of change risk becoming outmoded. Neither are they founded on fixed identities. Vibrant religious and artistic traditions constantly debate their aim and direction. Traditions that subject their self-understanding to critique constitute, to use MacIntyre's phrase, continuities of conflict. The importance of transmitted understanding is not its historical provenance but how it sustains and engulfs us in a community of debate. The self is not positioned over and against tradition. To the contrary, Williams argues, 'To be aware of the self is to be aware of something that bears the marks of otherness, not of a pristine independent subjectivity. My intellection is – in the Germanic phrase – "always already" addressed, impressed, illuminated and precisely by the traditions I find myself thrown within'.[47] The Cartesian aspiration to subject all received judgements to sceptical examination is, in Gadamer's view, nihilistic. The project is implausible; the range and depth of pre-understanding are so extensive as to be untheorisable. To condemn pre-understanding because it cannot be methodologically grounded devalues the very insights upon which any world orientation and creative practice depend. It is not that these insights are intrinsically valuable: they operate as way-markers along the journeys of understanding they enable. Debate and dialogue in practices enable participants to move on, to widen and transform acquired experience and, indeed, to bring many of the presuppositions of a traditional practice into critical review. The pre-understanding of tradition is the condition of hermeneutic movement and learning. As Richard Sennett observes, the lessons of experience emerge through a dialogue between tacit knowledge and explicit critique.[48]

Movement and development are intrinsic to the German word for tradition. *Überlieferung* has the active connotation of both transmitting and handing something on. What a tradition transmits from age to age are questions and issues. The importance of canonical works is not that they are peerless exemplars of an idiom but that they raise difficulties in an exemplary way. Traditions can check their self-understanding against their own historical projections.[49] A commitment to tradition is not a commitment to academic antiquarianism. It is, essentially, a commitment to a field of debate. Tradition is a resource and a provocation for thinking and creativity. Consider *Psalmlieder*, Peter Cornelius's astonishing adaption of Bach; or *Offertorium*, Sofia Gubaidulina's response to the *Ricercar* of Anton Webern, which is in turn his answer to Bach's own *Musical Offering*. Tradition is not only talked of but talked *with*.[50] Whereas sameness is the currency of a conservative conception of tradition, instability, questioning and the challenge of otherness are the drivers of Gadamer's more dialogical concept of tradition.

It has been argued against Gadamer that his revaluation of tradition does not really bring its content to a point of critical reflection. He acknowledges that, like any other temporal phenomenon, not all of its vistas can be adequately thematised or articulated. This does not mean, however, that tradition is beyond critical appraisal. Traditions can, as Wolfhart Pannenberg argues, check their normative assumptions against their self-projections. Other critics suggest that Gadamer's approach to tradition and aesthetics is overtly classical in its preoccupation with forms that maintain continuity through time rather than radically alter themselves. It does not allow for those radical intrusions or revolutionary interjections which alter the perceptual paradigm of an age. The charge overlooks not only Gadamer's embrace of Heidegger's quite radical phenomenological reworking of the classical philosophical tradition but also the requirement that for one paradigm to replace another there must be a certain relation between them. One must address an absence or a lack within the other. Without a degree of continuity within tradition, any radical emergence would lack critical bearing upon the received. Traditions are, unquestionably, continuities of practice but are driven by on-going debate about how their fundamental questions are best negotiated.[51] Furthermore, because practices are in a certain sense unknown to themselves (their creative potential is, historically speaking, never fully determined), they require *engagement* with the other precisely in order to test and extend their expectancies.

Nietzsche once remarked that we cannot understand an entity that does not have a history. A practice that had no internal conflicts or challenges would be a practice without history. It would endlessly repeat itself. What gives a practice or tradition its history (or, indeed, its histories) is precisely its encounters with the strange, the foreign and the new. In other words, the *continuity* of a practice (the history of its transformations) is provided by the provocative power of the new and not by the repetition of the old. The differential of the new is the proper location of productivity.[52] It is the new which prompts a practice or a tradition to transform the possibilities within itself.

2.5 THE 'SUBSTANCE' OF AESTHETIC SUBJECTIVITY

Gadamer's determination to reveal the cognitive content of aesthetic experience requires exposing the ontological grounding of subjectivity. To approach artworks solely on the basis of subjective responses to them or to read them only in terms of an artist's intentionality is, for Gadamer, always to miss the point. Hermeneutically speaking, the philosophical focus should be on the ontological fourfold that informs subjective experience and guides its experience, that is, play, symbol, language and tradition. This points to a speculative refiguring of aesthetic subjectivity in which 'we discover in all that is subjective the substantiality that determines it'.[53] We will later suggest that subjective responses to art are the epistemological mode of ontological interactions related to the fourfold mentioned above. In *The Relevance of the Beautiful* Gadamer elucidates substance as follows: 'substance' is understood as something that supports us, although it does not emerge into the light of reflective consciousness; it is something that can never be fully articulated, although it is absolutely necessary for the existence of all clarity, consciousness, expression and communication.[54]

Uncovering the ontological foundations of aesthetic experience does not undermine the primacy Gadamer gives to art's immediate address. The aim is to demonstrate the cognitive legitimacy of subjective experience by revealing how aesthetic experience is both involved in something larger than itself and, indeed, reflects (*speculum*) that larger actuality within itself. The ability of aesthetic experience to express trans-individual phenomenological structures and social imaginaries explains what is meant by substance and Gadamer's speculative attitude towards it. Gadamer's aesthetics is properly concerned with *experiencing* what underlies its more abstract concepts. This is not a matter of naming or describing the reality which manifests itself in aesthetic experience but of trying to say something about the experience an individual has of it.

2.6 SUMMARY

This chapter has examined the key arguments that characterise Gadamer's ontological deconstruction of the subjective dimensions of aesthetic consciousness. His reflections on what makes the experience of art possible gather around several signature arguments concerning the dialogical nature of art experience. To articulate the 'event' that is art, they draw famous analogies between the nature of play, the festival, the symbol and language. Each element is presentational in both the positive and negative sense, the positive bringing something into being and the negative making the presence of the withheld manifest. The capacity to bring something forth is also a feature of Gadamer's innovative renovation of tradition. In addition, the purpose of his reflections upon the experience of art is not to direct us to something beyond the artwork but to make us aware of what is at play it within it. This, in Gadamer's mind, reasserts the priority of meaning over the experience of aesthetic qualities.

In Chapter 1 of this study we concerned ourselves with the broad intellectual context of Gadamer's reform of aesthetics. In this chapter we have attended to the specific operational structures of his key arguments as manifested in his discussion of the objective ontological fourfold which sustains the substantiality of subjective consciousness. We have seen that the principal concern of Gadamer's meditation upon art is to bring attention to the transformative movement within aesthetic experience. It is to his understated account of aesthetic attention that we shall now turn. This will bring us to one of the major tensions in Gadamer's thinking about art. How is it possible to reconcile the interested nature of phenomenological experience with the disinterested nature of aesthetic experience? This question has a bearing not just upon discerning the nature of aesthetics but also upon how the transformative capacity of the humanities is best understood.

NOTES

1. Hans-Georg Gadamer, 'Aesthetics and Hermeneutics', in *The Gadamer Reader*, ed. R. E. Palmer (Evanston: Northwestern University Press, 2007), p. 126.
2. The earlier parts of this chapter are a reworked version of some of my essay 'Gadamer's Aesthetics', in *The Stanford Encyclopedia of Philosophy* (2007): http://plato.stanford.edu./entries/gadamer-aesthetics/
3. Hans-Georg Gadamer, *Kunst als Aussage, Gesammelte Werke*, Band 8 (Tübingen: Mohr Siebeck, 1993), p. 374.
4. Hans-Georg Gadamer, 'Classical and Philosophical Hermeneutics', in *The Gadamer Reader*, p. 70.
5. Hans-Georg Gadamer, 'The Universality of the Hermeneutic Problem', in *The Gadamer Reader*, p. 79. The priority of meaning over formal aesthetic impact is emphasised by the observation that the importance of aesthetic qualities relates to the question of whether they guide us to and enhance or distract from and obscure the meanings communicated.
6. Ibid.

7. Hans-Georg Gadamer, *The Relevance of the Beautiful* (London: Cambridge University Press, 1986), p. 130.
8. Ibid.
9. Gadamer, 'Classical and Philosophical Hermeneutics', p. 66.
10. Hans-Georg Gadamer, 'Autobiographical Reflections', in *The Gadamer Reader*, p. 25.
11. Gadamer, 'Classical and Philosophical Hermeneutics', p. 66.
12. Gadamer, *The Relevance of the Beautiful*, p. 69.
13. Ibid., p. 146.
14. Ibid., p. 71.
15. Ibid., p. 146.
16. Ibid.
17. Hans-Georg Gadamer, *Philosophical Hermeneutics*, trans. David E. Linge (Berkeley: University of California Press, 1976), p. 93.
18. Gadamer, 'Classical and Philosophical Hermeneutics', p. 67.
19. Gadamer, *Philosophical Hermeneutics*, p. 98.
20. Gadamer, 'Classical and Philosophical Hermeneutics', p. 102.
21. TM, p. 302.
22. Gadamer, *The Relevance of the Beautiful*, p. 78.
23. Friedrich Schiller, *On the Aesthetic Education of Man*, ed. and trans. E. M. Wilkinson and L. A. Willoughby (Oxford: Clarendon Press, 1982).
24. Gadamer, *The Relevance of the Beautiful*, p. 23.
25. TM, pp. 92, 98.
26. Ibid., p. 25.
27. Ibid., p. 103.
28. Christopher Lawn, *Gadamer: A Guide for the Perplexed* (London: Continuum, 2006), p. 91.
29. Gadamer, *The Relevance of the Beautiful*, p. 40. See also Josef Pieper, *In Tune with the World: A Theory of Festivity* (South Bend: St Augustine's Press, 1999).
30. Gadamer, *The Relevance of the Beautiful*, p. 60.
31. Ibid., p. 63.
32. Ibid., p. 31.
33. Ibid.
34. Ibid., p. 32.
35. TM, p. 356.
36. Ibid., p. 487.
37. Gadamer, *Philosophical Hermeneutics*, p. 226.
38. See Rowan Williams, *Grace and Necessity: Reflections on Art and Love* (London: Morehouse, 2006), p. 40.
39. TM, p. 89.
40. Gadamer, 'The Art Work in Word and Image', in *The Gadamer Reader*, p. 195.
41. TM, p. 401.

42. Joel Weinsheimer, *Philosophical Hermeneutics and Literary Theory* (New Haven: Yale University Press, 1991), p. 162.

43. Heidegger's argument concerning the temple in the essay 'The Origin of the Artwork' constructs a similar juxtaposition. The destiny or vocation of a people is transcendent to the individuals that constitute it. The temple neither pictures nor represents; it facilitates (hosts) a space whereby its presence becomes manifest. See Martin Heidegger, 'The Origin of the Artwork', in *Poetry, Language and Thought*, trans. Albert Hofstadter (New York: Harper, 1971), p. 42.

44. On the distinction between sign and symbol, the reader is referred to Joel Weinsheimer's excellent discussion of the topic in his book *Philosophical Hermeneutics and Literary Theory*, p. 162.

45. Gadamer, 'Word and Image: So True, So Full of Being', in *Kunst als Aussage*, p. 374.

46. A similar charge is made by Leszek Kolokowski against utilitarianism (only that which is measurable is valuable). See his *Positivist Philosophy: From Hume to the Vienna Circle* (London: Penguin, 1972), pp. 92–108.

47. Williams, *Grace and Necessity*, p. 24.

48. Richard Sennett, *The Craftsman* (London: Penguin, 2008), p. 51.

49. See Wolfhart Pannenberg, *Theology and the Philosophy of Science* (London: Darton, Longman and Todd, 1976), p. 197.

50. Don Paterson, *Orpheus: A Version of Rainer Maria Rilke* (London: Faber and Faber, 2006). See introductory essay.

51. Alasdair MacIntyre, *After Virtue* (London: Duckworth, 1993), p. 222.

52. Theodor Adorno, *Negative Dialectics*, trans. E. B. Ashton (London: Routledge and Kegan Paul, 1973), p. 38.

53. TM, p. 302.

54. Gadamer, *The Relevance of the Beautiful*, p. 78.

3. *Aesthetic Attentiveness and the Question of Distanciation*

attentive: 1. Concentrating; paying attention, observant awake, 2. Assiduously polite. Courteous, courtly, gracious accommodating, 3. Mindful, carefully, alert, heedful, assiduous.[1]

3.1 INTRODUCTION

Gadamer's reflection on the experience of art is vexed by a tension between the existential interests that dominate his phenomenological account of experience and his rejection of Kantian disinterestedness in aesthetics. How can Gadamer defend his phenomenological approach to experience and demonstrate how art supports its cognitive concerns, and yet proclaim the autonomy of art without losing its connectedness to the everyday world? Having examined Gadamer's critique of subjectivist aesthetics, we suggest that his approach to aesthetic attentiveness offers a persuasive reconciliation of the interested and the disinterested. The reconciliation is one of Gadamer's greatest unremarked contributions to contemporary aesthetics. Aesthetic attentiveness is no unthinking receptiveness but a complex interactive reflective practice capable of transforming understanding.

Gadamer's need to articulate the nature of aesthetic attention was stated at the end of the last chapter. He does not need a special hermeneutic method to access what is withheld within a work but a better account of contemplative engagement with the work. Being attentive to what an artwork says, learning to discern its enigmatic quality and acquiring a sensitivity to its speculative resonances are not instances of Gadamer submitting aesthetic experience to an externally imposed theory or method. However, the question of how aesthetic attention is understood is not directly approached in Gadamer's *magnum opus*. This chapter addresses it more fully.

The nature of attentiveness is important to Gadamer's reflections about art as it draws out the hermeneutic dynamics of aesthetic experience itself. Yet the theme poses two paradoxes. If aesthetics concerns the disinterested whilst phenomenology articulates the interested, is a phenomenological aesthetics a contradiction in terms? How can aesthetic experience embrace the particularities of an artwork and at the same time reflect upon the ideational content of that work's subject-matter? Aesthetic attention conceived within the parameters of Gadamer's thought can resolve these paradoxes. Aesthetic attention entails a hermeneutic poise, adopting a distance of regard that sees more closely.[2] Furthermore, these arguments extend his critique of the subjectivism of aesthetic response. Aesthetic attentiveness demonstrates that the receptiveness associated with aesthetic reception is not grounded in subjective preference but in subjects' participation in enabling cultural horizons that shape their being. Before we elaborate these claims, let us consider the broader issues which call for articulation regarding the nature of aesthetic attentiveness.

3.2 AESTHETICS AND THE DISINTERESTED

Gadamer's hermeneutical aesthetics is riven by a creative tension that marks it out as a *Zwischenspiel* (a play of the in-between). Baumgarten's initial description of aesthetics as 'sensible knowledge' frames the apparent contradiction: how can there be principled and unchanging knowledge of the indistinct and confused?[3] Kant circumnavigates the problem by insisting that the principled and unchanging lies not in the object of knowledge but in the way it is known within the forms of a subject's judgement. The price of Kant's avoidance of Baumgarten's conundrum is high. He denies that an aesthetic object can be brought under a clear concept and be equated with (in his terms) knowledge proper. It places the grounds of aesthetic judgement in subjective consciousness alone, a proposal which, as we have seen, Gadamer vehemently contends. Yet, Kant insists, though an aesthetic object is given sensibly – that is, subjectively – it is possible to adopt a disinterested posture towards it and take pleasure in it *for its own sake*. In Kant, aesthetic experience and the disinterested become inseparable and it is this equation that Gadamer attacks.

Is a phenomenological aesthetics a contradiction in terms? It depends upon how aesthetics and phenomenology are understood. The Kantian high canon emphatically associates the perception of the aesthetic object with disinterestedness. Taste is the faculty of estimating an object by delight or aversion *apart from any interest*.[4] Every interest vitiates the judgement of taste and robs it of its impartiality.[5] Aesthetic judgement

> is not based on any inclination of the subject (or on any other deliberate interest), but the subject feels himself completely free in respect of the liking which he accords to the object, he can find as reason for his delight no personal conditions to which his own subjective self might alone be party.[6]

Within the history of philosophical aesthetics these remarks are of incomparable importance. They point to both the incontestable value of striving to see things in their own right, free from the distorting influence of obvious prejudice and the discipline of allowing our attention to be held by a subject-matter. Sustained watchfulness is central to Gadamer's conception of aesthetic contemplation as 'tarrying' with a work. Nevertheless, the epistemological framework of Kant's comments poses a difficulty for Gadamer.

Despite his opposition to Kant's aesthetics, Gadamer's avowal of the evidentiary nature of aesthetic experience commits him (contrary to his own self-understanding) to a form of disinterestedness. A purely instrumentalist orientation excludes seeing utilitarian objects aesthetically. Whoever views an aircraft solely as mode of transport will be blind to the sculptural relations between wing, tail and fuselage. Such aesthetic disinterestedness is not alien to Gadamer's thought. It is implicit in Heidegger's distinction between *Zuhandenheit* and *Vorhandenheit*, which Gadamer adopts.[7] In the world which is to hand, we take for granted the purposes and acquired wisdom ingrained in a knife's handle: we fail to see the cooking knife *as* a knife. We just reach for it (unthinkingly) whenever a kitchen task calls for it. The tool is a vehicle of embodied intentionality. So long as an ends-orientated reasoning dominates consciousness, the world of accumulated experience and practical wisdom embodied in the knife's handle will be veiled from us. When we fail *to see* the tool as it is, that is, as a specific item of equipment with highly particular characteristics, we fail to perceive it aesthetically as an object in its own right, resonant with the practical insights which brought it into being. For the early Heidegger, mistaken expectancies or frustrated intentions initiate the shift from *Zuhandenheit* to *Vorhandenheit*. This alteration of consciousness can reveal the implicit interests of our practical world, disclosing insight and meaning not perceived before. Not taking such tools for granted enables us to appreciate them aesthetically, that is, as things both standing in their own right within their own world and as responding to that world. Heidegger inhabits Gadamer's mind when he celebrates the capacity of artworks to assert themselves contrary to our expectancies.

Aesthetic experience can force a change of disposition towards everyday things, allowing us to see them for their own rather than our sakes. This restates our problem.

Gadamer's commitment to aesthetics involves a commitment to a form of disinterestedness. However, the term has philosophical associations which conflict with his phenomenological loyalties. Gadamer follows Schiller in regarding Kant's philosophy of art as lifeless. If the aesthetic were actually concerned only with those themes that we might be truly disinterested in – geometric shapes or numerical symmetry – art would have no significant cognitive content regarding those concerns that define us as human beings; birth, death, love and loss. Gadamer insists that art does address these interests and can transform our understanding of them. The 'transformation into structure' argument contends that art's compelling power lies in its ability to clarify aspects of our everyday concerns which, without its intervention, would remain unresolved.[8] Unlike life, art offers meanings 'with nothing out of place'.[9] It is precisely because of the compelling interests which shape our human horizon that we are susceptible to art's claims. Gadamer's position is plainly opposed to Kant's but he requires an account of the aesthetic which allows the artwork to stand in its own right *and* challenge our interests. Gadamer's hermeneutical aesthetics does not resolve this tension but manages to present its contraries in a new way. Gadamer needs to reconcile the claim that art has a spontaneity and autonomy that is not irreducible to perspectival interests alone with the argument that it is precisely because we have existential and cultural interests that we are vulnerable to art's cognitive claims. The doctrine of aesthetic attention offers a compelling resolution between the interested and the disinterested. It emerges from a critique of aesthetic consciousness and differentiation.

Gadamer's unswerving belief in art's cognitive content dominates his critique of Kantian aesthetics. Kant, he claims, denies 'taste any significance as knowledge' and 'reduces [the] *sensus communis* to a subjective principle'.[10] Taste 'imparts no knowledge of the [its] object' and is concerned only with the inward pleasure associated with the free interplay of imagination and understanding.[11] By establishing the possibility of 'communication of feeling without concepts',[12] Kant's *sensus communis* may lead aesthetics away from the purely subjective but only to point it toward a community of subjects based on the contingent possibility of shareable pleasures. Kant allegedly subjectivises the *sensus communis* and fails to recognise its ontological grounding in tradition and, hence, its cognitive orientations. In consequence, this deprives both the artwork and its grounding traditions of practice of any cognitive status: 'Is there to be no knowledge in art?'[13] Gadamer fears the nihilism in a negative reply.

If subjective consciousness is judged to be without cognitive significance, it is because scientific knowledge has been valorised as *the* legitimate model of knowledge. This condemns insights acquired through social practice as unfounded subjective prejudice or collective bias. What Michael Polyani describes as 'tacit knowledge' (those enabling stocks of cultural reference laid down by virtue of practising a given form of life) is formally marginalised.[14] This demonises accrued 'know-how' as superstition or, worse, as meaningless. For Gadamer, however, artworks have a trans-subjective legitimacy precisely because they are ontologically grounded in received historical conventions and social practices. Yet, the challenge which Kant's aesthetics poses for Gadamer's hermeneutical operation is enormous. The epistemological orientation of Kant's aesthetic threatens to undermine the ontological foundations upon which Gadamer's account of art's cognitive legitimacy depends. Gadamer cannot prove Kant wrong without assuming the premises of the argument he contests. What he can do is question whether the Kantian model of aesthetic consciousness (i.e. a subject taking pleasure in a beautiful object for its own sake) provides a plausible route to understanding art's content. Can art be understood in terms of aesthetic consciousness?[15] Is the aesthetic approach to a work of art the appropriate one? Or, is what Kant calls aesthetic consciousness an abstraction?

Gadamer suggests that, 'in order to do justice to art, aesthetics must go beyond itself and surrender the purity of the aesthetic'.[16] The stance is emphatic. He refers to the impotence of the subjective[17] and to the need to transcend subjective consciousness in order to discern its ground. Gadamer's strategic hermeneutic mission statement refers to the need to discover in all that is subjective the substantiality that determines it.[18] The difference between Gadamer's and Kant's aesthetic orientation rests on contrasting conceptions of mind.

Gadamer rejects Kant's doctrine of sovereign subjects who internally generate the laws and forms of their own judgements. He displaces the Kantian position with a Hegelian model of consciousness, in which a subject's awareness is *not* transparent to the subject but requires the other and otherness, be they cultural or historical, to bring it to a dialogical form of self-awareness. This vision of subjective consciousness being awoken to itself by the provocation of the other that is beyond its immediate grasp prompts Gadamer's strategic question: is the aesthetic (i.e. subjectivist) approach to a work of art the appropriate one? Gadamer's response is unequivocal: aesthetic subjectivity as envisaged by Kant is a rarefied form of consciousness which, because of an overestimation of its epistemic autonomy, has both devalued and dulled its awareness of the ontological preconditions which make both art's expressive content and, indeed, its own selfhood possible. The charge that aesthetic subjectivity is a rarefied form of consciousness is elaborated within Gadamer's strategic distinction between two conceptualisations of experience: *Erlebnis* and *Erfahrung*.

3.3 THE AESTHETICS OF *ERLEBNIS* VERSUS THOSE *ERFAHRUNG*

For Gadamer 'the experience of art is an experience of meaning' and is, therefore, to be absorbed within hermeneutics. This distinguishes Gadamer's position from descriptions of the aesthetic as offering a special kind of pleasure. In *The Relevance of the Beautiful* Gadamer suggests that the onlooker who indulges in aesthetic or cultural enjoyment for its own sake succumbs to escapism. An encounter with the work of art is regarded as a liberation from the pressures of reality.[19] This divorces Gadamer from any *Erlebnis-Ästhetik* in which artworks are proclaimed the site of intense momentary experiences, to be enjoyed independent of their cognitive content. Such aesthetic hedonism severs the individual observer from communal networks of meaning capable of illuminating his or her personal experience. For Gadamer, art stands witness to the fact that understanding always occurs through understanding something other than the self, and not through the contemplation of inward states.

Gadamer's critique of aestheticism turns on a distinction between *Erlebnis* and *Erfahrung*, both German words for the term 'experience' but with very different connotations. *Erlebnis*, a term favoured by Wilhelm Dilthey, emphasises the distinctness and singularity of the perceived moment. *Erfahrung*, preferred by Gadamer, emphasises the cumulative and formative character of experience, as when one speaks of an 'experienced' artist or musician. The developmental, open-ended and on-going nature of experience is emphasised with the latter, whereas *Erlebnis* stresses the intensity of the lived moment. *Erlebnis* is associated with the qualities of sensation and their refinement; the education of taste and discernment does not reflect on the significance or meaning of the objects of sensation, only on their qualitative nature.[20] *Erfahrung*, by contrast, implies an involvement in the meaning and significance of what is experienced.

Gadamer's critique of *Erlebnis* extends arguments expressed by Heidegger in the epilogue to his essay 'The Origin of the Work of Art'.

Almost from the time when specialised thinking about art and the artist began, this thought was called aesthetic. Aesthetics takes the work of art as an object, the object of *aisthesis*, of sensuous apprehension in the wide sense. Today we call this apprehension experience. The way in which man experiences art is supposed to give information about its nature. Experience is the source that is standard not only for art appreciation and enjoyment, but also for artistic creation. *Everything is an experience. Yet perhaps experience is the element in which art dies.* The dying occurs so slowly that it takes a few centuries.[21]

What concerns Gadamer about subjectivist aestheticism is its blindness to the hermeneutical dimensions of its experience. In consequence, everything given to it becomes an object for its diversion and consumption. This mode of consciousness neither feels that it is shaped by what addresses it, nor that its being is implicated in what is revealed to it. Gadamer's critique seeks to prevent art and our experience of it from being turned into hypothecated possessions, a falsification which neutralises art's transformative dimension. *Erlebnis* is judged to be a mode of experience in which 'art dies', whereas *Erfahrung* is considered to be that experiential mode in which art thrives. *Erlebnis* embraces the momentary, whilst *Erfahrung* brings forth the momentous.

Erlebnis has clear subjectivist connotations. Even Dilthey struggled with the subjectivist connotations of the term and sought in his hermeneutic to overcome them.[22] It could be argued that a sensationalist approach to art has the virtue of by-passing convention and expectancy. However, apart from whether there can be an innocent eye, Gadamer insists that such 'living in the moment' leads to experiential fragmentation and relativism:

> The work of art is only an empty form, a mere nodal point in the possible variety of aesthetic experiences (*Erlebnisse*), and the aesthetic object exists in these experiences alone. As is evident, absolute discontinuity – i.e. the disintegration of the unity of the aesthetic object into the multiplicity of experiences – is the necessary consequence of an aesthetics of *Erlebnis*.

Gadamer goes on to note that, following Luckas's idea, Oskar Becker:

> has stated outright that in terms of time the work exists only in a minute (i.e. now); it is now this work and now it is this work no longer. Actually, that is logical. Basing aesthetics on experience leads to an absolute series of points, which annihilates the unity of the work of art, the identity of the artist with himself, and the identity of the person understanding enjoying the work of art.[23]

Referring to Kierkegaard, Gadamer claims that aestheticism reveals 'how desperate and untenable existence is in pure immediacy and discontinuity'.[24] He challenges the epistemological presuppositions that the experiencing subject is inviolate and that artworks are given over to the subject as objects solely for entertainment, distraction and consumption. For Gadamer, the encounter with art is valuable precisely because it subjects subjects to something other than themselves and their states: 'Our experience of the aesthetic too is a mode of self-understanding. Self-understanding always occurs through understanding something other than the self.'[25] This is Gadamer's fundamental objection to aestheticism: aestheticism's wilful refusal to consider anything other than the *qualities* of sensation blinds itself to the transformative horizons of meaning that underwrite the subject's very being. The subject becomes saturated in 'the absorbing presence of the momentary aesthetic impression'.[26]

What makes Gadamer's critique of aesthetic consciousness so powerful is its insistence that profound experience is not momentary in nature. Were it a genuine characteristic of aesthetic experience, we could only say that a work exists in this 'now', is, and then is no longer.[27] Were this so, the temporal coherence of the work and of the person seeking to understand it would be destroyed. The continuity of meaning characteristic both of an artwork and of a hermeneutic subject depends upon the ability of a community of spectators to bring such moments into relation with others, past and present.

Gadamer's differentiation between momentary aesthetic sensationalism and the continuities of aesthetically apprehended meaning has other implications. To think that the experience of the new is equivalent to the immediacy of the 'instantaneous flash of genius' is also to treat the new as a passing diversion. If so, the new possesses the power of fragmentation, destroying the continuity of aesthetic experience, in Gadamer's hermeneutical sense of the term. For substantive change to take place within a practice, genuine exchange with another perspective is required. As Gadamer remarks, 'self-understanding always occurs through understanding something other than the self, and [this] includes the unity and integrity of the other'.[28] Moments of transformative newness maybe momentary in their occasional emergence but can be momentous in their implication. They are a result of an engagement with other practices or traditions that has, in consequence, become decisively different to itself. Newness requires engagement with traditional or different practices in order to acquire a comparative sense of its inherent distinctiveness, implications and possibilities.

It is clear that the aesthetic does refer to the sensual, but what if it were to refer to *Erlebnisse* alone? Extending the discussion of this question from Chapter 1, the meaning of aesthetic experience would be weakened by reducing its scope of reference to the sensually momentary.[29] Without the capacity to transcend perceptual immediacy, aesthetic experience is rendered fragmentary and is prevented from contributing to the continuities of meaning which shape self-understanding. An exclusively sensual aesthetic would be an anaesthetic. Closing the differential space between the sensual and the ideational renders impossible the movement upon which understanding and its transformational capacities rest.

Gadamer's objections to *Erlebnis-Ästhetik* stem from the phenomenological empiricism that he derives from Heidegger. Being-in-the-world is saturated with the pre-understandings of *Dasein*. Rarely do we confront brute sensation: because of our received interpretative dispositions, things are already imbued with significance. We do not hear unpleasant noises and then notice a baby crying. Understanding depends upon the given fact that we are already moving within currents of meaning. Phenomenologically speaking, aestheticism's appeal to *Erlebnisse* invokes an abstraction, an experience of things stripped of meaning, leaving only a qualitative residue of pleasant (though inconsequential) sensations. The substantive charge against the *Erlebnis-Ästhetik* is that, because of its privileging of the sensual, it severs the objective connections between an artwork and the hermeneutical world upon which its cognitive significance depends.

Gadamer does not doubt that the work of art and its importance for us relate to what he terms the hermeneutic imperative of continuity:

> We recognise that even the phenomenon of art imposes an ineluctable task on existence, namely to achieve that continuity of self-understanding which alone can support human existence, despite the demands of the absorbing presence of the momentary aesthetic impression.[30]

Later, he observes:

> There remains a continuity of meaning which links the work of art with the existing world and from which even the alienated consciousness of a cultured society never quite detaches itself.[31]

Gadamer does not suppose that life has an intrinsic meaning. His thinking accords with Dilthey's conviction that:

> Every expression has a meaning in so far as it is a sign which signifies or points to something that is part of life. Life does not mean anything other than itself. There is nothing in it which points to a meaning outside it.[32]

For Gadamer, the meaningfulness of existence resides in its relationality, in how different aspects of being illuminate and inform others in ever-shifting patterns. It is not so much a particular symmetry that is significant but how changing relations establish and transform emergent continuities of significance. Such alterations trace the self-forming process of *Bildung*, the weave of which shapes the narratives of self-understanding. It is not that life reflects or re-presents a set meaning but rather that participation in life, with its joys and risks, gives rise to meaning and vulnerability to it. This establishes a telling contrast between *Erlebnis* and *Erfahrung*.

Erlebnis is touristic in nature. Foreign places are visited, exotic dishes consumed, not because they are vital to a person's religious or cultural persuasion but because they are regarded as sites to be seen and 'collected'. Such a traveller neither changes in outlook nor sensitivity but just becomes heavier with accumulated new sensations. No framework of meaning is challenged, none is exchanged.[33] *Erfahrung*, however, demands immersion in a (new) *Lebensform*.

Gadamer's commitment to hermeneutic continuity is not an apologetics for the essentialist supposition that life and tradition have a single meaning. Life interests operate variously and not always consistently.[34] Traditions are, in MacIntyre's phrase, 'continuities of conflict', which do not require complete internal unanimity.[35] Continuity, for Gadamer, has little to do with fixity but with movement and transformation. The ability of a work to transform understanding demands that it be related to those horizons of meaning which shape our being. The continuity to be defended is not a continuity of view but a continuity of relatedness. The substantive charge against the *Erlebnis-Ästhetik* is, then, that, because of its privileging of the sensual, it severs the objective connections between an artwork and the hermeneutical world upon which its cognitive significance depends. It does not allow us to see 'the world at work' within its disclosures.[36]

The foregoing argument strongly implies that an *Erlebnis-Ästhetik* destroys what is conventionally meant by art. By regarding artworks as significant on the basis of the intensified sensations they produce, the argument concedes that it is not the content of art that is important but the degree to which and the kind of sensation it generates. By focusing on a private condition, the *Erlebnis-Ästhetik* divorces the onlooker from the public horizons which inform a work and are central to his or her self-understanding. Here, Heidegger's remark takes on its full weight: 'Everything is an experience. Yet perhaps experience is the element in which art dies.'[37] Art and the transformation of the self wither because the *Erlebnis-Ästhetik* fails to recognise that 'understanding always occurs through understanding something other than the self, and includes the unity and integrity of the other'.[38]

It should not be concluded that Gadamer is anti-sensualist. He adopts the Hegelian view that, through art, subject-matters gain a sensual presence in the world. What Gadamer objects to is the insistence that the artwork be treated *only* as sensual phenomena, that its what-ness is separate from its about-ness. This amputates the artwork from its subject-matter and enforces, to use Ernst Bloch's phrase, 'the darkness of the lived moment'.[39] Sensual presence is severed from that which illuminates its intelligible content. Bloch argues in parallel fashion to *Truth and Method*: 'if life is understood as the totality of merely lived moments, it dissolves into the unreality of these moments'.[40] Gadamer's response to sensual reductionism is anticipated by Franz Rosenzweig; the subjective experiences of presentness must show their meaning and warrant in history and its lived continuity.[41] When Gadamer talks of the continuity of experience (*Erfahrungen*), he seeks the continuities, symmetries and patterns of subject-matters which manifest themselves over historical time in and through sensible experience.

Underlying these criticisms of *Erlebnisse* is, perhaps, the Platonic anxiety that the sheer intensity of sensual experience distracts the onlooker from discerning the continuity and transformation of an artwork's contents. A key element in Gadamer's critique of aestheticism is its blindness to the hermeneutic aquifers of meaning that shape its concerns. This is why philosophical hermeneutics needs to establish a hermeneutically aware mode of aesthetic attentiveness. However, Gadamer does not attempt to grasp an essential content beyond or behind sensible experience but seeks to discern intelligible content (*Sachen*) in and through the temporal range of experience.

Is Gadamer fair to Dilthey in his critique of *Erlebnisse* as sensation without cognitive content? Dilthey uses the term differently, attributing to it affective, conative and cognitive dimensions. All *Erlebnisse* entail, at least to a degree, a mood or feeling towards an object of experience, an inclination to act in one way or another towards that object and an immediate apprehension of the meaning or significance of the same. The horizon of experience includes rather than opposes 'willing, feeling and thinking'.[42] This gives sensation a cognitive element, pointing beyond the immediacy of the sensation itself. Nevertheless, Dilthey's *Erlebnisse* remain subject-centred and lack the ontological foundation of *Erfahrung*en. Whilst Dilthey proposes common empathetic structures as a bridge between cognitive subjects, Gadamer avoids psychologism by arguing that understanding derives from a common mode of being in the world (*Dasein*).

Gadamer absorbs one aspect of *Erlebnisse* within his own position. Although he opposes the reduction of an artwork to its sensual properties, he suggests that the isolation of a work from the provenance of its world allows the work to be seen as a work in the first place. Gadamer differentiates between viewing a work as a representative of the world in which it was produced, as opposed to a work that presents a world from within itself:

> What we call a work of art and experience (*erleben*) aesthetically depends on a process of abstraction. By disregarding everything in which a work is rooted (its original context of life and the religious or secular function that gave it significance), it becomes visible as the 'pure work of art'. In performing this abstraction, aesthetic consciousness performs a task that is positive in itself. It shows what a pure work of art is, and allows it to exist in its own right. I call this aesthetic differentiation.[43]

The autonomous work is not reducible to 'the experiencing (*erlebende*) centre from which', as in the case of the *Erlebnis-Ästhetik*, everything considered art is measured.[44] The perception of autonomy requires that the artwork is freed from its historical horizons. Without such abstraction, artworks would retain importance only as signs or symptoms of their original environment. An artwork is clearly an object in its world but it is not just of its world: it is connected to traditions of meaning that differentiate it from its immediate surroundings. For an artwork to address the world beyond itself, it must be differentiated from its original environment. By abstracting a work from its initial context, an *Erlebnis-Ästhetik* opens the way to perceiving the ontological autonomy of work by recognising its operational capacity over and above the circumstances of its production. Both the *Erlebnis-* and the *Erfahrungs-Ästhetik* break the link between a work and its immediate horizon, but with different outcomes. Whereas for the sake of individuating pleasure, an *Erlebnis-Ästhetik* marginalises the trans-individual operations of an artwork, an *Erfahrungs-Ästhetik* endeavours to maximise them.

Transcending aesthetics as articulated within the framework of *Erlebnisse* does not leave it behind but transforms what it has been understood as being. Transcendence is neither denial nor negation but affirmation: it brings us to understand that what we thought we understood is in fact different. Gadamer's critique of aesthetic subjectivism portrays it (*pace* Hegel) as a form of 'alienated spirit',[45] closed off from its substantive historical content. For aesthetic consciousness to discern the hermeneutical continuities that flow through it, a change in its mode of awareness is required. In Gadamer's words, 'to do justice to art, aesthetics must go beyond itself and surrender the "purity" of the aesthetic'.[46] 'Aesthetics has to be absorbed into hermeneutics'.[47] The key claim is that aesthetic consciousness as conceived by Kant is blind to its hermeneutic anterior.

If artworks speak meaningfully, they and their addressees must participate in a shared form of life that establishes the communicative practices governing the intelligibility of such speaking. The occasion of an artwork addressing us can be shocking not so much because it reveals the existence of a hitherto unknown world but because it shows that what we thought we knew we did not know at all. Major aspects of the hermeneutical substantiality that informs consciousness do not necessarily come to awareness. Language provides a poignant example.

The vocabulary that a language user recognises is huge compared with that which can be deliberately recalled. Aesthetic reflection has, therefore, the double aspect of rediscovery and transcendence. When an artwork addresses us, we rediscover our prior involvement in the world of meaning disclosed by it. This can effect a transcendence regarding how we grasp ourselves: 'the work of art that says something confronts us with ourselves'.[48] In the language of traditional hermeneutics, Gadamer's conception of aesthetic reflection oscillates between part and whole: an individual consciousness grasps its individuated nature more fully when aware of the broader life-world it belongs to.

The second way of explicating how aesthetic reflection recognises an externalised dimension of its existence concerns both what art makes known and the being of what it makes known. Hermeneutical excess is at issue. For aesthetic reflection to meet an externalised dimension of its existence in the world implies that aesthetic consciousness must be ahead, be anterior to and, indeed, be in excess of itself. In the essay 'The Scope and Function of Reflection' (1967), Gadamer writes:

> Hermeneutical reflection fulfils the function that is accomplished in all bringing something to a conscious awareness. . . . Reflection on a given pre-understanding brings before me something that otherwise happens behind my back . . . *Bewusstsein* is inescapably more *being* than consciousness.[49]

Being situated in the world means (*pace* Heidegger) that we are pre-reflectively shaped by an understanding of what it means to be (*Dasein*). Weinsheimer observes, 'being is never wholly assimilated to consciousness'.[50] Finite mind can never grasp the totality of linguistic and cultural relationships that informs it. This hermeneutic anterior is not in principle unknowable. It is not a Kantian thing-in-itself but is that which is yet to be understood, always present within what Heidegger describes as the withheld. Aesthetic consciousness, then, as Kant conceives it, does not know what it (already) knows.

> Aesthetic consciousness . . . no longer admits that the work of art and its world belong to each other, but on the contrary, aesthetic consciousness is the experiencing (*erlebende*) centre from which everything considered art is measured.[51]

There is an important parallel between Gadamer's claim that 'we are always more than we know ourselves to be' and his argument that as 'art cannot present the full truth of what it experiences in terms of definitive knowledge', 'there is no final exhaustion of what lies in an art work'.[52] An artwork can never exhaust what it presents. Yet what it does not present (the undisclosed aspects of its hermeneutic substratum) is reliant upon what is presented. Only the presented reveals the presence of the as-yet-to-be shown. Within hermeneutical aesthetics, consciousness and being are not epistemological opposites (Kant) but elements of a dialogical relation in which each element reflects and co-inheres in the other. The character of this relationship is illuminated by that between an artwork and its subject-matter.

The subject-matter of a work is always larger than the work itself. Though a work cannot capture the totality of its subject-matter, it insinuates that which exceeds it. This gives to words and images a speculative capacity to point beyond themselves. The realm of the excess does not exist independently of the works that make its presence discernible. Artwork and subject-matter, consciousness and being, are folded into and reflect each other. The primary shortcoming of Kantian aesthetic consciousness is its unawareness of its co-inherence in its hermeneutic anterior.

Gadamer's account of the hermeneutic anterior and its effects on aesthetic reflection explains his hostility to modern subjectivism. Any passage to a more hermeneutically astute aesthetics must recognise, to use Adornos's words, that 'subjective experience is only the outer shell of philosophical experience, which develops beneath it and then throws it off'.[53] The subtitle to Part One of *Truth and Method* is telling: 'Transcending the Aesthetic Dimension' ('*Die Transzendierung der ästhetischen Dimension*'). Gadamer claims that Kant's account of aesthetic consciousness assumes a sovereign 'experiencing centre from which everything considered art is measured'.[54] It directs itself towards what is supposed to be the work proper and ignores 'the extra-aesthetic elements that cling to it', that is, the work's hermeneutic substrate. This is an instance of what Heidegger refers to as that 'modern subjectivism' which postulates a timeless subjectivity as the ground of both artistic spontaneity and the norms of aesthetic reception.[55] Kant's account of aesthetic consciousness is charged with supposing meaning to be an act of subjectivity rather than a reflection of belonging to a tradition and its projects,[56] with holding that aesthetic judgements are ones whose determining ground cannot be other than subjective, and with believing that every aesthetic judgement has its determining ground in the feeling of the subject and not in any conception of the object. Being unaware of the hermeneutic substrate that sustains it, Kantian aesthetic consciousness is accused of not knowing what it is and of not being able to say what it is.[57] This is why Gadamer insists that, in order to do justice to an experience of art, aesthetics has to be absorbed into hermeneutics.[58]

This does not deny the sensual but recognises that sensual appearance is the ontological mode through which art's subject-matters manifest themselves. Gadamer utilises the Hegelian notion of making concrete: abstract ideas without sensual embodiment could have no epiphany within actuality. To separate the sensual from what it makes discernible deprives the sensual of the ability to refer to its intelligible content. This is not a reference to a metaphysical world of pure ideas but to other constellations of meaning, in relation to which subject-matters gain their general poignancy. The ability of the sensually given to refer beyond itself links the experience of art to hermeneutic consciousness.

Within hermeneutic consciousness 'knowledge of oneself can never be complete'.[59] Accordingly, 'the experience of art acknowledges that it cannot present the full truth of what it experiences in terms of definitive knowledge'.[60] The range of reference for both is infinite. The shift from aesthetic (sensualist) to hermeneutic attentiveness attributes aesthetic differentiation with its proper weight and significance. In summary, this shift enables Gadamer to attribute a cognitive content to aesthetic experience by grounding it not in the feelings of a subject (*Erlebnisse*) but in the interplay of cultural horizons, which form the basis of a subject's existence. By fragmenting experience, an *Erlebnis-Ästhetik* severs the spectator from that continuity of movement between part and whole which sustains experience conceived as *Erfahrung*. Gadamer's claim that 'the experience of art . . . cannot present the full truth of what it experiences in terms of definitive knowledge' reinforces his argument in favour of *Erfahrungen*. By blinding spectators to the hermeneutic hinterlands of their experience, the *Erlebnis-Ästhetik* cuts them off from engaging with the interplay of those part–whole relations which simultaneously provide the ground for any meaningful experience of art and set the conditions for any transformation of understanding.

This allows us to engage with the next phase of our argument. Speaking of the experience of an artwork, Gadamer comments,

> What unfolds before us is so much lifted out of the on-going course of the ordinary world and so much enclosed in its own autonomous circle of meaning that no one is prompted to seek some other future or reality behind it. The spectator is set at an absolute distance, a distance that precludes practical or goal orientated participation. But this distance is aesthetic distance in a true sense, for it signifies the distance necessary for seeing, and

thus makes possible a genuine and comprehensive *participation* in what is presented before us.[61]

The issue that must now concern us is the paradox of an attentive distance which inaugurates a deeper involvement in the subject-matter of aesthetic experience.

3.4 AESTHETIC ATTENTIVENESS AND THE QUESTION OF DISTANCIATION

We have proposed that Gadamer does not need a better hermeneutic method to access meanings within an artwork but a more sophisticated account of what is entailed in engaging with their interplay. Contemplative involvement with a work and being attentive to what it 'says', discerning its enigmatic qualities and its speculative resonances, is central to Gadamer's aesthetic practice. How is aesthetic attention to be understood? Attentiveness is strangely neglected in much philosophical and hermeneutical literature. We propose that attentiveness is double in nature and that such doubledness assumes different forms.

Attention is both active and passive, passive in that it is vulnerable to the unprovoked address of subject-matters and active in the sense that it attends to their address with patience and focus. Being attentive to a work implies that one knows one is being addressed and that one's self-understanding is caught up in the entailments of that address. Pre-understanding and prior experience make one hermeneutically susceptible to such an address, so that one is almost predisposed to follow its direction. On the other hand, aesthetic attention is active, a disciplined following through or tarrying with the paths that a subject-matter may open. The active–passive nature of attention is consistent with what is termed the *pathos* of hermeneutical experience.[62]

Aesthetic attention is a doubled form of attentiveness, involving a mental space which simultaneously holds apart and yet joins the immediate sensual particularities of an artwork with the general resonances of its meaning. Aesthetic attention is doubled in that it has the hermeneutical ability to see in the particular the embodiment of a general subject-matter and to see subject-matters instantiated in particulars. Goethe characterises this as a part–whole relationship: '*das Allgemeine und Besondere fallen zusammen: das Besondere ist das Allgemeine, unter vershiedenen Bedingungen erscheinend*'.[63] Gadamer is acutely aware of the movement between particular and universal but is wary of privileging either:

> Must we not also allow of aesthetic 'experience' what we say of perception, namely, that it perceives truth – i.e. remains related to knowledge. It

is worthwhile to recall Aristotle here. He showed that all *aisthesis* tends toward a universal. . . . The fact is that we see sensory particulars in relation to something universal.[64]

Aesthetic attention can neither pass fully from the singular to the universal (that would reduce the aesthetic to the purely philosophical) nor completely renounce the conceptual in favour of the sensual (without reinvoking the aesthetic distanciation from intelligible content it seeks to avoid). Aesthetic attentiveness must (like hermeneutical consciousness) dwell in the in-between and maintain the relational movement between sensual particular and conceptual universal. Aesthetic attention requires a differential space which simultaneously distinguishes the sensual and the cognitive and yet holds them together in an articulate relationship. This point is pertinent to our later discussion of Kant's aesthetic idea, which is neither concept nor sensible intuition.

Aesthetic attentiveness must be disinterested with regard to and yet affectionate towards its object. Gadamer's approach to aesthetic experience avoids the detachment of Clive Bell's approach to 'significant form' and must do so in order to make good the claim that art addresses us cognitively. At the same time, Gadamer's participatory account of our concern with art's subject-matters cannot permit a level of intimate involvement such that we become incapable of distinguishing them from matters which do challenge interests. The Heideggerian would argue that to treat an object as mere object would prevent it from being treated as an artwork. Nothing would appear from within it. Mikel Dufrenne extends the thought: 'the aesthetic object differs from the non- aesthetic object because it offers itself up as a world in itself'.[65] This suggests that an artwork can be perceived as such only if it stands out from or challenges horizons of commonplace expectancy. It implies a dispassionate mode of apprehension not governed solely by interest. Indeed, it can be argued that such an aesthetic way of viewing (the ability to attend to an object as a world-in-itself) is vital for any creature who lacks a generic essence and is what it is by virtue of its becoming. For such a creature, it is imperative that it review and test what it has learned experientially. This is an argument central to Gadamer's account of self-formation (*Bildung*).[66] Furthermore, it offers a riposte to the claim that phenomenological aesthetics is concerned only with what interests us and not with aesthetics as offering a detached mode of attention.

It can be counter-argued that it is in the interest of *homo bildung* to have a capacity for detachment, since, without it, chances for development are jeopardised. Such detachment is not indifference. Probing and testing the assumptions that inform life interests is far

from a matter of indifference. It is, in effect, a matter of life enhancement (*Lebensteigerung*). Habermas grasps the point in his distinction
between the species' interests that govern the possibility of practically
effective knowledge (that concerning the exchange and expansion of
existential possibilities) and the methodological detachment necessary
for the pursuit of such knowledge.[67] It is a feature of aesthetic attention that its detachment is very much 'interested', a source of action-
orientated knowing. Such detachment serves its interests, that is, it
dispassionately opens itself to new sources of existential understanding.

This argument supposes that practical knowledge acquired through
experience requires movement, transformation and transcendence.
Movement is the essence of what Gadamer calls 'spirit'.[68] The life of
the spirit requires constant challenge and testing. If life requires movement, transformation is essential to its continuance. Now, attentiveness
to the subject-matters of experience can initiate such movement. It is
not a question of a spectator wilfully imposing himself or herself on
an inert subject-matter. Mark McIntosh notes that 'it is not so much I
who am knowing but that the known has drawn me into an encounter
with itself'.[69] It is *experience* (*Erfahrung*) rather than any instrumentalist theory that initiates such movement. Gemma Fiumari suggests
that attention animates thought and assists openness, whilst theory
de-animates it.[70] This concurs with Gadamer's claim that 'experience
is always actually present only in the individual observation'.[71] If
transformation is of the essence, the achievement of new orientations
and perspectives is vital not just to confirm received experience but
to test it. Within this framework of argument there is no opposition
between interestedness and disinterestedness. The need for detachment
is, in effect, a mode of interestedness in the testing of old experience
against new. This quest leads via the negativity of experience to the
transformation of perspectives. Detachment in Gadamerian form is that
'readiness for experience that distinguishes the experienced man from
the man captivated by dogma'.[72] The equation of detachment with the
undogmatic is suggested in the following passage:

> The experienced person proves to be someone who is radically undogmatic;
> who, because of the many new experiences he has had and the knowledge
> he has drawn from them, is particularly equipped to have new experiences
> and to learn from them. The dialectic of experience has its proper fulfilment
> not in definitive knowledge but in the openness to experience that is made
> possible by experience itself.[73]

Gadamer's argumentation accounts for how detachment can remain
consistent with the interests of tradition and its cultural horizons.
Objectivity is, in this context, not a question of methodology but of

attentive openness: it has little to do with any culturally affected indifference but embodies a species interest in learning. Before the argument is developed, we will briefly comment on related approaches to attentiveness.

The theologian Daphne Hampson links attentiveness to the development of spirituality. She does not suggest that attentiveness leads to spirituality but rather that spirituality – attending to the movement in things – is inherent in attention itself. Attentiveness is allied to the fostering of human becoming, to allowing others to flourish and to the creation of circumstances whereby this becomes possible. Her remarks are congruent with Gadamer's commitment to *Bildung*: attentiveness has reverence for the concrete details of life and its affirmation.[74] Attending is also profoundly ethical: it is a practice through which the one who attends changes. Crucially, she notes the distance essential to attentiveness: it entails the capacity not to be swallowed up by involvement with another. It retains a critical distance whilst caring deeply for that to which one attends.[75] Attentiveness involves an availability (*disponsibilitié*) or receptiveness to others but, whereas Hampson speaks of a critical distance, Gadamer does not. He suggests that:

> this kind of being present is a self-forgetfulness to what one is watching, Here self-forgetfulness is anything but a private condition, for its arises from devoting one's full attention to the matter at hand.[76]

He speaks of being taught by the thing itself and of 'being totally involved in and carried away by what one sees'.[77] Yet this restates Gadamer's problem: how to reconcile participation and critical distance.[78]

Simone Weil emphasises attentiveness as a developed practice. What is learned through attentiveness is learnt by dint of practice and not methodological application. For Gadamer, attention is not a matter of subjective conduct but of being influenced by the nature of the subject-matter contemplated. Weil also argues that it is not a matter of will but a question of giving oneself up to that to which one attends. The 'I' disappears and, when it does, beauty appears to those freed from wishing and longing. 'Beauty is a fruit which we look at without trying to seize it.'[79] This approach to attentiveness has certain attributes of aesthetic experience itself. It is a practice pursued without extrinsic purpose, other than the maintenance of the practice itself. The value of attentiveness resides in its nurturing the possibility of sustaining further attention. Teaching for Weil should have no aim other than to train for greater aptitude in attentiveness. The parallel with Gadamer's advocacy of experience as a route to enhanced experience is clear.

Iris Murdoch speaks of the need for a 'new vocabulary of attention' which gives careful and just consideration to persons and things. Her idea of a patient, loving regard directed upon a person presents the will not as unimpeded movement but more like obedience.[80] In the essay 'The Sovereignty of Good Over Other Concepts', she comments on 'attentiveness' as being unpopular with recent philosophers, who prefer to talk of reasons rather than of 'experiences'.[81] Adhering to her preference for using philosophy as a means to deepen experience, she holds that attentiveness shares with art the ability to change the quality of an experience to such a degree that a change of consciousness can be achieved:

> I am looking out of my window in an anxious and resentful state of mind, oblivious of my surroundings, brooding perhaps on some damage done to my prestige. Then, suddenly I observe a hovering kestrel. In a moment everything is altered. The brooding self with its hurt vanity has disappeared. There is nothing now but kestrel.[82]

Attentiveness entails the transformation of everyday consciousness into a non-possessive, almost *aesthetic* mode of contemplation, in which we surrender to that which has won our attention and free ourselves from the selfishness of everyday consciousness. George Steiner senses in attentiveness an ethical dimension. He speaks of a civility towards 'the inward savour of things', and of that courtesy of mind which is both a 'scruple of perception' and indicative of a well mannered understanding.[83] Murdoch emphasises how attention also entails a regard for what is truly other:

> Attention is rewarded by knowledge of reality. [It] . . . leads me away from myself towards something alien to me, something which my consciousness cannot take over, swallow up, deny or make unreal.[84]

She shares Gadamer's attention to the proper complexity of human experience and wanting to do it justice:

> In fact, any experience is infinitely rich and deep. We feel it to be intrinsically significant because we can brood upon it, but at the same time brooding shows it to be *endlessly various in its meaning*.[85]

These approaches to attention expand the implications of the term. Gadamer offers a dialogical structure to the attentive. 'Anyone', he suggests, 'who listens is fundamentally open. Without openness there is no genuine human relationship' and no responsiveness to an artwork's address.[86] Attentiveness nurtures receptivity and preparedness for exchanges of outlook. Nevertheless, despite the affinity between Gadamer's position and the positions of Weil and Murdoch, there is no articulated account of aesthetic attention as such in Gadamer's hermeneutics. Two points remain pertinent. First, if Gadamer's defence of art is to remain plausible, the tension between aesthetic disinterestedness and phenomenological participation requires an account of aesthetic attentiveness. Second, there is sufficient material in Gadamer's argument to establish such an account and it is to this that we shall turn.

3.5 AESTHETIC ATTENTIVENESS AND THE QUESTION OF MOVEMENT

> The essence of what is called spirit lies in the ability to move within the horizon of an open future and an unrepeatable past.[87]

Hermeneutics can be conceived of as 'thinking' (along) with a philosophy, not merely reconstructing its principal thoughts but moving them on. This does not have anything to do empathy, nor is it a reflection of Collingwood's tactic of reiterating the order of a previous philosopher's thoughts. For Gadamer, 'thinking with' is 'thinking beyond': it involves an intuitive sense of what lies undeveloped within a position. We shall apply this to his comments on attentiveness.

We propose that aesthetic experience involves partaking in a hermeneutical experience of movement. Movement is invoked by Gadamer in six ways.

1. *Ontological movement.* Indicating that he wishes to move away from traditional, substance-based metaphysics, Gadamer argues that 'understanding is not just one of the various possible behaviours of the subject but the mode of being of *Dasein* itself. . . . It denotes the basic being-in-motion of *Dasein* that constitutes its finitude and historicity'.[88] In the essay 'Classical and Philosophical Hermeneutics', he states, 'Understanding is no longer meant as one process of human thinking among others . . . rather, it means something that constitutes the basic being-in-motion (*Bewegtheit*) of the existing human being (*Dasein*)'.[89] Gadamer claims that 'Heidegger . . . tried to see the *on he on* . . . that is the "being-question", through Aristotelian eyes. . . . [W]hat ever *Sein* (being) is, a movedness must pertain to it that belongs to *Sein*. Indeed, nobody can doubt that in the world around us we see moved beings in their movedness.'[90]

2. *Perceptual movement.* Aristotle's *Physics* proves a seminal text for Gadamer. 'For there, in the basic character of movedness, the *Da* of *Sein* becomes visible – and exactly through this it is concealed. In the puzzling miracle of mental wakefulness lies the fact that seeing something and thinking something is a kind of motion, but not the kind that leads from something to its end. Rather, when someone is looking at

something, this is when he or she truly sees it, and when one is directing one's thinking at something, this is when one is truly pondering it. So motion is also a holding oneself in being, and through this motion of human wakefulness, there blows the whole breath of the life-process, a process that ever and again allows a new perception of something to open up.'[91]

3. *Reflective movement.* Again following Aristotle, Gadamer specifically speaks of the realm of motion which is called philosophical thought.[92] 'Our thinking is never satisfied with what one means in saying this or that. Thinking constantly points beyond itself.'[93]

4. *Experiential movement.* Experience, Gadamer contends, 'moves by expanding into the manifoldness of [its] contents or as the continual emergence of new forms of mind'.[94] The movement of travel is invoked in the remark that 'hermeneutic philosophy, as I envision it, does not understand itself as an absolute position but as a path of experiencing'.[95] Experience is dynamic: 'both art and the historical sciences are ways of experiencing in which our own understanding of existence is immediately brought into play'.[96]

5. *Subject-matters and movement.* Subject-matters (*Sachen*) are for Gadamer the intelligible themes and issues of concern pointed to by perception, language and thought. They can be described as cognitive agencies, in that they inform independently a subject's way of thinking and the ways that idioms of speech or styles of thinking evolve within a *Weltanschauung*. Charles Taylor names such entities social imaginaries.[97] Subject-matters evolve and subject us to their motions. Gadamer observes, 'In . . . the language of conversation, of poetry and also of interpretation – the speculative structure of language emerges, not as the reflection of something given but as the coming into language of a totality of meaning. This drew us toward the dialectic of the Greeks, because they did not conceive understanding as a methodic activity of the subject, but as something that the thing itself (*Sache*) does and which thought "suffers". The activity of the thing itself is the real speculative movement that takes hold of the speaker.'[98] In ordinary language, we speak of being drawn into a painting and of finding a novel compelling reading. Such idioms of speech indicate that, in the experience of an artwork, it is not the subject's eye that scans the painting or the subject's cognitive attention that analyses the text. It is, rather, that eye and mind are led. As Wolfgang Iser argues, 'painting follows the motion . . . of the *Sache*', prompting a 'continual dispersal of perceptual and conceptual description'.[99] Subject-matters contain elements of uncontrollability, producing their own shifting forms of organisation and as such are autopoietic in nature.[100] As the intelligible

content of an issue, *Sachen* are in effect immeasurables – multifarious and yet particular, inexhaustible and unfathomable.

6. *Movement and understanding*. To understand something is to experience a movement from not knowing to knowing, from existing in a state of deception or forgetfulness to becoming aware of something in a new light. The transitive nature of hermeneutical understanding is well stated. 'In this most authentic realm of hermeneutic experience, the conditions of which a hermeneutic philosophy tries to give an account, the affinity of hermeneutics with practical philosophy is confirmed. First of all, understanding, like action, always involves risk and is never just the simple application of a general knowledge of rules to the statements or texts to be understood. Furthermore, where it is successful, understanding means a growth of inner awareness, as a new experience enters into the texture of our own mental experience. Understanding is an adventure and, like any adventure, is dangerous. Because it is not satisfied with simply wanting to register what is there or said there but goes back to our guiding interests and questions, one has to concede that the hermeneutical experience has a far lower degree of certainty than that attained by the methods of the natural sciences. But when one realises that understanding is an adventure, one realises that it affords unique opportunities as well. It is capable of contributing in a special way to the broadening of our human experiences, our self-knowledge and our horizon, for everything that understanding mediates is mediated through ourselves.'[101] This conception of experience (not unlike Dilthey's) is animated by conative, affective and cognitive movement. Although Aristotle inspires his comments on the 'movedness' of living things, an aspect of Hegel's thought remains decisive for Gadamer. True, he makes use of Aristotle's claim that perception tends to a universal[102] but he recognises that, for Aristotle, experience is essentially mimetic: the forms of experience (and the concepts they point to) are ontologically prior to experience itself. Education is not developmental but a question of attuning oneself to pre-established norms and ideals. Hegelian thought travels in the opposite direction: the universalising tendency within perception is formative, anticipatory and mimetic, not because it refers back but because it points forward to a greater consolidation of its subject-matters. *Bildung* for Hegel and Gadamer is progressively accumulative.

It is not the experience of movement *per se* that is important but the notion that intense experience is itself a site and an expression of colliding perceptual and reflective movements. This is at the heart of Gadamer's reworking of aesthetic experience and informs his conception of aesthetic attentiveness.

Contemplative attentiveness can be considered as being open to and participating in a form of movement. The model is Aristotle's *Ethics*: it treats contemplation as a practice, as an activity with no end other than itself. The ability to contemplate the proper order and movement of logical ideas is appraised by Aristotle as being akin to God's continuous reflection upon the order of Being.[103] However, for Gadamer, contemplation is not fixed upon a static object, nor aims at complete stillness, but strives to be open to the movement within the subject-matters of reflection themselves. Receptiveness to such movement is not itself the point but what participation in it sets into play within the spectator. The speculative dimension of language provides an example. Reflecting hermeneutically on a word or image is not applying a method of interpretation to it but a matter of attuning oneself to where the sense of that word or image can take us. Opening to the speculative movements of words and images extends horizons of communication already in play. Attentiveness to such speculative movements is an acquired practice. Extending thought by following nuanced meaning within words or images is to engage not with demonstrable certainties but with reasonable, persuasive probabilities held within lines of meaning.[104]

Such a mode of aesthetic attentiveness does not commence *ex nihilo*. It is historically situated and attunes to established movements within *Sachen* and their images. It assumes the hermeneutical situatedness of the spectator. Having located itself within such movement, the task of hermeneutical reflection is to extend it. The spectator or contemplative must awaken 'the intuitive power' (its speculative dimension) 'already resident in language and thereby extend the possibilities for meaning and its communication'.[105] This is opposite to 'that rigid fixing of things in terminology which is fully appropriate in the realm of modern science'. It is, however, particularly appropriate to the 'realm of motion called philosophical thought'.[106] Aesthetic attentiveness does not just observe movement, it *induces* it so the spectator comes to think and feel differently about a *Sache*.

Aesthetic attentiveness emerges as an important condition of change within a spectator's horizon of understanding. This account of aesthetic experience does not concern the experience of static forms but the experience of unfolding movement. Such movement is central to the further hermeneutic question of what an artwork *does* and *how* it does it. The ontological and cognitive senses of being-in-movement and being-moved are central to our extended hermeneutical reconstruction of aesthetic experience. Images produced by the Scottish artist Ian Hamilton Finlay offer examples of the practical consequences of attentiveness. Hamilton Finlay's works have a simplicity that reveals the economy of hermeneutical elements they set in play. They provide a straightforward example of how artworks affect and effect movement in the experience of art. Weaponry is a favoured motif. His art handles complex subject-matters with an obvious directness and has a neo-classical ambivalence signifying order *and* chaos, destruction *and* renewal.

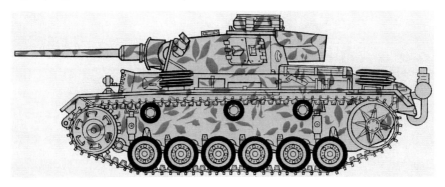

Ian Hamilton Finlay and George Oliver, *Arcadia (photograph Judy Dean).*

In my study hangs Hamilton Finlay's print *Arcadia*. It invokes master-pieces of the same name by Nicolas Poussin (1594–1665). They derive from Virgil's poetic work *Eclogues* V 42. Finlay's title immediately places the image into various fields of classical meaning. The consequent discord prompts a range of questions. We might ask, 'Death and destruction are supposedly absent from paradise but, on reflection, can death actually be absent from Arcadia?' If, according to neo-Platonic myth, the primordial types of all creatures are formed in an *Ur*-Arcadia, then so too must be that of the military beast. If such machines roved Arcadia's glades, what caused their subsequent exile? In Poussin's paintings, shepherds stare into a grave. Does the tank, too, stare at the abyss? Does it serve as spiritual symbol of overcoming the provocation of the negative? A remark by Hegel is pertinent:

> But the life of Spirit is not the life that shrinks from death and keeps itself untouched by devastation, but rather the life that endures it and maintains itself in it . . . Spirit is this power . . . [of] looking the negative in the face, and tarrying with it. This tarrying with the negative is the magical power that converts it into being.[107]

By inserting the image of an armoured vehicle into a set of herme-neutical horizons rich in classical nuance, Hamilton Finlay prompts a rethinking of the meaning of Arcadia. This is made possible by the speculative dimensions of the print's visual language, which builds on various hermeneutical associations: the choice of forest green for the tank's colouration, the leafy camouflage on the vehicle invoking Arcadia's glades, the irony of olive leaves as a mode of military disguise and the form of the image itself, so reminiscent of late eighteenth-century folios of flora and fauna illustrations. The association with documenting primal archetypes is clear.

Finlay's images do not invent the meanings identified: they invoke them and establish an aesthetic space in which they appear. An effective artwork does not merely draw on the pre-understood (the implicit assumptions of our mode of thinking) but seeks to reconfigure it in unpredictable and perhaps disturbing ways. What, for example, is the relationship between art and violence? Finlay's works are not great art but they offer simple and effective visual aphorisms which explicitly reveal their hermeneutical workings. Their effectiveness presupposes the existence of an established set of semantic horizons (tradition). Because they are inherently unstable, the well placed word or the carefully honed image can effectively disturb webs of established meaning and facilitate new ones. Though Gadamer tends to down play it, the constructive role of the receiving horizon is emphasised once again.

Gadamer's account of attending to the movement of subject-matters formally requires distanciation. The ability to contemplate such movement is a condition of the possibility of the spectator's own horizon being brought into in play. Without distanciation, a significant condition for setting a spectator's individual horizon of experience into movement disappears. The passage cited above is telling: 'seeing something and thinking something is a kind of motion. . . . this is when he or she truly sees it, and when one is directing one's thinking at something, this is when one is truly pondering it.'[108] Seeing what is in motion in the perceived subject-matter draws the spectator's horizon itself into a transformative movement. A clear sequence of ideas in Gadamer's reasoning is discernible.

A condition of an artwork speaking is the prior existence of established sets of semantic horizons. When an artwork addresses its spectator, the power of its address will be synonymous with its ability to seize and hold attention. The emergence of the artwork from the flux of everyday phenomena – the moment of aesthetic distanciation – establishes a level of reflective distance, in that the spectator becomes aware of something acting contrary to expectation, will and doing. A work's address is never complete. Attending to the work allows the enigmatic within its address to unfold. Aesthetic attentiveness requires a reflective gap between what a work points to and how it addresses it. It is in this space that movement between the horizons of a work's address and the horizons of the spectator's reception can occur. Within philosophical hermeneutics, the artwork serves as a guarantee against becoming overly circumscribed within the perceptual horizons of the everyday. An ability to see movement in subject-matters independent of our immediate concerns has to be supposed. Without the possibility of such detachment, openness to the intrinsic movements of subject-matters becomes limited, as do the possibilities for transformational change in the spectator's horizon. Such distanciation opens the spectator to unanticipated movements within a subject-matter. These irregular movements can unexpectedly realign and transform the horizon of a spectator's understanding. Here, Gadamer's position becomes less concerned with the serendipitous moment of art's address and more with the development of attentive practice, understood as a deliberate putting of oneself in the way of hermeneutical risk. There is not, therefore, an opposition between disinterestedness and phenomenological involvement within Gadamer's reasoning. Detachment and distanciation are an internal feature of aesthetic attentiveness. In conclusion, Gadamer's commitment to open attentiveness is a commitment to a disciplined aesthetic practice. The practice entails contemplative exposure to the movement of art's subject-matters. As a movement which can fuse and re-fuse the horizons out of which art emerges and into which it is received, it is a movement capable of transforming the spectator's understanding. The case for aesthetic attentiveness as participation in a form of cognitive movement finds support in Kant's analysis of the aesthetic idea.

Whereas Gadamer's notion of the *practice* of aesthetic attentiveness is indebted to Aristotle's conception of contemplation, his conception of that practice's object owes more to Kant's aesthetic idea. The latter suggests that subject-matters are also areas of cognate movement. It has been argued that Gadamer's discussion of subject-matters should differentiate more strongly between a determinate concept and an indeterminate field of cognate meanings.[109] If the suggestion of cognate fields of subject-matters is upheld, a parallel with Kant's aesthetic idea emerges.

3.6 AESTHETIC IDEAS AND SUBJECT-MATTERS

Kant insists that aesthetic ideas are not determinate concepts.

> But, by an aesthetic idea I mean that representation of the imagination *which induces much thought, yet without the possibility of any definite thought whatever, i.e. concept, being adequate to it, and which language, consequently, can never get quite on level terms with or render completely intelligible.* It is easily seen, that an aesthetic idea is the counterpart (pendant) of a rational idea, which conversely, is a concept, to which no intuition (representation of the imagination) can be adequate.[110]

This suggests that aesthetic ideas and subject-matters are, by association, open cognate structures which no particular work or interpretation can exhaust. Furthermore, Kant's remark emphasises the cognitive instability of both notions. Gadamer uses such lack of determination to good effect: it can promote further determinative movement in the understanding of a subject-matter. In consequence, aesthetic ideas, like subject-matters, always reach beyond their particular instantiation and suggest transcendent cognate structures: the aesthetic idea/subject-matter which informs a work, and is in turn illuminated by it, will always be in excess of what appears in that work.

Aesthetic ideas and subject-matters alike induce cognitive movement. Both are given within fields of meaning which reach into previous determinations of thought and anticipate new ones. When we perceive an aesthetic idea or subject-matter we do not simply perceive it as given but as something given within a horizon of opportunity.[111] It promises to inform what we already partially know but do not fully know, and to extend the possibilities of what might yet be known.

> Aesthetic ideas . . . serve . . . as a substitute for logical presentation, but *with the proper function, however, of animating the mind by opening out for it a prospect into a field of kindred representations* stretching beyond its ken.[112]

Though aesthetic ideas and subject-matters transcend their perceptual instantiations, the poet or interpreter seeks to illuminate what is given in singular experience by 'transgressing' it, by using the imagination 'to body them [aesthetic ideas] forth to sense with a completeness of which nature affords no parallel'.[113]

Subject-matters and aesthetic ideas have an unstable cognitive content. As historically open constellations of meaning, subject-matters have no fixed logical identity. Because both subject-matter and aesthetic idea have no essential core, particular instantiations require appraisal in terms of how they have been previously understood and might yet come to be understood. Kant speaks of a speculative rational impulse 'to body out an aesthetic idea'. By this he means the multiplication and unification of its diverse determinations within a part–whole dynamic. This reappraises previous understandings of an aesthetic idea in the light of present experience, and re-envisions what it might come to mean as a consequence of that reappraisal. Kant's reference to a speculative rational structure which endeavours to draw the determinations of an aesthetic idea within a unified whole resonates with Gadamer's invocation of language's speculative capacity. It is with a clear Kantian nuance that Gadamer speaks of the speculative in relation to the 'poetic word':

Language itself, has something speculative about it . . . as the realisation of meaning . . . Such a realisation is speculative, in that the finite possibilities of the word are orientated towards the sense intended, as towards the infinite . . . Someone who speaks in this way may well use only the most ordinary and common words and still be able to express what is unsaid and is to be said . . . All this is found, in an intensified way, in the poetic word . . . in that the event of the poetic word expresses its own relationship to being (i.e. to the disclosure of an infinity of unspoken meaning in the spoken or written word).[114]

To grasp what a statement might mean, or to fathom its profundity, is to pass from what is stated *per se* – the word as statement – to what is expressly suggested, that is, an unspoken totality of meaning. The task of interpreter and poet is to bring the part (the spoken word) to full life in the context of the unspoken whole of meaning that informs it. In other words, the nature of x is illuminated by revealing its place within $x+$.

The continuous speculative movement from part to whole and back again indicates to Kant that the aesthetic idea cannot be resolved into a determinate concept. No intuition will suffice to capture the idea, as 'no expression indicating a definite concept can be found for it'.[115] Gadamer refers to the argument himself: 'conceptual explication is never able to exhaust the content of a poetic argument'.[116] Kant consequently devalues the cognitive status of the aesthetic idea, but for Gadamer the fact that a subject-matter cannot be reduced to a concept is, hermeneutically speaking, advantageous. Whereas aesthetic ideas strain to be what they are not – determinate conceptual identities – subject-matters strain to be more than themselves. Concepts require fixity and stability, whilst subject-matters can achieve different determinations of themselves precisely because they lack a fixed identity. Indeed, their historical effectiveness and potential for extensive application depend upon their lack of rigid meaning. As Gadamer argues, when confronted with a subject-matter or aesthetic idea we do not meet with something in isolation. We meet in that subject-matter a world already interpreted, yet the meanings and nuances of that world are always unstable. Gadamer says appropriately of the poetic word: 'it can never stop consisting of meanings that arise out of the words, or parts of words' that have meaning or which point to a meaning.[117]

Whereas for Kant the indeterminacy of aesthetic ideas weakens their status in relation to concepts, the indeterminacy of subject-matters strengthens their cognitive status. The fullness or richness of a subject-matter depends upon how its presentational particularity can be located in the speculative 'whole' which sustains its meaningfulness. The meaning of a subject-matter or aesthetic idea does not reside in a specific language system or discourse, nor is it constrained to the particular context in which the subject-matter presents itself. As Gadamer argues, 'its meaning is never completely separated from the multiple meanings it has in itself . . . other things are co-present and it's the presence of all that is co-present there that comes to make up the evocative power of living speech'.[118] The speculative quest to achieve fuller determinations of meaning for subject-matters or aesthetic ideas initiates a cognitive movement from part to whole. In Kant's words,

> Aesthetic ideas . . . put the faculty of intellectual ideas *into motion* – a motion, at the instance of representation, towards an extension of thought, that, while germane, no doubt to the concept of the object, exceeds what can be laid hold of in that representation or clearly expressed.[119]

The infinite synchronic relations between actual and possible determinations of meaning attached to a subject-matter imply that though interpretation will never arrive at a fixed determination of that subject-matter, it will thicken and intensify accumulated meanings associated with the notion and thereby strengthen its cognitive power.

That the meaning of an aesthetic idea cannot be resolved into a fixed concept suggests to Kant that decisions concerning its possible combinations of meaning are arrived on the basis of subjective preference. The theologian John Milbank argues that this is a false dichotomy, indicative of a mesmerising distinction between pure and empirical reason. Milbank implies that Kant's aesthetic ideas should be accorded the status of what Giambattista Vico identified as *poetic* or *concrete* universals. Milbank argues tersely,

> Because metaphorical *poesis* does not appear to be bound by the principle of non-contradiction – which is not to say that it denies it as a principle of logic for established meanings, but that *poesis* is a logic for the establishment of meanings – it is easy to imagine that it disallows any stability of meaning.[120]

If the proliferating alignments of meaning associated with the aesthetic idea cannot be reduced to a determinate concept, is an instability of meaning for aesthetic ideas (and, by implication, subject-matters) unavoidable? On one level, such instability is advantageous to hermeneutics, as it allows for a proliferation of meaning. However, the burden of the question remains. Is any clustering of meaning arbitrary and subjective? This strikes at a fundamental issue for philosophical hermeneutics. Does the open, irresolvable nature of interpretation suggest that there is no knowledge in art? After all, in Gadamer's words, this question 'can hardly be recognised if, with Kant, one measures the truth of knowledge by the scientific concept of knowledge and the scientific concept of reality'.[121] However, Milbank notices what Kant does not, namely, that aesthetic ideas have the formal characteristics of Vico's poetic or cultural universals. Subject-matters, aesthetic ideas and poetic universals share key ontological characteristics: each transcends its material sensual instantiation, each emerges in history and each is subject to historical and cultural mediation. Furthermore, Milbank's observation provides Gadamer with the cognitive force needed to be attributed to subject-matters in order to demonstrate that the opposite of Kant's rigid notion of conceptual knowledge is neither subjectivism nor relativism. Poetic or concrete universals may not be logically *a priori* but they are culturally *a priori*: they 'invoke the specific ways in which human beings commonly appropriate their experience'.[122] Aesthetic ideas and subject-matters are thus historically transmitted concrete universals that ground tradition and its *sensus communis*. Reasoning within the boundaries of such universals, 'while less definable than abstract reason . . . [is] no less exacting according to its own mode'.[123] This strengthens Gadamer's argument concerning the reasonableness of debate surrounding the experience of art.

Milbank's argument illuminates another aspect of Gadamer's thesis. With specific reference to von Balthasar, Milbank distinguishes between the aesthetic and poetic (*poesis*) dimension of cultural universals. Aesthetic ideas or subject-matters are *aesthetic* insofar as they are presented sensually in conjunction with material objects. They are *poetic* in that they are built in and through 'our collective making' and continue to be reborn and transfigured. Their speculative dimension has 'a stability' (though not fixity) 'of meaning . . . guaranteed by an appropriate *sensus communis* . . . corresponding to the transcendental subjectivity of the depth of origination which *must* accompany any meaningful artefact'.[124] The speculative dimension is also given aesthetically: it manifests itself as 'a temporal occurrence through us'. And yet, though so given, it cannot be so had. It is, Milbank argues, 'only there at all' as something to be contemplated. The positive plenitude of meaning which appears in and through its temporal occurrence within specific texts and artworks operates as a hermeneutical sublime. It is a fullness of possible meaning which, though given in and through the individual work, remains an *inascibilitas* never to be fully determined. Precisely because it is beyond conceptual grasp, it is discernible to the speculative sensibilities of aesthetic attentiveness and contemplation.[125] Here, a signature argument of a hermeneutical approach to aesthetics unfolds.

If, following Milbank's case, the image leads to a contemplation of meaning that reaches beyond the image itself, it can be objected that our argument has only succeeded (once again) in repeating the subjection of art to philosophy in the manner of Baumgarten and Hegel. The objection would have some substance if what these two philosophers assumed about art were actually true, namely that the image refers to an object independent of its representations. Philosophical hermeneutics makes no such assumption. The objective referent of the image, its aesthetic idea or subject-matter, is not a concept with an essential identity but an open, fluid, indeterminate field of meaning. That aesthetic attentiveness leads to a contemplation of the aesthetic idea or subject-matter does *not* suggest, *pace* Hegel, that aesthetic attentiveness passes its idea over to philosophy. As we have shown, aesthetic ideas or subject-matters are not concepts: they cannot be grasped by reflection as determinate intelligibles. As Milbank's argument implies, the fields of meaning that these entities embody are only there at all as something to be contemplated. The argumentation of philosophical hermeneutics further implies that the movement from sensual image to field of meaning is recursive, returning the spectator to a new consideration of the image *ad infinitum*. We have noted the centrifugal motion of hermeneutic reflection: in the perception of a singular image, the spectator passes from a particular to the more universal field of meaning that that image belongs to. We move from x to $x+$.

As a field of speculative meaning, $x+$ is necessarily more than x but $x+$ does not exist apart from the many particular instances of x. Though x can never be commensurable with $x+$ and though $x+$ can never be reduced to a singular concept or image, x and $x+$ co-inhere, so that all possible hermeneutical entailments relating to $x+$ are, ontologically speaking, implicit in every different instance of x. The centrifugal aspect of hermeneutical experience involves a spectator's established understanding of x being significantly extended by coming into contact with other bodies of relations included within or that embrace $x+$. In being significantly extended, the horizons associated with x draw the spectator into further connections of meaning. As aesthetic ideas and subject-matters are not concepts, these movements do not resolve in a clear conceptual determination but in a further realignment of meaning, which is of significance not as a proliferation of meaning *per se* but as a reshaping of particular meanings which can now be newly associated with the initial image of x. The centrifugal impetus of new insight which drives the spectator into new relations of meaning becomes a recursive centripetal movement: a new body of associations connects with and feeds back transformatively into the framework of meaning that initiated the movement in the first place. In partaking in the movement that constitutes the fields of meaning associated with aesthetic ideas and subject-matters, aesthetic attentiveness does not lead to a mode of philosophical reflection that detracts from the artistic image but to one which, by extending the connectivity of meaningful associations around it, enriches and enhances the image. Aesthetic attentiveness does not participate in the speculative movements generated by an artistic image in order to become philosophy, but in order to extend the effectiveness of the image by anchoring it in new and unanticipated networks of meaning.

3.7 CONCLUSION

To conclude, this chapter has approached the question of how Gadamer can reconcile the phenomenological interests that govern his account of understanding with the disinterestedness that is central to what is understood as the aesthetic. He can do so by replacing disinterestedness with distanciation. Aesthetic attentiveness demands the practice of spectorial and reflective *distance*, the achievement of which is the opposite of 'the extinction of our interest' in a subject-matter.[126] Spectorial distance is not a posture of indifference but a 'kind of being present' 'to what one is watching', a devoting of one's full attention to the matter in hand.[127] This distance 'precludes practical or goal orientated participation'. It is 'aesthetic distance in a true sense for it signifies the distance necessary for seeing'.[128] The practice requires us to detach ourselves from a practical concern with a subject-matter and to open ourselves towards its speculative movement in order bring our pre-understanding into play. We return once again to the threefold figure of Gadamer's doubled hermeneutics: (1) an artwork addresses us; (2) reflection upon what is entailed in that address subjects the spectator to the movement of the subject-matters within it; and (3) that movement brings the pre-understanding of the spectator into play and, in so doing, potentially transforms his or her understanding.

The dynamics of aesthetic attentiveness offer an insight into three of Gadamer's major arguments. First, aesthetic attentiveness requires that the spectator is grounded in enabling horizons of cultural meaning. The basis of aesthetic response no longer resides in spectators' feelings but in their participation in the play of meanings that ground and circumscribe their being. Second, the thesis that aesthetic attention involves exposure to the movement of cultural universals offers further insight into what is meant by art's cognitive claim. Third, the threefold analysis of address, reflection and transformation provides an answer to the question of how artworks work. Understanding art's transformative effects is central to Gadamer's claim that 'An education by art becomes an education to art'.[129] However, aesthetic attentiveness is a practice that can be maintained only so long as it remains in play: movement is central to its being. Any attempt to reduce the speculative content of a word or image to a determinate concept is inimical to maintaining the contemplative movement on which the possibility of transformational understanding rests. The dynamic of interpretation itself indicates that aesthetic attentiveness involves not only an experience of constant movement between part and whole but also generates movement itself. Aesthetic attentiveness establishes itself as a critical involvement in a *perpetuum mobile*, a concerned standing-apart from the movement of a subject-matter in order both to engage with it and to sustain it. We are not merely 'played' by such hermeneutical movement but are 'players' in bringing forth what emerges from within it. Gadamer's critique of the subjectivist attitude of modern aesthetics culminates in the reconstruction of aesthetic experience as a participatory act.

NOTES

1. *New Oxford Dictionary of English* (Oxford: Oxford University Press, 1998).
2. Nicholas Davey, *Unquiet Understanding* (Albany: New York State University Press, 2006), pp. 244–8.
3. See Karsten Harries, *The Meaning of Modern Art* (Evanston: Northwestern University Press, 1968), pp. 16–27.
4. Immanuel Kant, *The Critique of Judgement*, trans. J. C. Meredith (Oxford: Oxford University Press, 1978), p. 50.
5. Ibid., p. 64.
6. Ibid., p. 51.
7. Martin Heidegger, *Being and Time*, trans. John Macquarrie (London: Blackwell, 1960), pp. 102–4.
8. TM, pp. 111–12.
9. Ibid.
10. Ibid., p. 43.
11. Rudolf A. Makkreel, *Imagination and Interpretation in Kant: The Hermeneutical Import of the Critique of Judgement* (London: University of Chicago Press, 1990), p. 92.
12. Ibid., p. 164.
13. TM, pp. 92–7.
14. Michael Polyani, *The Tacit Dimension* (Chicago: Chicago University Press, 2009).
15. TM, p. 144.
16. Ibid., p. 92.
17. Ibid., p. 489.
18. Ibid., p. 302.
19. Hans-Georg Gadamer, *The Relevance of the Beautiful* (London: Cambridge University Press, 1986), p. 30.

20. The translator of Dilthey, H. P. Rickman argues that 'In German *Erlebnis* is contrasted to *Erfahrung*, while English uses experience for both. The latter has the sense which the *OED* gives as the actual observation of facts or events, considered as a source of knowledge. . . . *Erlebnis* corresponds to the meaning defined by the *Oxford English Dictionary* as "the fact of being consciously affected by an event. Also an instance of this; a state of or condition viewed subjectively: an event by which one is affected".' See Wilhelm Dilthey, *Selected Writings*, ed. H. P. Rickman (London: Cambridge University Press, 1976), p. 29.

21. Martin Heidegger, 'The Origin of the Art Work', in *Poetry, Language and Thought*, trans. Alfred Hofstadter (New York: Harper, 1971), p. 75 (emphasis added).

22. Dilthey, *Selected Writings*, p. 186.

23. TM, p. 95. For a counter-argument to Gadamer's position, see Galen Strawson, 'Against Narrativity', *Ratio*, Vol. 17, No. 4, Dec. 2004, pp. 428–52.

24. TM, p. 96.

25. Ibid., p. 97.

26. Ibid., p. 96.

27. Ibid., p. 95.

28. Ibid., p. 97.

29. See Chapter 1, Section 3, above.

30. TM, p. 96. It would be wrong to suppose that Gadamer is committing himself to a single continuity of self-understanding. It is clear that the latter can embrace a number of related narratives. See Anthony Giddens, *Modernity and Self-Identity* (London: Polity Press, 1995).

31. TM, p. 134.

32. Dilthey, *Selected Writings*, p. 236.

33. See Hans Peter Duerr, *Dreamtime: Concerning the Boundary Between Wilderness and Civilisation* (Oxford: Blackwell, 1985), Chapter 12.

34. Nietzsche comments: 'The wisest man would be the one richest in contradictions', in *The Will to Power*, trans. Walter Kaufman and Roger Hollingdale (London: Weidenfeld and Nicolson, 1968), Section 259.

35. Alasdair MacIntryre, *Whose Justice? Which Rationality?* (London: Duckworth, 1988), Chapters 17, 18, 19.

36. See Chapter 1, Section 1, above.

37. Heidegger, 'The Origin of the Art Work', in *Poetry, Language and Thought*, p. 75.

38. TM, p. 97. It could be argued that this passage offers the basis of a prescient critique of the self-centred preoccupations of much so-called Brit Art.

39. Ernst Bloch, *The Spirit of Utopia* (Stanford: Stanford University Press, 2000), p. 199.

40. Ibid.

41. Franz Rosenzweig, *Understanding the Sick and the Healthy: A View*

of World, Man and God (Cambridge, MA: Harvard University Press, 1999), p. 16.

42. Dilthey, *Selected Writings*, p. 162.

43. TM, p. 85.

44. Ibid.

45. Ibid., p. 84.

46. Ibid., p. 92.

47. Ibid., p. 164.

48. Hans-Georg Gadamer, 'Aesthetics and Hermeneutics', in *The Gadamer Reader*, ed. R. E. Palmer (Evanston: Northwestern University Press, 2007), p. 129.

49. Hans-Georg Gadamer, *Philosophical Hermeneutics*, trans. David Linge (Berkeley: University of California Press, 1976), p. 38.

50. Joel Weinsheimer, *Gadamer's Hermeneutics: A Reading of Truth and Method* (New Haven: Yale University Press, 1985), p. 12.

51. TM, p. 85.

52. Ibid., p. 100.

53. Theodor Adorno, *Hegel: Three Studies* (Cambridge, MA: MIT Press, 1993), p. 138.

54. TM, p. 85.

55. Heidegger, 'The Origin of the Work of Art', in *Poetry, Language and Thought*, p. 76.

56. TM, p. 296.

57. Ibid., p. 100.

58. Ibid., pp. 144, 116, 164.

59. Ibid., p. 302.

60. Ibid., p. 100.

61. Ibid., p. 128.

62. Davey, *Unquiet Understanding*, p. 239.

63. Johann Wolfgang Goethe, *Maximen und Reflexionen* (Munich: Deutscher Taschenbuch Verlag, 1968), p. 68.

64. TM, p. 90.

65. Mikel Dufrenne, *The Phenomenology of Aesthetic Experience* (Evanston: Northwestern University Press, 1973), p. 51.

66. See Davey, *Unquiet Understanding*, Chapter 2.

67. Jürgen Habermas, *Knowledge and Human Interests* (London: Heinemann, 1972), pp. 191–3.

68. Gadamer, *The Relevance of the Beautiful*, p. 10.

69. Mark McIntosh, *Mystical Theology* (Oxford: Blackwell, 2006), p. 70.

70. Gemma Corradi Fiumari, *The Other Side of Language: A Philosophy of Listening* (London: Routledge and Kegan Paul, 1990), p. 167.

71. TM, p. 351.

72. Ibid., p. 362.

73. Ibid., p. 355.

74. Daphne Hampson, *After Christianity* (London: SCM Press, 2002), p. 262.
75. Ibid., p. 260.
76. TM, p. 12.
77. Ibid., p. 125.
78. For Paul Ricoeur's reading of this problem, see 'Distanciation and Appropriation', in *Hermeneutics and the Human Sciences*, trans. John Thompson (London: Cambridge University Press, 1981), p. 183.
79. Simone Weil, *Gravity and Grace* (London: Routledge and Kegan Paul, 1972), p. 109.
80. Iris Murdoch, *Existentialists and Mystics* (London: Chatto and Windus, 1997), p. 331.
81. Ibid., p. 369.
82. Ibid.
83. George Steiner, *Real Presences* (London: Faber and Faber, 1989), p. 148.
84. Murdoch, *Existentialists and Mystics*, p. 89.
85. Ibid., p. 54.
86. TM, p. 324.
87. Gadamer, *The Relevance of the Beautiful*, p. 10.
88. TM, p. xxx.
89. Gadamer, 'Classical and Philosophical Hermeneutics', in *The Gadamer Reader*, p. 57.
90. Gadamer, 'Hermeneutics and the Ontological Difference', in *The Gadamer Reader*, p. 366.
91. Ibid., p. 367. James Risser offers an excellent account of Gadamer's assimilation of Aristotle's conception of life as movement in his *Hermeneutics and the Voice of the Other: Re-reading Gadamer's* Philosophical Hermeneutics (Albany: State University of New York Press, 1997), pp. 125–9.
92. Gadamer, 'Autobiographical Reflections', in *The Gadamer Reader*, p. 34.
93. Ibid., p. 31.
94. TM, p. 355.
95. Gadamer, 'Autobiographical Reflections', p. 35.
96. Ibid., p. 23.
97. Charles Taylor, *Modern Social Imaginaries* (Durham, NC: Duke University Press, 2004).
98. TM, p. 474.
99. Wolfgang Iser, *The Range of Interpretation* (New York: Columbia University Press, 2000), p. 195.
100. Ibid., pp. 194–5.
101. Gadamer, 'Hermeneutics as Practical Philosophy', in *The Gadamer Reader*, p. 245.
102. TM, p. 90.
103. Aristotle writes, 'Finally, it may well be thought that the activity of

contemplation is the only one that is praised on its own account, because nothing comes from it beyond the act of contemplation.' See Aristotle's *Ethics*, ed. J. A. K. Thomson (London: Penguin, 1975), p. 304. He also says, 'But if from a living being there is taken away action, not to mention creation or production, what is left him but contemplation? And from this it follows that among human activities that which is most akin to God will bring us the greatest happiness.' Ibid., p. 305.

104. Gadamer, 'Autobiographical Reflections', p. 27.

105. Ibid., p. 36.

106. Ibid., p. 35.

107. Hegel's *Phenomenology of Spirit*, Section 27, cited by Robert B. Pippin, *The Persistence of Subjectivity: On the Kantian Aftermath* (Cambridge: Cambridge University Press, 2005), p. 77.

108. Gadamer, 'Hermeneutics and the Ontological Difference', p. 367.

109. See Christopher Smith, 'Plato as Impulse and Obstacle in Gadamer's Development of a Hermeneutical Theory', in *Gadamer and Hermeneutics*, ed. Hugh Silverman (London: Routledge, 1991), pp. 23–41.

110. Kant, *The Critique of Judgement*, pp. 175–6 (emphasis added).

111. See Samuel Todes, *Body and World* (London: MIT Press, 2002), pp. 202–30.

112. Kant, *The Critique of Judgement*, pp. 177–8 (emphasis added).

113. Ibid., p. 177.

114. TM, pp. 423–7.

115. TM, p. 179.

116. Gadamer, 'Autobiographical Reflections', p. 37.

117. Gadamer, 'On the Truth of the Word', in *The Gadamer Reader*, p. 147.

118. Ibid., p. 107.

119. Kant, *The Critique of Judgement*, p. 177. Emphasis added to draw attention to the theme prominent in Gadamer's thought, that is, the movement of Being exhibited in thought and sensation.

120. John Milbank, *The Word Made Strange: Theology, Language, Culture* (Oxford: Blackwell, 1998), p. 128.

121. TM, p. 87.

122. Milbank, *The Word Made Strange*, p. 128.

123. Ibid.

124. Ibid., pp. 136–7.

125. Ibid., p. 142.

126. TM, p. 298.

127. Ibid., p. 126.

128. Ibid., p. 128.

129. Ibid., p. 83.

4. Theoros *and Spectorial Participation*

4.1 INTRODUCTION

Methexis actually means 'participation'.[1]

Methexis . . . is a wholly formal relationship of participation; based on mutuality . . . one thing is there together with something else. Participation, *metalambanein*, completes itself [*erfüllt sich*] only in genuine being-together and belonging-together, *metechein*.[2]

Gadamer's reconstruction of aesthetic experience as a participatory act offers a new valence to the part–whole relationship within hermeneutics. The emphasis given to experiential movement and transformational understanding implies participation in a part–whole nexus. In traditional literary hermeneutics, the part–whole relationship is deployed by the knowing subject as a contextualising procedure of understanding: a section of a text is explained by being set into an exposition of the whole. For Gadamer, however, the part–whole structure is not a fixed epistemological device utilised by the interpreter to set a work into a given context but an ontological framework, the motions of which inform the interactions of an artwork's subject-matter and its spectator. Critical discussion of the part–whole relationship in hermeneutics tends to concentrate upon definitions of part and whole, disputes which Gadamer wisely avoids.

The dominant term in philosophical hermeneutics is *participation*. One cannot participate unless one is a part of what one participates in, and what is participated in cannot *be* without its participants. A principle of reciprocal original dependence is asserted: on the one hand, I could not utter the meanings I do were it nor for my dependence upon linguistic frameworks that transcend my individual consciousness; on the other, those meanings whose extent transcends my awareness

cannot maintain their being unless I participate in their play. This gives
to participation a double interactive valence: by virtue of its participation, the part is both informed by the semantic horizons in which it is
placed and informs those same horizons when engaged with its meanings. These remarks point once again to the ontological co-inherence
of x and $x+$ as a part–whole structure. The notion of participation
also strengthens the emphasis given to *Erfahrung* and the movement
of understanding it articulates. Hermeneutical part–whole structures
cannot be understood from the 'outside', as it were, but only by being
participated in. This implies that any understanding of a given part and
its place within a related whole is dependent on the subject's position
within that field. To understand more of either part or whole requires
a shift of spectorial position within the given field, a shift that will also
alter the character of that field as the spectator participates in it.

The artwork addresses a subject only because the addressee already
participates in the horizons of meaning out of which the artwork
speaks: presentation demands participation. Participation can also
be transformational. Interpretations and images not only bring complexities of past experience to summation but open possibilities for
new forms of experience and creative interaction. 'What moves [the
disclosures of a subject–matter], moves us [allows the emergence of new
associations of meaning]. Through continued dialogical participation,
new associations "move along" the cultural dialogue which grounds
the possibility of collective transformation and transcendence.'[3] As we
shall argue, achieving alteration and movement in part–whole relationships gives art its visionary power: if art moves, understanding moves.

The shift within Gadamer's aesthetics to what Wolfgang Iser has
called an 'epistemology of participation' is a consequence of the
primacy it gives to meaning in the experience of art. The apprehension of meaning requires participation in cognitive and behavioural
structures that transcend individual subjects. In Wittgenstein's terms,
to understand a language game requires partaking in a form of life.
Participation is a condition of meaning's emergence, a point established
in Gadamer's discussions of play, festival and dialogical engagement.
We have argued accordingly that aesthetic attentiveness is not best
conceived as the disinterested observation of an aesthetic object but
as that detached though attentive involvement in the play of meaning
that shows itself as, or, rather, is the 'eventing' of, art. The primacy
Gadamer gives to meaning has an important corollary that bears on the
question of participation.

Gadamer accepts that an experience of meaningfulness is dependent
upon the effective operation of part–whole relationships in a semantic

field. This strictly denies any essentialist account of intrinsic meaning because such fields are constantly shifting and it is impossible to survey them as a totality. Meaningfulness, albeit transient, is established *within* part–whole relationships. The part–whole relationship which traditional hermeneutics understands as a tool of analysis becomes in Gadamer's hands a figure for mapping the interactions of participatory engagements. The character of this transition is simply outlined.

The speculative axiom of philosophical hermeneutics is that of incommensurability: *x* is never equal to *x* but equates to *x+*. For Gadamer, 'to be' is always 'to be more': the meaning and being of both object and subject are beyond immediate grasp. 'To be' is to admit to transcendent ontological dependence. The promise of becoming more graspable depends upon continued and extended participation in fields of hermeneutical relations which enable meaningfulness and its understanding. The wholes in which we participate are, as Pannenberg stresses, necessarily incomplete.[4] Participation facilitates a completer understanding of subject and object by generating further mediations of the part–whole relations upon which they depend. This supports the argument that aesthetic attentiveness involves 'the distance necessary for seeing and thus makes possible for a genuine and comprehensive *participation* in what is presented before us'.[5] Aesthetic attentiveness extends the subject-matters one participates in. Gadamer's discussion of *theoros* is a case in point.

4.2 *THEOROS*: A DIALOGICAL APPROACH TO ART

Gadamer's hostility to purely theoretical accounts of art and aesthetic experience gains its impetus from his phenomenological *Destruktion* of the term 'theory'. He returns the modern notion of theory as a general-ising explanatory framework to the ancient sense of *theoria* as witness and participation.

> To be present means to participate ... here we can recall the concept of *theoria*. *Theoros* means someone who takes part in a delegation to a festival. *Theoria* is a true participation, not something active but something passive (*pathos*), namely being totally involved in and carried away by what one sees.[6]

The statement 'A festival exists only in being celebrated',[7] indicates the ontological argumentation underlying the assertion. (1) The audience member, a visitor to a worshipping congregation, an unexpected guest at a party is not an adjunct to an occasion but participates in bringing

an event into being. (2) Constitutive participation reinforces the ontological argument that art is an 'event'. (3) Though the artwork happens
to us independent of our willing and doing, there is a sense in which art
cannot happen without us. Gadamer's ontology of the artwork implies
a reciprocal dependence between work and spectator. After closing,
there are no works of art in an art gallery, only objects. For an artwork
to 'happen' and become culturally effective, it has to 'present' itself
to (address) a spectator.[8] Art, like the religious festival, exists in and
through continuous participation.

Gadamer's reworking of the notion of *theoria* is one of his most
important contributions to contemporary aesthetics and aesthetic
education. The account of *theoros* undercuts views that theory involves
a mode of interpretation external to art and that its use of words and
concepts is inimical to the experience of art. The affinity between the
Gadamer's approach to aesthetic contemplation and *theoria* is a powerful one.

Stressing the participatory involvement of the *theoroi*, Andrea
Wilson Nightingale observes:

> The *theoros* was thus encouraged to adopt a broader, more encompassing
> perspective. The gaze of the *theoros*, then, is characterised by alterity: the
> pilgrim brings his foreign presence to the festival, and he interacts with
> people from other cities and cultures. He thus returns home with a broader
> perspective, and brings information and ideas from foreign parts of the city.[9]

By participating in a festival, the *theoroi* enhance the being of the event
in the same way that a visitor to a church congregation not merely
bears witness to worship but swells it. By analogy, when an artwork
addresses the spectator, its being is enhanced by the observer's involvement in its annunciation of meaning.

Nightingale's stress upon alterity exposes an interesting tension in
Gadamer's argument. If an artwork speaks so directly, why does the
need to interpret arise? There is a similar *aporia* in Heidegger's aesthetics. Sophie Vlacos has suggested that Heidegger's attempt to assert
an absolute singularity for the authentic artwork in order to avoid its
nature being caught up in the customary 'metaphysics' of language
(form and content etc.) places the work beyond any meaningful communication.[10] Gadamer's position avoids the problem of singularity
as identified by Vlacos. No matter how forcibly a work announces
itself, it remains an appearance: other aspects of it remain undisclosed.
There is always more to be drawn from within the disclosed, for,
wherever meaning is experienced, the hermeneutical principle of x
$= x+$ will apply. Understanding the declarative sense of a work does
not rule out the need for interpretation. The profundity and richness

of a work require 'the test of time' not to reveal its supposed essence but to unfold its withheld capacity for expression. Interpretation allows a work 'to become more', in the sense of realising its undisclosed aspects and increasing the range of its potential historical effectiveness.

To return to the theme of *theoros*, the confrontation between theoreticians and practitioners over an artwork can be deeply estranging for both parties. Gadamer's participatory account of subject-matters suggests a reconciliation capable of enhancing mutual understanding. The key to this concerns the idea of a supplementarity of horizons. Theoretician and practitioner often share more than their professional demarcations permit them to recognise in terms of their perspectives on the same subject-matters and artworks. Hermeneutical exchange promises to expand these horizons of mutual concern and enhance the reality of the subject-matters at the core of the exchange. This is not to be understood as asserting the supremacy of the word over the experience of the visual, as critics such as Derrida have implied.[11]

Gadamer is sympathetic to the view that commentaries on poetic and visual works often lack the vividness of the original referent. However, he is right to imply that experiences which cannot be talked about rancour, become taboo, lose significance or become inconsequential. Yet to talk about an artwork is not to put it into words. The challenge of description that complex and profound works always pose their interpreters does not concern their suggested incommensurability with the linguistic. Such words do not 'capture' a work but allow it to unfold in wondrous and unexpected ways. The theologian Dale Wright points out that Buddhist hermeneutics recognises, usefully, what are called 'turning words':

> 'Turning words' are words that fit into a context in such a way that they open that context to view in some revealing way . . . what they pointed to was less a meaning than an opening or fissure in the network of meanings.[12]

Artists, such as Franz Marc and Paul Klee, who write eloquently about their work are not translating it into another medium but attempting to draw the spectator into the play of their works. The phrase 'bringing a work to life' suggests not just achieving vividness but participating in the *movement* of that work. Effective hermeneutical exchange between practitioner and theoretician requires a work's advocate to draw his or her counterpart into the subject-matter that both parties are both already grounded in. Participation in different aspects of a subject-matter's movement is, as we shall see, central to Hans Herbert Kögler's analysis of the theoretician–practitioner exchange.

4.3 THEORETICIAN–PRACTITIONER EXCHANGE

Exchange between theoreticians and practitioners can be exasperating. The theoretician often overflies the particular details of a work whilst the practitioner can become obsessed with them. A phenomenological perspective suggests that the opposition between theory and practice is misleading; after all, theoretical contemplation has its roots in aspects of observed particulars and sensual experience is mediated by concepts. Practitioner and theoretician may seem epistemological outsiders to each other but hermeneutical ontology insists that both are participants in a shared subject-matter. Such mutuality is often hidden because, as Hans Herbert Kögler argues, both parties think on the basis of largely implicit and unreflective (ideological) pre-understandings about the epistemological superiority of their own perspective. The theoretician claims to see a work as a whole, whilst the practitioner proclaims an intimacy with its particular material genesis.

Kögler realises that the stance of epistemological outsider relative to another participant has an initial advantage. Each party is capable of reciprocally revealing 'the other's subject-symbolic practical background'.[13] The 'outsider' potentially holds the key to what the 'insider' does not, as yet, know explicitly of his or her position. Once recognised, the alterity of each party becomes hermeneutically productive: a mutual dependence is revealed. The practitioner requires the theoretician's methodological and conceptual skills to articulate the context of his or her operation. To talk about an artwork is not to put it into words. The right words do not 'capture' a work but allow it to unfold in unexpected ways. On the other hand, the theorist needs the practitioner to reveal characteristics of artistic production which he or she could otherwise overlook. It was artists such as Roland Penrose who pointed out to military camouflage theorists that, in matters of deception and disguise, the texture of a surface is more important than its colour.[14] Practitioners possess knowledge about the context of an artistic presentation which can force theorists to review their initial assumptions. Kögler in effect reworks Kant's argument: without the theoretician, the practitioner's endeavour is blind; without the practitioner, the theoretician's models are without content.[15] The attainment of reciprocal understanding confirms that both parties are mutual participants in sets of aesthetically productive relations that transcend them both. It establishes the basis of an emergent aesthetic community.

Theoretician and practitioner invariably share a common situatedness with regard to the historically constituted subject-matters which constitute a work and the horizons within which it appears. That the two parties can have different perspectives on the *same* body of cultural meaning is veiled from them by the illusion of privileged epistemological access at the heart of their individual claims to disciplinary autonomy. An ontological recognition of common situatedness with regard to an artwork's subject-matters significantly undermines the standard opposition between theory and practice. Theoretician and practitioner are mutually involved in the quest to '*Begreifen, was uns ergreift*'.[16] Kögler's case can be taken further. Like Hegel's argument concerning the priest and the disciple, it suggests that, once it is recognised, neither party can lay claim to the truth (though each party is situated perspectivally within it); both parties emerge as part of a hermeneutic community and bring to it different but related aspects of the truth (subject-matter), around which its emergence takes place. A community with a shared open faith in the truth emerges: the theoretician is no longer dominant over the practitioner but shares with him or her a vulnerability and awe in the face of a transcendent truth that binds their common concern. Common involvement emerges when both parties realise they are not epistemological opponents laying siege to the truth of a work but participants in the emergence of its truth. Each brings to the dialogue different but reciprocal understandings of a common involvement in the part–whole relationships which sustain a work. Unlike Kantian aesthetics, which looks to the possibility of the formation of a civilised community (*Bildung*) arising from the suspension of competitive interests in the objective referent of a work, Gadamerian aesthetics implies that the mutual recognition that each party has different but supplementary interests in the truth of a subject-matter establishes the basis of a 'commonwealth' of mutually supplementing interpretations. The ontological significance of the theoretician–practitioner exchange is, then, that it not only allows the understanding of each party to 'become more' but that, by bringing each participant to recognise their common situatedness in relation to the subject-matters of art, it also promises the emergence of a non-competitive hermeneutical community which delights in and celebrates the mutual complementarity of their different interests. Philosophical hermeneutics lends support to the argument that the effects of aesthetic exchange are humanising: *my* interest in the truth of a subject-matter and its fulfilment *requires* engagement with the other.

> The capacity to transcend and to reflect on one's situated self as such opens up a transgressive space of self-creation that avoids deterministic or reductionist pitfalls. The reflexive self takes an attitude toward self that does not reify self into an object or atom of social life but that understands the self as a relation in social networks.[17]

Kögler's account expands beyond the conditions of self-reflexivity to those that can establish a hermeneutical community. His analysis of the theoretician–practitioner debate has greater formative ontological implications than those he imagines. The revaluation of the *theoros* suggests that the role of theoretician and practitioner within the arts is genuinely supplementary. Both partake in art's subject-matters in different ways and reciprocally extend their effective reality. This argument has notable consequences for aesthetic education.

Many students arrive at art schools unknowing of the character of the cultural horizons that have shaped their understanding of what constitutes 'great' painting or sculpture. Such students are often unaware of the degree to which their visual understanding is ideologically shaped. Art educators often respond to the influence of (conservative) tradition either with an assertion of modernist values which bluntly denies any value to the past or with a deconstruction of it so as to reveal its uncomfortable social bias. Both tactics attempt to restore a supposedly more natural, more spontaneous eye. This is not the place to take issue with the overtly nineteenth-century romantic assumptions that underpin these contemporary appeals to individuality and originality. As E. H. Gombrich observes, 'the innocent eye, sees nothing'.[18]

The task of the hermeneutic educator is to make explicit what lies implicit within a student's normative assumptions. This is often best undertaken by contrast and comparison. It is axiomatic in philosophical hermeneutics that understanding begins at that precise point whereby the differences between our own position and that of another show themselves. Working with other traditions and genres quickly exposes previously unseen alternative approaches to subject-matters. What initially appear as paradigmatic ways of dealing with an issue in painting can be revealed as just one of several plausible responses to a subject-matter. Not only does this increase a student's awareness of the repertoire of available responses but it allows students to take ethical responsibility for their own engagement with that subject-matter. Hermeneutic analysis of the traditions which underlie a student's perspective can uncover how that perspective is indebted to other artists' approaches. It poses a question too. How can practitioners (whether student or professional) contribute to the enhancement and historical effectiveness of the subject-matters that ground their practice? The relationship between teacher and student within this argument is analogous to Hegel's dialectical reshaping of the priest–disciple relationship. The master practitioner may possess what the student does not, namely a long practical experience of a working tradition, a mastery of the 'tricks of the trade' and a clear assimilation of 'know-how'. But, despite

the acquisition of such skills, the master practitioner does not, logically speaking, possess any more 'superior' knowledge of a truth than
a student does. Indeed, the master practitioner sometimes needs the
naiveté of the 'young Turk' to see aspects of long-established practices
in a new way. On the other hand, the apprentice needs the practical
'know-how' of the master practitioner in order to acquire the skills
required to negotiate the specific challenges that certain subject-matters
pose. In effect, the model of art education that philosophical hermeneutics suggests is not one of power (and revolt) but of a dialogical
reciprocity in which both parties engage, on the basis of a mutual need:
a recognition that the other can open his or her partner's horizon to
possibilities which require a fresh pair of eyes to see. The authoritarian
dimensions of the classic master–apprentice relation dissolve, and can
be replaced by a mutuality of common involvement in art's subject-
matters. The master–apprentice relation is not as restrictive as Richard
Sennett sometimes implies.[19] The transition from a proprietorial struggle over the 'truth' of a work to the mutual recognition of practitioner
and theoretician as agents in bringing that truth forward promises to
initiate a non-competitive aesthetic collegiality. Both parties draw out
aspects of a work's subject-matter which previously remained withdrawn from the other. We come to see otherwise by seeing how others
see. The argument puts a very persuasive case for interdisciplinarity
within the humanities.

4.4 SUMMARY

The participatory nature of aesthetic attentiveness accords *theoria*
with an ontologically constructive role. The positive evaluation of
theoria leads to a deconstruction of the classic theory/practice distinction. The transition from proprietorial struggles over the 'truth' of
a work to the mutual recognition of practitioner and theoretician as
complementary agents in bringing the truth of a work into being offers
the basis of a non-competitive aesthetic collegiality. We have argued,
furthermore, that Gadamer's critique of the subjectivist attitude of
modern aesthetics culminates in the reconstruction of aesthetic experience as a participatory act. This immediately involves the spectator
in a network of objective part–whole relationships which inform the
subject/spectator and yet transcend him or her. Gadamer's reform of
aesthetics aims to free it from the charge of inconsequential subjectivity to the end of demonstrating that the experience of art does have a
cognitive content. The claim that the experience of art *is* an experience
of meaning forces a complete change in the structure of the argument:

the subject's experience of art no longer stems from isolated personal responses but from participation in shared fields of meaning, which sustain aesthetic ideas or subject-matters whose core meanings are historically established. The assertion of meaning as primary redefines subjective response as participatory interaction within a nexus of cultural relationships that informs but transcends the being of individual participants. It is in this context that the hermeneutic axiom of surplus meaning, $x = x+$, comes into its own.

The principle $x = x+$ asserts that the meaning of a word or image can never be propositionally contained, since the totality of semantic relationships to which it is connected cannot be captured in the logic of statements: x always means (intends) more than itself, hence $x = x+$; or, alternatively expressed, x and $x+$ are incommensurables. Nevertheless, the meaning of x depends on its relationship to $x+$, that is, the meaning of the part is dependent upon the wider field of relationships it belongs to. Indeed, the meaning of x will depend upon from where within the field of $x+$ it is viewed. Gadamer's assertion of the word's ontological primacy is co-extensive with an assertion of the original ambiguity and opaqueness of meaning. Such vagueness confirms that a word or image can act has a placeholder in different horizons of meaning and facilitate movement between them. References to subject-matters and aesthetic ideas as bodies of part–whole relations neither imply that they are timeless essential structures nor that they have a closed meaning or identity. Subject-matters and aesthetic ideas are not Platonic forms or eternal archetypes that somehow stand outside the cognitive relations that point to them. As they transcend a spectator's individual perspective, they are historically emergent forms established by fluid, interconnected, open frameworks of meaning which gather a consistency of reference over time. No spectator can claim definitive knowledge of an aesthetic idea or subject-matter: the idea is historically fluid and, as a participant in its particular field of meaning, it is impossible for the spectator to view its totality. Within the perspective of hermeneutic thought, these arguments do not suggest a negative conclusion.

If definitive knowledge of a form requires that it be conceived as an essential identity, it can never be known. All that can be known of it is, in effect, what it is: a transient field of historically established part–whole relationships. Though final or complete knowledge of a subject-matter or aesthetic idea is impossible, the possibility of further knowledge is not. At this point in our argument, the themes of participation and movement coalesce: within a part–whole structure, participating subjects can only increase their knowledge of that which circumscribes them by changing their perspectival position within the whole in which they are situated. Knowledge and understanding of x become 'more' when significant movement relating to the spectator occurs in field $x+$. Since hermeneutics stresses that self-understanding is also dependent upon interaction with an external environment, a change in the nature of how x is understood can induce change in how spectators understands themselves. Furthermore, as the discussion of the practitioner/theoretician debate indicated, both types of participant can allow their individual perspective on a subject-matter or work of art to be expanded by the other. In consequence, the work becomes 'more'.

It might be argued that participation in a part–whole field of meaning limits one's understanding of x, in that one's historical and cultural location within a field inevitably curtails one's perspective. This is true but having a perspective is a condition of it being expanded or changed. The subject's participation in a collectively established field of meaning is important. More important, however, is the fact that such participation is the precondition of a transformative movement within one's understanding, which we described above as Gadamer's doubled hermeneutics: in the experience of an artwork, modes of a part–whole relationship can come to permeate a customary perspective in such a way as not to displace it but to achieve a new and significant permutation of it, permanently altering its initial configuration. Movement between part–whole relationships is key and, once again, justifies the stress we have placed upon movement within aesthetic attention.

The primacy Gadamer accords to the word implies that ambiguity and opaqueness of meaning are also original. The relationship between the clear and the vague, the confused and the distinct, affirms the multiplicity of part–whole relationships that words and images exist within. Gadamer's position is not unique. His account of the confused and the distinct echoes the relationship as differently articulated in Cartesian aesthetics, as well as in Baumgarten's and Leibniz's aesthetics. What is experienced as ambiguous in one framework is so only in relation to an experience of clarity in another. Vagueness and ambiguity confirm that a word or image can act as a placeholder for different meanings in various horizons of meaning and facilitate the possibility of movement between them. A spectator does not live in a single unified horizon but amongst many part–whole relationships, be they literary, philosophical, linguistic or historical. Being placed within multiple horizons is an important condition of transformative understanding. A spectator might not be initially aware that a meaning in one field of relationships connects with another. However, accident, in the form of an unexpected confrontation with a new artwork, simply hearing an unexpected turn of phrase, or undergoing fresh experiences, can prompt unpredicted movement between two sets of part–whole relationships. They can realign in such a way as allows the placeholder meanings held in common to operate as revolving semantic gateways, by means of which one part–whole relationship starts to inflect another, altering its pattern and configuration. The movement between the part–whole relationships in which a spectator participates is key to transformational understanding.

The assertion of meaning as primary has far-reaching practical con-sequences for Gadamer's aesthetics. Meaning is both participatory and grounding. It positions a spectator's responses to art in shared fields of meaning which, though metaphysically contingent, are far from arbi-trary in historical terms. The spectator's experience of art expresses a cognitive element: it reflects the collective part–whole relationships out of which it emerges. The fluid meanings generated by the part–whole relationships that constitute both subject-matters and aesthetic ideas are upheld and extended by the movement between field participants. Transformational understanding is not a matter of acquiring knowledge of an additional aspect of x but concerns a poignant experience of move-ment, an experience of a familiar framework of references undergoing significant permutations of form or content. Gadamer's reconstruc-tion of aesthetic experience as a participatory act within part–whole relationships confirms that the experience of art has a 'substantiality' that does not reduce to matters of personal feeling. To the contrary, aesthetic experience is an expressive manifestation of that 'substantial-ity' of framework (tradition, personal horizon, discipline perspective) which precedes, informs and transcends such subjective experience. The argument leads to another set of fundamental questions. What mode of being is it that one participates in when one engages with an artwork? How is the *being* of the latter to be understood and how does participa-tion in that being reciprocally affect participant and participated in? It is to these questions and their relationship to matters of presentation and appearance within aesthetics that we now turn.

NOTES

1. Hans-Georg Gadamer, 'Plato as Portraitist', in *The Gadamer Reader*, ed. R. E. Palmer (Evanston: Northwestern University Press, 2007), p. 311.
2. Hans-Georg Gadamer, 'The Art Work in Truth and Image', in *The Gadamer Reader*, p. 317.
3. Nicholas Davey, 'Truth, Method and Transcendence', in *Consequences of Hermeneutics: Fifty Years After Gadamer's* Truth and Method, ed. J.

Malpas and S. Zabala (Evanston: Northwestern University Press, 2010), p. 37.

4. Wolfhart Pannenberg, *Theology and the Philosophy of Science* (London: Darton, Longman and Todd, 1976), p. 309.
5. TM, p. 128 (emphasis added).
6. TM, pp. 124–5. Richard Sennett observes, '*Theoria* shares a root in Greek with *theatron*, a theatre, which means literally a "place for seeing." The philosopher can pay a certain price in the theatre of ideas for durable ideas that the craftsman in the workshop does not.' See *The Craftsman* (London: Penguin, 2008), p. 124.
7. TM, p. 124.
8. Ibid., p. 164.
9. Andrea Wilson Nightingale, *Spectacles of Truth in Classical Greek Philosophy: Theoria in Its Cultural Context* (Cambridge: Cambridge University Press, 2005), p. 35. Nightingale is well aware of the dangers of being a *theoros*, returning home to an environment which becomes hostile to what was witnessed. A telling contemporary example is the fate of those Soviet citizens who fought for Stalin in the Spanish Civil War only to return to labour camps and execution.
10. Sophie Vlacos, *Paul Ricoeur and the Theoretical Imagination*, PhD Thesis, Cardiff University, September 2011.
11. See J. M. Bernstein, *The Fate of Art: Aesthetic Alienation from Kant to Derrida and Adorno* (London: Polity Press, 1992), Chapter 3.
12. Dale S. Wright, *Philosophical Meditations on Zen Buddhism* (London: Cambridge University Press, 1998), p. 103.
13. Hans Herbert Kögler, *The Power of Dialogue* (Cambridge, MA: MIT Press, 1996), p. 257.
14. See Tim Newark, *Camouflage* (London: Thames and Hudson, 2007), pp. 92–3. See also Peter Forbes, *Dazzled and Deceived: Mimicry and Camouflage* (London: Yale University Press, 2009), plate 18.
15. Immanuel Kant, *Critique of Pure Reason*, trans. Norman Kemp Smith (London: Macmillan, 1970), A 51, B 75.
16. Hans-Georg Gadamer, 'Classical and Philosophical Hermeneutics', in *The Gadamer Reader*, p. 61.
17. Kögler, *The Power of Dialogue*, p. 270.
18. Ernst Gombrich, *Art and Illusion: Studies in the Psychology of Pictorial Representation* (Oxford: Oxford University Press, 1983), p. 271.
19. Sennett, *The Craftsman*, Part 1, Section 2.

5. Presentation, Appearance and Likeness

5.1 INTRODUCTION

Gadamer's critique of aesthetic subjectivity insists that, phenomenologically speaking, an involvement with art demonstrates that the experience of meaning has primacy over the experience of aesthetic properties. If meaning results from the conveyance of significance within bodies of semantic relations (which Gadamer describes collectively as linguisticality), meaning's mode of being, whether visual or literary, is *presentational*. With characteristic restraint, this simple move in Gadamer's aesthetics prompts a major ontological shift in thinking about the ancient but nonetheless continuingly contentious question of art's relation to reality. The prominence of word and image in the experience of meaning attests to the ontological primacy of presentation: the disclosive attributes of art exhibit the processural nature of Being itself. This supports the additional claim that the transformative effects of art allow the real to become more real. The linkage of Being, art and meaning as disclosure prompts a reappraisal of the ontological significance of appearance. Establishing 'appearance' as the ontological mode of a subject-matter grounds the argument that temporal appearances add to, rather than detract from, the reality of their subject-matters. This argument prompts a revaluation of the ontological status of both 'likeness' and image as potentially transforming the part–whole relationships from which they spring. Likenesses become visualisations of future possibilities within part–whole relationships and images assume in art a cognitive significance by allowing their objects 'to become more what they are' (*Werden zum Sein*). Such arguments rework the classical distinctions between *mimesis* and *imitation*. They are the consequence of a commitment to art as presentation (*Darstellung*) and reveal the importance of the ontological categories of participation and relationality in philosophical hermeneutics. The arguments culminate in a novel reappraisal of the part–whole relationship in hermeneutics which points, in its turn, to the argument that what art discloses is not the actual *per se* but analogous patterns of reasoning which intimate different readings of how the actual might be understood.

5.2 THE PRIMACY OF PRESENTATION

If word and meaning are original, then so too is presentation: presentation is meaning's mode of being. In the experience of art, meaning *presents* itself. One might speak of onto-*logos* – the being that both is and which presents itself through the word or image. Following Heidegger, Gadamer adopts the thesis that the fundamental characteristic of Being is self-presentational. Being is self-presentation for 'what presents itself in this way is not different from itself in presenting itself'.[1] There is no hidden reality, no thing-in-itself, behind the presentation: *appearing* is of the essence. With this simple assertion, the reality/appearance distinction of much European aesthetics is swept aside, but not without the consequent need for philosophical hermeneutics to revalue the meaning of aesthetic appearance. If Being and art are both modes of presentation, what distinguishes the artwork from the actual? The need for revaluation suggests three points.

First, aesthetic appearance as disclosure no longer represents an obstacle to an understanding of its intended objects (subject-matters). Though the event of disclosure can only ever be partial, that which denies it completeness, that is, time, grants the possibility of a fuller understanding as each newly revealed aspect of a work adds to those already experienced. Something that a previous generation of spectators could not have seen within a subject-matter becomes discernible to participants with a different orientation. We, for example, might consider medieval landscapes as 'picturesque' in way that Renaissance viewers would not. Such a visual *epistemé* was not available to them. Not so for us, and so the temporality of aesthetic appearance ceases to be a hindrance and contributes to an enhanced understanding of a subject-matter.

Second, the temporality of aesthetic appearance suggests an ontology of revealment and concealment, a continuous alternation between what has appeared and what has yet to appear. Gadamer appreciates that Heidegger's celebration of disclosure is allied to his rejection of 'total objectifiability', hence his awareness of the concealment that accompanies every disclosure.[2]

> Revealment and hiddenness are an event of being itself. To understand this
> fact helps us in our understanding of the nature of the artwork. There is
> clearly a tension between the emergence and the hiddenness that constitute
> the being of the work itself ... its truth is not its simple manifestation of
> meaning, but rather the unfathomableness and depth of meaning. Thus by
> its very nature the work of art is a conflict between world and earth, emer-
> gence and hiddenness.
>   The conflict between revealment and concealment is not the truth of the
> work of art alone but the truth of every being, for as unhiddenness, truth is
> always such an opposition of revealment and concealment. The two belong
> necessarily together.[3]

Heidegger's argument supports Gadamer's assertion that 'the experience of art acknowledges that it cannot present the full truth of what
is experienced in terms of definitive knowledge. There is no absolute
progress and no final exhaustion of what lies in a work of art. The
experience of art knows this of itself.'[4] The positive corollary of this
negative insight is that the finitude of an artwork's disclosures permits
others at other times. The artwork becomes an inexhaustible source of
wonderment that always promises to reveal more than it has shown.

    Third, the oscillation of revealing and concealing within the event
of presentation involves a subtle reworking of the part–whole relationship. The emergence of a powerful image is in terms of the hermeneutic
axiom of $x = x+$, a forceful presentation of x (part) to the spectator.
That revelation gains its power because it is also an enigmatic and
partial disclosure of $x+$, the speculative field (whole) from which x gains
its resonance. The presence of $x+$ in x can be only partially disclosed,
since the totality $(x+)$ cannot be rendered in either image or conceptual
form. Yet that disclosure makes manifest within the image the presence of the yet to be revealed. Such oscillation gifts an artwork with
greater historical effectiveness. That a work can never be fully objectified implies that it can come constructively to mean different things to
different historical audiences. J. S. Bach heard by and reconstructed by
Ferruccio Busoni will not be the Bach heard and rearranged by Edward
Elgar or Luigi Berio.[5] Like Nietzsche, Gadamer rejects the notion of
work-in-itself as a pure abstraction, as if interpretation were an ines-
sential overlay.[6] Furthermore, what a work is capable of presenting
depends on the nexus of cultural relationships in and through which
it shows itself. What is accordingly disclosed or withheld will be relative to the horizons in which the work is received. The still-life and the
surreal image are emergent historical forms which can influence the
reception of works in ways unimaginable to their original creators and
audiences. This lends Gadamer's notion of a contemplative dwelling-
with a work a specific poignancy. It is a matter of 'watching-with' a

work not just so as to allow its different aspects to come forth but also to allow ourselves to adjust categories of interpretation so that works come to life in unexpected ways. This is central to the notion of aesthetic attentiveness proposed in Chapter 3. The hermeneutic process of soliciting undisclosed aspects from a work increases the latter's reality by multiplying the range of its historical effectiveness.

On one level, Gadamer's approach to the question of art's relation to reality dissolves the distinction. Art considered as 'presentation' or 'disclosure' simply is what Being is, that is, a perpetual process of appearance and disappearance. This gives rise to a question considered below: if art and Being are both modes of disclosure, what distinguishes art from actuality? As 'presentation', Being discloses itself through word and image not because either captures it but because both exhibit its processural features: both show and hide simultaneously and in their showing show that they hide. The interconnection of Being, word and image is illustrated by the argument that what Being is cannot be asserted, only shown. It is shown by what the word makes manifest and by what the image reveals though the symbol. When used in a sentence, the word 'Being' calls forth a certain meaning or orientation and yet such meaning always remains opaque and leaves something yet to be said. The symbol operates in a similar manner, summoning a specific set of meanings and hiding others. Insofar as word and image function annunciatively (simultaneously showing and hiding), they not only participate in Being but show (do) what Being is. This is perhaps what Gadamer means when he comments on 'Being as the word in which truth happens'.[7] The word and, indeed, the image *do* what Being is: it is an ever-present waxing and waning of disclosure.[8] This interplay of disclosure and withholding enables Gadamer to equate art and what it brings into appearance as the real. Art neither provides us with images nor pictures of the real but, insofar as it is eventual, it is a bringing into being of the real. This ontological perspective attributes to art a transcendental capacity. Art exhibits generative processes which extend beyond the seen. Indeed, it is the artwork which makes discernible that which is, logically speaking, anterior to the work, beyond the work and yet cannot be seen other than through the artwork, that is, the showing that is Being itself. What is more, as we shall see, insofar as the image can draw attention to as yet unrealised possibilities within Being, the artwork also adds to the effective reality of Being.

This language of disclosure and uncovering should not suggest that art's processes of revealing are mere spectacle. To the contrary, not only are we 'played' by these processes (shaped by their subject-matters), but we participate in and play with these processes and, thereby, uphold their being. Gadamer's ontology of art is participatory: experiencing art (interacting with it) is a mode of art's being. Indeed, it is engagement with the subject-matter of a work that allows an aspect of something withheld to be brought forward. This supports our principal claim that aesthetic attentiveness contributes to the actualisation of the real. Aesthetic distance, Gadamer claims, is 'the distance necessary for seeing and thus makes possible a genuine and comprehensive *participation* in what is presented before us'.[9] To participate is to bring to life what we are *already* part of.

Though Gadamer inexplicably underplays the point, presentation presupposes participation. What presents itself as an image to the spectator is a part of a wider part–whole nexus concerning a subject-matter that also intersects the horizons within which the spectator stands. Such asymmetry allows the spectator to bring different perspectives to the image, thereby increasing the range of its hermeneutic effectiveness. This is consistent with the argument that, within an open part–whole structure, further knowledge is made possible only by a change in the perspectival position of the spectator. The experience of art becomes less a subjective and more a participatory act in what is presented. Participation increases the effective Being of the image. However, the general argument is not without difficulty. If art and Being are both modes of presentation, what distinguishes art from the mode of disclosure that is Being? This is a complex question which we shall consider by reflecting on the nature of the likeness.[10]

5.3 ON THE LIKENESS

> I have, among other things, also tried to refute the idea that the art image is a mere copy of something.[11]

It is an irony (not uncharacteristic of his corpus) that the ontological characteristics of one of the more conservative art forms – portraiture – intimates the more radical side of Gadamer's thinking about art's effective being. The question of the portrait has a direct bearing on the relation of art to actuality, on the nature of a likeness, and concerns the cognitive value of such an image. How does the portrait increase the being of a sitter? What does the portrait add to the original and what comes to presence in the picture that cannot be understood simply by *looking* at the sitter?

Reflecting on the case of the portrait may seem unrewarding from the perspective of philosophical hermeneutics. If the portrait is understood as offering only a visual memento of the sitter, Gadamer questions whether such a work can be considered art: portraits are copies, likenesses or *mementos* of a person and *cannot* be treated as artworks, for the commonsensical reason that the person copied 'has a being that is independent of the copy of it – so much so that the picture seems ontologically inferior to what it represents'.[12]

If the portrait is intended as a commemorative copy of the sitter, success depends on achieving a resemblance to the original. This requires the self-erasure of the image. In bringing the beloved to mind, the memento's status as artefact disappears. Of course, the lover would prefer to be in the presence of his beloved but, in her absence, the memento suffices as a means of recollection. In other words, the portrait as visual record does not have the ontological impact of the original. An artwork, however, is never destined to be self-effacing. It protests its presence. It has something to say about the original and can thereby affect it.[13]

Discussions about the success of a portrait often make comparisons between the nature of its representation and the perceived nature of its objective correlative, the sitter. Such considerations do not fit with Gadamer's efforts to abandon representational conceptions of art. Proclaiming the priority of an external correlative, such conceptions demote art's cognitive status to the secondary, precisely the devaluation resisted by philosophical hermeneutics. Given Gadamer's commitment to an ontology of flux, any attribution of representational status to portraiture also reinvokes a negative concept of aesthetic appearance. The fixity of the portrait image can only present an idealisation of the sitter; insofar as the latter is in a condition of constant, albeit hardly perceptible, change, the portrayed 'likeness' can only ever be a misleading appearance.

Even if the argument is reversed and portraiture is considered art proper, challenging questions remain. Art proper involves 'the joy of knowing *more* than is already familiar'[14] and effects an increase in the being of its subject-matter. How does portraiture effect 'a new event of being', permitting the sitter to experience an increase in his or her being? To suggest that a portrait adds something to my being implies something outside of myself which, when linked to my present self-understanding, allows me to become more than I presently am. How is this possible? Furthermore, for a mode of thought which celebrates becoming, any pictorial ambition to 'capture' the immutable essence of a person might appear naive, if not contemptible.[15] The portrait image is surely an arrested moment within the vital temporal flow of a living person.[16] To draw such conclusions is premature, since Gadamer's aesthetic reasoning moves towards an unarticulated but highly original theory of portraiture grounded upon a phenomenological conception of 'likeness' pertinent to the claim that the presentational artwork increases the reality of its subject-matter.

Appreciating Gadamer's approach to 'likeness' requires abandoning any sense of the term as corresponding to a fixed thing, essence or object. In neo-Platonic aesthetics we might say that the likeness moves away from its original, whereas for Gadamer the likeness moves towards or anticipates the coming of its original. In philosophical hermeneutics, the likeness is ontologically constructive, a presentation, an object of aesthetic epiphany and not an object of epistemological reconstruction (re-presentation). A picture is no mere copy of a subject-matter but a visual medium in which a subject-matter comes forth pictorially. Presentation is more than a copy.[17] The original referent suffers no diminution of being by being pictorially represented. The picture, rather, occasions the ontological emanation of the original or, in Gadamer's words, the original comes to presentation in the image and, as such, presents itself there.[18] If the portrait is not a copy but a picture, from the point of view of the sitter it follows that, in the portrait image, sitters await in a consummate way 'the heightened truth of their being'. That a sitter might experience discomfort at the prospect of his or her likeness arriving would not be unsurprising. The force of that discomfort relates to the epistemological power that an image or likeness acquires within a realm of becoming. How is this to be understood?

Knowledge of both ourselves and reality 'always stands in a horizon of undecided future possibilities'. Reality is that which 'is untransformed'.[19] Self-knowledge is fragmentary, incomplete and mutable, depending upon changes in personal context and circumstance. In a realm of continuous flux, such knowledge appears elusive. As Nietzsche emphasises, knowledge and becoming mutually exclude one another.[20] However, Gadamer's point of reference is not Heraclitus or Nietzsche but Hegel and Husserl. Reality need not remain untransformed but can be raised up into its truth.[21] In this respect, Gadamer is sympathetic to Husserl's perspectivism: objects in the world are not so much the (external) objects of experience but are constituted by experience. He notes the argument of Husserl's *Ideen*: what we understand as a 'thing' is the continuity with which the various perceptual perspectives of an entity shade into one another and adumbrate themselves. Although 'every shading of the object of perception is exclusively distinct from every other, each helps co-constitute the "thing-in-itself" as the continuum of these nuances'.[22] This implies that what we perceive as a person is not an empirically given totality but aspects of a unity constructed over time, drawn from the continuities of experience itself. The question of whether an image is a good likeness or not does not concern verisimilitude between it and the 'real' sitter (as in the classical copy–original relationship) but whether it is congruent with the field of perspectives which forms the sitter in the mind of the spectator. The question is whether the portrait image or likeness brings the fragmentary perspectives held in the spectator's mind to a greater coherence, such that the sitter as imaged gains a greater effective presence. By bringing the fragmented parts of the sitter as experienced into an effective whole, the likeness lends a coherence to what was initially experienced as incoherent and incomplete, allowing sitters to become 'more essentially' what they are.[23] They 'become' more like themselves. The image is essentially constructive, anticipating more than what is initially given. It is clear that when Gadamer speaks of likeness in this manner he is not thinking of *mimesis* as *imitation* in the Platonic fashion (the likeness is at a remove from and a distortion of the original) but more in the manner of Aristotle, and presents *mimesis* as *Vollendung* (a bringing to completion). This gives rise to crucially different shadings in the meaning of the word 'likeness'.

Gadamer is conscious that, for Plato, there is an insuperable ontological difference between the thing that is a likeness (the sign or reference) and the thing which it is a likeness of (referent). Yet, without seeing it, Gadamer's repudiation of the portrait-as-copy thesis places extraordinary pressure on the more conventional meaning of likeness. If the portrait is not a copy of an actual objective co-relative, what is the portrait a likeness of? What if, as etymology permits, to look for a likeness can mean *to seek an image for*? Seeking an image or likeness *for* a subject suggests a philosophical orientation different to that which regards a likeness as a re-presentation or duplication *of* an original. *Mimesis* is not *imitatio* for Gadamer but the creative anticipation of as yet unrealised possibilities within a perceived subject-matter, an image of a reality which is yet to be.[24]

The emergence of a likeness presupposes that the spectator to whom it presents itself is situated in a horizon of visual and cultural references that allows it to be recognised as such. In other words, the emergence of a likeness assumes prior experience of a set of relations which hold the key as to whether the likeness achieves truthfulness or not. A pictorial image can bring an unformed and inarticulate state of affairs to an articulate truth in the sense that when seen as a pictorial image or likeness, that multiple state of affairs is visible in all its singularity, perhaps for the first time. Likenesses are not propositions stating how things are but visual anticipations of how hitherto unseen possibilities in a field of experience can be brought to culmination in such a way as to transform a previously experienced disparate set of affairs into an image of what that set more essentially is or, rather, can be seen as becoming. To find an image or likeness is not just to describe or reproduce the perceived but to endeavour to say something about it which renders it singular, to bring it into a visual summation such that were it not translated into an image, it would remain incoherent and inarticulate. The image achieves for its subject-matter a new mode of relationality. The skill of the portrait painter is, then, to summon from a host of present and previous observations, an image or likeness which unifies, gives sense and identity to a singular multiplicity. Two observations can be made here.

First, the description of the image or likeness as visual summation of what is at play within a state of affairs is analogous to Gadamer's transformation-into-structure argument.[25] The potent image produces cohesiveness in an experiential field which would otherwise have remained hidden and withdrawn:[26] the successful image raises an untransformed reality to its truth. The original (the experiential field which constitutes the sitter in the spectator's phenomenological field) suffers no diminution of being by being pictorially presented; rather, the picture is the ontological transformation of what was held in the original as untransformed.

Second, the congruence of the image-as-visual-summation with the transformation-into-structure argument suggests that the quest for a likeness is not a search for visual equivalence but for that image which reveals and articulates that which we have not, in effect, yet seen. We should also note that the argumentation suggests a response to a question raised above: if art and Being are both modes of disclosure, what distinguishes art from actuality? Modes of gradation would appear to be the answer. The likeness is a mode of appearance that unifies and coheres other appearances, whereas the appearances of actuality are open ended, awaiting their transformation into a unified multiplicity by the image. No wonder, then, that the art image allows us to see actuality otherwise.

To return to the questions that concern us. (1) How does the picture portrait increase the being of the sitter? (2) What does the portrait add to the original referent which was not originally within it? (3) What comes to presence in the picture that cannot be understood simply by *looking* at the sitter? The function of the image is to bring the contingent and variable aspects of how a sitter is perceived into a coherent and as yet unseen whole. It is in this sense that the being of the sitter is increased: she or he acquires something not previously possessed, namely, a likeness. The portrait's likeness allows us to know more of the sitter than we were previously familiar with. Replace the phrase 'work of art' with the word 'likeness' and the following passage makes Gadamer's central Aristotelean point:

> What we experience in a work of art [likeness] and what invites our atten-
> tion is how true it is, to what extent one knows and recognises something
> and oneself. . . . *The joy of recognition is rather the joy of knowing more*
> *than is already familiar.* In recognition what we know emerges, as if illumi-
> nated, from all the contingent and variable circumstances that condition it:
> It is grasped in its essence.[27]

The likeness does not correspond to an actual property but allows us to make sense of, or bring out the truthfulness of, an unnoticed mul-tiplicity of properties. Seeing a likeness is not seeing a *thing* that is a whole but seeing a set of relationships *rendered whole* by the image. What comes to presence within the picture that is not in the original set of experienced relations is the likeness itself. A likeness brings a new coherence to our seeing of a person not possible prior to its disclosure in the portrait.

Our everyday mode of being is one of dispersal. We are to a degree absent from ourselves, passing from task to task without catching sight of ourselves. Rooted in actuality, we bear the marks of its untrans-formed nature: everything about us is undecided, incomplete and fragmented. There are, of course, implicit patterns and open lines of continuity in what we do but, because of our immersion in everyday projects, rarely do we see ourselves, albeit provisionally, as coherent wholes. When capturing a likeness, the artist enables a transformation of our being. The portrait increases my being by giving it something I did not previously have, namely, a likeness. The experience may be pleasurable or disconcerting because of a challenge to established self-conceptions but in either case a confrontation with my likeness can be a transformative moment of reflexive awareness not possible prior to the emergence of the likeness. My own sense of reality can brought into question by what my likeness presents me as being. Of course, I can be subject to several likenesses but the fascination of the portrait derives from its ability to reveal that we are, indeed, absent from ourselves and hope for points of consummate return and arrival. The portrait likeness occasions one such moment of return. Portraiture also adds another dimension to Gadamer's dialogical conception of art: the likeness demonstrates my dependence upon the gaze of the other in order to discern what I could not otherwise see of myself. In Gerard von Honthorst's portrait of the Queen of Bohemia, Elizabeth, the subject of the painting, not only returns the artist's gaze but seems to scan it as if only through what the artist sees in his experience of her can she can grasp something of herself. It is a strikingly modern portrait, not so much of a likeness but of someone waiting upon her likeness.[28]

5.4 *WERDEN ZUM SEIN*: THE COGNITIVE SIGNIFICANCE OF LIKENESS AND IMAGE

In the essay 'The Art Work in Word and Image', Gadamer observes:

> Art can be overwhelming for us when it appears to be a copy of something but also when it is a complete departure from all copiedness, as can be the case in abstract painting and sculpture. Clearly, we are dealing here with something quite different from the relationship of original and copy. Works of art possess an elevated rank in being, and this is seen in the fact that in encountering a work of art we have the experience of something emerging – and this one can call truth![29]

The reference to 'something emerging' links with subsequent references to 'coming into being'.[30] Gadamer's observation on the emergence of the image prompts a revaluation of the category of becoming.

> Becoming is no longer simply some kind of nonbeing, that is, something seen as the becoming of something different; now [in the image] it signifies coming into being [*Werden zum Sein*]. Being emerges from becoming![31]

This passing comment by Gadamer indicates a pivotal move in his aesthetics, the character of which can be illustrated by a brief contrast with Nietzsche's argumentation. Both philosophers are subject to the gravitational pull of Plato's concepts. Gadamer is sensitive to this:

> It is of course true that the ancient doctrine of imitation dominates poetic theory. . . . Yet it seemed to justify itself more compellingly in the visual arts, for it is here that all talk of image and original most forcefully suggests itself. There is something immediately convincing about the claim that *a fundamental distinction remains between the original and the image . . . which does not move.* So, Plato employs the concept of *mimesis* in order to emphasize the ontological distance between the original and the image.[32]

In Nietzsche's framework (which he himself describes as an inverted Platonism[33]) the image is an appearance of an appearance, an artistic simplification of what is already a perceptual interpretation of actuality, that is, that endless chaos of interactions between different *Kraftzentren* or *Willenspunktationen*.[34]

> The apparent world, i.e. a world viewed according to values; ordered, selected according to values, i.e. in this case according to the viewpoint of utility in regard to the preservation and enhancement of the power of a certain species of animal.[35]

Nietzsche retains an inverted form of the Platonic reality/appearance distinction: flux is actual, whilst appearance is the lived-in, phenomenal world. As a further simplification of phenomenality, the aesthetic image constitutes an appearance of an appearance. The portrait within Nietzsche's framework is a simplification abstracted from a realm that is already a distillation of what is in itself judged to be unintelligible. In Gadamer, a more poignant reversal takes place: the image is not an impoverishment of the real by the apparent but an enhancement of a pre-given state of affairs. The art image does not refer to actuality as it presently is but to its unrealised potentials, and, by transforming them visually, allows them to be recognised perhaps for the first time: an image of completeness promises that which in actuality has yet to be.[36] In other words, it is its completeness that marks out the aesthetic disclosure from the incompleteness of the everyday disclosure.

Gadamer's philosophical hermeneutics is free of the neo-phenomenalism which defines Nietzsche's approach to the question of appearance. He adopts Heidegger's more positive valuation of appearing: actuality *is* appearing; it does not lie behind or beyond appearance but is the endlessness of appearing itself.

> For us, however, what is essential is that we have to do here with an appearing [*Er-Scheinen*]. As a shining forth [*Scheinen*] this is in keeping with its essence as shifting appearance. And yet there is still the unique shining-forth of the beautiful that is the magic of art, whether it be in our seeing or our hearing, in our experiencing of the sculpture, poetry, or music.[37]

This indicates a further difference between the artistic appearance or likeness and uncomposed appearance. The artistic image refers to something before or beyond, that is, to the withheld, the untransformed or the yet to find completion. Every artistic image emerges from the before (of previous experience) and looks towards the beyond (of that which has yet to be experienced). Gadamer also distinguishes the living object or referent of the image (the subject-matter) from the artistic image itself: the 'image does not move'.[38] This should not mislead us: there is no absolute dualism between the original (an experienced set of affairs) and the image, since the latter, as an additional mode of appearing, brings forth what is already held within an original set of appearances. Portraiture is not an instance of an image–original relationship but of an image allowing its original referent to achieve a notable singularity by unifying the previously experienced set in a new and original manner. By bringing a process of becoming to image, the artist potentially transforms and enhances that process by lifting it on to another level, allowing it to become graspable in a way that the previous cluster of experiences was not. The likeness or image is, therefore, not a duplication but a projective summation and, as such, effects a change in the ontological status of the original. It becomes something different to what it was before, that is, singular, cohesive, referencible, more than it was. *Mimesis* is a term that implies, for Gadamer, a looking forward rather than a looking back.

> All true *mimesis* is a transformation that does not simply present again something that is already there. It is a kind of transformed reality in which the transformation points back to what has been transformed in and through it. It is a transformed reality because it brings before us intensified possibilities never seen before.[39]

This is the basis of Gadamer's claim that the 'work of art effects an increase in Being'.[40]

> Even when one is dealing with a portrait, and the person portrayed knows and finds the picture to be a likeness, it is still as if one had never seen the person before in quite this way. . . . So much *is* the person. . . . One has, so to speak, been seen into, and the more one looks, the more 'it' comes forth. Certainly the portrait is a special case. However . . . the image has its own sovereignty. One says this even about a wonderful still life or a landscape, because in the picture everything is just right. This causes one to leave behind every relation to what is copied. This is its 'sovereignty' as a picture.[41]

The ability of artistic images to both regulate and encapsulate a complexity of experiences redeems a major claim of hermeneutical aesthetics: art has a cognitive significance. It allows us to know something of the world in a way that we did not know it before. Nietzsche is once again a useful counterfoil. He speaks of how a constructed world of appearances (images of things and objects) is projected back onto the world of appearances from which they were drawn, so much so that we mistake images of things for the things themselves. Gadamer, of course, makes no reference to an unintelligible noumenal world behind sensual appearance. Neither do his references to *Sachen* (subject-matters) refer to Plato's eternal ideas or a changeless rational structure of intelligible being. For Gadamer there is but one actuality – the constantly altering and multiply tiered actuality of phenomenological reality. Neither as image nor as concept can that reality be given in its totality: it can only ever be suggested speculatively by the poetic word or the artistic image. The cognitive significance of images and likeness within this framework is evident.

Within the ontological primacy of becoming, the emergence of the image serves as a stabilising and summative point within experience, allowing memories to be preserved, permitting comparisons across time and bringing partial coherence and identity to sets of significant experience. The argument applies to the significance of the portraiture image and to those artworks that create landmark images capable of capturing and articulating communal feelings by rendering them visible, communicable and shareable. Henry Moore's drawings of Londoners sheltering from the Blitz in London's underground stations or the apocalyptic bleakness of Paul Nash's First World War battle-scapes not only speak to the moods and anxieties of those times but allow those times speak well beyond themselves. Images and likenesses might be described as the visual half-lives of the events that give rise to them. That which initially presents itself as inchoate feeling is, when transformed into image, rendered relatively intelligible. As 'that which does not move', the image effects and enhances the movement of under-standing out of which it emerges and, hence, it acquires its cognitive significance. Once established as a likeness, the image enters a world of other images, in relation to which it can acquire different meanings. Images and likeness not only have an 'effective being' amongst them-selves but affect the becoming of Being by achieving further mediations of meaning amongst the disclosive relations which constitute the latter.

5.5 THE DISJUNCTIVE IMAGE

Gadamer's discussion of presentation, likeness and image strengthens his critique of subjective aesthetic consciousness. The occasion of presentation might be metaphysically arbitrary but, hermeneutically speaking, its occurrence is far from coincidental. Its emergence presup-poses that the spectator is already placed within networks of meanings compatible with the form of the presentation itself. The notion of likeness also presupposes that a spectator is associated with a network of meanings which are recognised as transformed subsequent to the appearance of the image. When so aligned, the direction of Gadamer's argument is consistent. However, discussion of the image or likeness introduces a dialectical twist into his argument which is of considerable importance in the account of art's transformative hermeneutic power.

We have suggested that Gadamer's dialogical thinking produces a third emergent element. Aesthetic experience considered as the experi-ence of transformative meaning is not just a matter of the spectator's horizons confronting those of an artwork. Gadamer's aesthetic theory is far from academic: it is not a matter of decoding the specific discourse of an artwork. Within such an exercise, no matter how worthy, no *Erfahrung* occurs. In Hans-Peter Duerr's words, 'to understand is not the same as to translate'.[42] For philosophical hermeneutics, the point would be that within such an exercise no moment of realisation or application would have occurred: the code might have been broken but without any sense of what it meant or pointed to. Here, the opposition of philosophical hermeneutics to discourse theory is most manifest:

speculative meaning is not constrained to the internal elements of an assertion or proposition but spills out into related fields of meaning, as the axiom $x = x+$ insists. Neither is hermeneutic exchange a matter of replacing one way of seeing with another. Hermeneutic doubling is not a logic of substitution. In the experience of art, the mode of relations that constitute an artwork come to permeate those that form a customary way of seeing in such a way as not to displace it but, rather, to achieve a new and significant permutation of it, permanently altering its initial configuration. Becoming acquainted with Van Gogh's pine trees does not turn pine trees into paintings but it guarantees that, because of the painting, they will be seen differently. This entails, as we have suggested, an obversion of form: because of exposure to a foreign set of visual relations, a home perspective effectively becomes a qualitatively different world.

The claim is, then, that the experience of art enables us to see otherwise. How is this possible when the fixity of an image represents something that Gadamer acknowledges does not exist? In response to this, it can be argued that the *reality* of our experience of art – its power of transformative application – depends upon recognising that the image or likeness is disjunctive: it does not reflect actuality. To the contrary, the image celebrates the ontic priority of unrealised possibilities.[43] In this, philosophical hermeneutics follows the inspiration of Heidegger: 'higher than actuality stands possibility'.[44] The hermeneutic power of the image lies in its suggestion of possibilities that *could* become actualities.[45] The positive power of the image therefore requires a disjunctive relationship to actuality.

That the positive power of the artistic image resides in its disjunctive relationship to actuality seems counterintuitive, especially when Gadamer insists upon the ability of the image or likeness to reveal the essential truth of its subject-matter. Yet, on three levels, a disjunctive relationship between the image and actuality is clearly implied. (1) Within an actual world of Becoming, the image is proclaimed as that which does not move.[46] (2) The pictorial image has an autonomy that does not refer to anything but itself. As James Risser argues, 'a picture is not itself a copy since it is not intended to be cancelled out . . . one is not directed away from it to some anterior or posterior presentation'.[47] (3) The likeness argument suggests, by default, that a crucial aspect of the portrait image is that it cannot refer to anything actual. If the likeness is a mere repetition of something actual, it could not present an increase in the being of the sitter but only something that the sitter already possessed. What, then, is the relationship between the image and our experience of actuality?

The ability of an artistic image to transform our experience of the actual presupposes some form of effective relationship. Yet the declared incommensurability of image and Becoming, and the assertion of a purely self-referential image threaten to enclose the artwork in a world of its own. How is this conundrum to be resolved? We should look more closely at the representation/presentation distinction.

Gadamer's aesthetics rests on an ontological distinction between the representational and the presentational. Whereas representational terminology is dualist (the artistic image is judged secondary to its objective correlative), presentational concepts are monistic (the emergent character of art is of the same ontological order as the eventual nature of Being itself). Presentational terminology has advantages: it attributes a positive status to aesthetic appearance and it celebrates art as a mode of Being: 'coming into appearance' is no longer understood as a copying or devaluing of the real but as its emergence. This attributes to 'appearing' a positive value. It is a 'coming forth'. 'Art has its "being" in the vital event of its appearing'.[48] Compare these points to the ontological corollaries of representation.

(1) Representation supposes an objective correlative, in relation to which the image is mere appearance. Whether the correlative is understood as a natural or a metaphysical form is irrelevant: an external referent is supposed. The supposition is problematic for presentational ontology. In a world of Becoming, the image cannot refer to a stable empirical object or to a stable form of objectification, giving rise, once again, to one of our questions – what does an image manifest? (2) The representational image is, as image, placed at one remove from 'real Being' and is ancillary to its objective correlative, whereas in presentational ontology the coming-into-appearance of an image is of the same order of eventual Being. (3) By referring to an unchanging form, the representational image seems to assume a completeness of Being. There is nothing that the image can add to its referent. Presentational aesthetics implies, by contrast, that Being is incomplete, allowing an image a constructive ontological valence by magnifying its subject-matter. (4) The representational image acquires artistic status by being seen as a fabricated appearance of a different order to the things of actuality. This raises, as we have seen, a difficulty within presentational aesthetics: if the emergences of art and Being are of the same ontological order, what distinguishes art from Being? (5) Because the representational image is retrospective and refers back to what is ontologically prior, the language of representation is invariably nostalgic, invoking an imagined, unchanging completeness. The language of representation echoes that ancient Greek epistemé which esteems Being as complete and in so

doing condemns the art image to duplicating or reconstructing something ontologically anterior. These points clarify the force of an earlier question: if, within presentational aesthetics, the artistic image does not re-present actuality, what does it present? Consider the following.

What the artistic image within presentational aesthetics depicts is not an actual state of affairs but a future possibility, capable of transforming what we thought we had come to understand. The incommensurability of image and Becoming asserts that, as something fixed, the image cannot depict the actual. What it does represent, to the contrary, is the precedence of the possible over the actual. This commitment is not unique to Gadamer. Ernst Bloch speaks of the 'ontology of the not yet' and of 'real possibilities' as objects of hope.[49] Paul Ricouer proposes that human existence is not a fatalistic being-before-death, as Heidegger argues, but an optimistic being-before-possibility. Artistic fictions are not simple repetitions of either past or present circumstances but the creation of genuine new possibilities for existence. How is it that an image can represent the priority of the possible over the actual?

The image cannot be an image of anything actual for, as we have seen, it presents a fixed or stable identity. This marks it out as something fabricated, lacking correspondence to anything in actuality. This endorses the claim that within presentational ontology, for an image to be recognised as an *art* image, it cannot refer to any actual state but only to a state of affairs that does not *as yet* exist. What comes into appearance through the art image is a vision of completion that does not correspond to anything in actuality.

> An experience of art is like this: it is not a mere copy of something. Rather one is absorbed in it. It is more like a tarrying that waits and preserves in such a way that the work of art is allowed to come forth than it is like something we have done.[50]

Gadamer recognises that, on one level, a work of art is never complete (finished): 'there is no absolute progress and no final exhaustion of what lies in a work of art'.[51] The very notion of bringing something into appearance suggests that what appears is not the whole truth: 'the artwork withholds the very truth that it embodies and this prevents it from becoming conceptually precise'.[52] Gadamer's later writings point at a similar but differently grounded conception. The artwork, like nature, is alive through its being in motion,[53] through its constant bringing forth and hiding. Gadamer hints that the artwork has an *energeia*, a self-regulating process which continually re-organises the composite multiplicity of elements that enter into it.[54] It can be said of the artwork that, 'so long as it is ongoing, it is not completed. What is being moved is still under way, has not yet arrived. It is still becoming.'[55] 'Art has its "being" in the *Vollzug* – the vital living event of its *appearing*, or its performance.'[56] To put it another way, we might say that the very being of the artwork (its moving vital nature) is the process whereby it seeks to bring to completion what will in actuality never come to complete fulfilment. Returning to the theme of the possible and the actual, as well as the question of what the image represents, our argument suggests the following development.

Philosophical hermeneutics recognises the 'thrownness' of our existential predicament: we exist amongst a plethora of part–whole relationships, open and indeterminate in nature. The play of these relationships constitutes the being of our cultural and historical horizons. In the flux of everyday experience we pass from one alignment of meaning to another, remembering some and forgetting others. It is the character of these relationships to remain open and indeterminate so that, in actuality, their play is never resolved or completed. The genius of the image is, then, that it distils from patterns of meaning at play within our lived cultural horizons a fixed form which draws the open-ended nature of that play into a closed, intelligible structure, such that nothing is left out of place. Experience, as Gadamer argues, is shaped by horizons of desired, feared and undecided future possibilities.[57] The image envisages what is at play within those horizons as a completed circle of meaning, in which 'no lines of meaning break off or scatter in the void'. Possibilities at play within the actual achieve in the image an imagined completeness not possible without art's intervention. The image affords 'a transformation into structure', permitting a set of experiential sequences to be seen as never before, that is, as a structured whole. Word and image allow a sequence of experience to become relatively intelligible, transforming it into a *vision* of fulfilled meaning. The artistic image affords a moment of transcendence which permits seeing as whole part–whole relationships that are normally experienced as fragmented.

The aesthetic realisation of possibilities held within actuality confirms the disjunctive relationship between the image and actuality. The contained completeness of meaning within a work of art will never obtain within the open temporality of actuality. This lends the image its aesthetic autonomy: the unity of its part–whole relationships marks it off as both a 'finished work' and a work of fiction, since there is no actual state of affairs that it corresponds to. The disjuncture remains. Does this mean that, because what the image conveys does not actually exist, the artwork remains a chimera or an escapist folly?

By invoking a complete part–whole relationship, the art image refers not so much to what does not exist but to what does not *as yet* exist. This distinguishes the art-image-as-emergence from the event-as-emergence. Whereas the event-as-emergence is the coming to be of what is actual, the event as art image invokes the not-as-yet, envisioned but un-actualised possibilities within the real. No image can make actual the not-as-yet but it can breech the enclosures of perceived actuality with a vision of what it might become. Were the art image merely a representation of the actual, it would only endorse present actualities. Philosophical hermeneutics, however, insists on the precedence of the possible over the actual. Its presentational ontology suggests that the image refers to a future reality and in so doing is capable of presently transforming our understanding of what is possible within human reality.[58] As we saw in the case of the portrait, the sitter will never become his or her image but the emergence of his or her likeness can transform the sitter's understanding of what he or she might as yet become and how we too might come to understand him or her. Perhaps Adorno appreciates better than Gadamer the tragic element within this dialectic.[59] The world is not art and yet the world requires art in order for us to discern what worldly action is possible. The world can never become as complete and coherent as an artwork but the vision of a possible completeness can inspire practical action towards making the incomplete more complete. It is not a question of translating the image into actuality but of allowing that image to transform one's understanding of what is plausible or possible within actuality. This returns us to the doubled hermeneutics of Gadamer's style of thought.

In the experience of aesthetic completeness, the mode of relations that constitute an artwork come to permeate those that form an established perspective, in such a way as not to displace it but to achieve a new and significant permutation of it, permanently altering its initial character. This obversion of form prompts the home perspective to become, effectively, a qualitatively different world. Like a literary fiction, the portrait image of what a person could be (but never will actually be) flows back into the multiplicity of experiences which constitute our understanding of that person, reorganising it and allowing us to perceive that person differently. The experience of art enables us to see actuality otherwise, not by making us see it as art but by allowing art to reveal its unseen possibilities. The *reality* of our experience of art – its power of transformative application – depends upon recognising that the image or likeness is disjunctive not so much because it does not reflect actuality *per se* but, rather, because its very disjunctiveness reveals actuality's future possibilities.[60]

In conclusion, Gadamer's ontology of presentation resolves the paradox of the fixed image within an actuality of flux. Only because it does not represent anything actual can the image alter rather than repeat actuality. This it does by giving that which is at play within actuality greater coherence and intelligibility. The image allows an experiential sequence to become singular, more essentially what it is and was indeed capable of becoming. Philosophical hermeneutics has plainly transposed aesthetics into an altogether different framework of ontological categories. No longer does it address the emotional condition of the spectator but the ontic possibilities of the world in which the spectator is located. No longer is the role of the image to be spell-bindingly beautiful. Neither is it to offer a glimpse of the timeless. Rather, the image offers to what is in play within the actual a glimpse of transformation. It visualises a possible completeness and offers the actual a transformative future. Coming to see otherwise shows what can in actuality become otherwise. The disjunctive image is, in other words, a call to practical action. Art reveals our world as an unfinished world.

5.6 CONCLUSION

Gadamer's ontology of art is directly connected to his critique of the subjectivism of aesthetic consciousness. To deny that the transformations of consciousness achieved within our experience of art are not reducible to the subjective alone, he has to demonstrate their ontological status. This is done by claiming that the disclosive power of both word and image reveals the processural nature of reality itself and that, furthermore, the transformative capacities of art allow the real to become 'more real' (i.e. achieve a greater historical effectiveness). This achieves a major ontological shift in the relation of art to reality: art becomes a mode of Being's self-presentational nature. As 'showing', Being discloses itself in word and image, not because either capture it but because both exhibit its processural features. Gadamer's ontology of art is participatory: experiencing art (interacting with it) is a mode of art's being. This supports the claim that aesthetic attentiveness contributes to the actualisation of the real.

These ontological claims are of considerable consequence: they invert the customary negative relationship in aesthetics between appearance and reality, they show how the participatory nature of aesthetic attentiveness accords *theoria* with an ontologically constructive role and, as was suggested in the last chapter, the positive evaluation of *theoria* leads to a deconstruction of the classic theory/practice distinction. The transition from proprietorial struggles over the 'truth' of a work to the mutual recognition of practitioner and theoretician as complementary agents in bringing forth the truth of a work promises a basis for non-competitive aesthetic collegiality. In addition, Gadamer's turn from representation to presentation allows a pictorial likeness to disclose as a singular truth what would remain without its intervention an unformed, inarticulate state of affairs. This promotes the argument that, as in the case of the portrait, the likeness increases the being of the sitter. The genesis of the 'likeness' parallels Gadamer's account of concept formation: both image and concept bring into a coherent whole not what is seen but a visualisation of what the seen infers or suggests. Nor is the likeness or image a reproduction but a projective summation of what is held as possible within an original set of relationships. The emergent image allows its original referent to become more than it was. Furthermore, the *Werden zum Sein* argument consolidates Gadamer's central claim that art has a cognitive content. Within the ontological primacy of becoming, emergent images serve as stabilising and summative points, permitting comparisons across time, allowing memories to be preserved and bringing relative stability to fields within the flux of experience. The ability of the presentational image to achieve ontological increments to the reality of its subject-matter demands from Gadamer a much stronger distinction between *mimesis* (producing a new likeness) and *imitatio* (making an imitation). Imitations are secondary and defer to the ontological primacy of an original. A likeness, however, does not duplicate reality: that would not increase the latter's being. This raises the question of how the image allows us to see actuality differently when what the image presents cannot be seen as an actual object within actuality. From the reworked mimesis/imitation distinction a vital ontological distinction between the actual and the possible arises. If the artwork has a disclosive autonomy, it cannot represent (be a visual surrogate for) anything that is actual. Were it to do so, it would merely reproduce rather than transform the actual. The issue is not whether the world presented in the image is possible or not but whether new possibilities for relating to actuality differently arise when the relations that constitute actuality are re-read in the light of those that constitute the image. Gadamer's ontological approach to aesthetic disclosure culminates in the question: what more of our world is disclosed as possible when viewed in terms of the relations that constitute the non-actual world of the image?

Two final observations are pertinent. (1) Gadamer's position demonstrates that the capacity of an image to transform a subject's understanding of his or her existential perspective requires participation in the same part–whole structures that the image brings to aesthetic summation. (2) Such summations and the transformations they initiate alter in turn the part–whole structures out of which they emerge. This confirms that presentational ontology requires aesthetics and its traditional philosophical basis to be rethought. It exposes the extent to which traditional aesthetics has been too long in the thrall of an ancient Greek metaphysical assumption: Being is complete, without any need to regenerate its forms. Presentational aesthetics is Promethean in nature. The movement of Being is disclosed in the bringing forth and the withholding of aesthetic presentation. Aesthetic presentation demands spectorial participation in the movement of subject-matters, such that when the latter achieve a transformation of understanding in the spectator, the change effects alteration in the being of subject-matters. If transformation requires participation in what comes to presentation, what is the medium of interaction? We turn, accordingly, to the theory of linguisticality underwriting Gadamer's reflections on aesthetic understanding.

NOTES

1. TM, p. 487.
2. Hans-Georg Gadamer, 'Heidegger and Marburg Theology', in *Philosophical Hermeneutics*, trans. David E. Linge (Berkeley: University of California Press, 1976), p. 203.
3. Gadamer, *Philosophical Hermeneutics*, p. 226.
4. TM, p. 100.
5. Busoni, *Bach Piano Transcriptions 1*, Nikolai Demidenko, Hyperion, CDA66566; *Bach Transcriptions*, Esa-Pekka Salononen, Los Angeles Philharmonic, Sony, SK89012; *Bach, Orchestral transcriptions by Respighi and Elgar*, Gerard Schwarz, Seattle Symphony Orchestra, Naxos 8.572741.
6. TM, p. 156.
7. Hans-Georg Gadamer, 'On the Truth of the Word', in *The Gadamer Reader*, ed. R. E. Palmer (Evanston: Northwestern University Press, 2007), p. 137.
8. Nicholas Davey, 'Lest We Forget: The Question of Being in Philosophical Hermeneutics', *Journal of the British Society for Phenomenology*, Vol. 40, No. 3, Oct. 2009, p. 251. It should be noted that Gadamer's general equation of word and image within hermeneutics finds support in Joseph Margolis's arguments presented in *The Arts and the Definition of the Human: Towards a Philosophical Anthropology* (Stanford: Stanford University Press, 2009), Chapter 3.
9. TM, p. 128.
10. I first raised the question of how philosophical hermeneutics approaches the problem of portraiture in the article 'Sitting Uncomfortably: A Hermeneutic Reflection on Portraiture', *Journal of the British Society*

for Phenomenology, Vol. 34, No. 3, Oct. 2003, pp. 231–46. The present discussion approaches the same question but from a substantially different tangent.

11. Gadamer, 'On the Truth of the Word', p. 196.
12. TM, p. 138.
13. Ibid., p. 140.
14. Ibid., p. 114.
15. In addition to the some of the portraits by Francis Bacon, those by Frank Auerbach seem not to impose an image of a person over the temporal flow which is their life but rather to suggest an image of a person-in-flow. What is important is not just the way he works and reworks the same portrait but the way in which the reworked spatial planes gain a suggestive vibrant vagueness of edge which somehow indicates a living space which the sitter is simultaneously coming to occupy and vacate. See Frank Auerbach's *Catherine Lampert Seated* (1994) and *Head of J. Y. M.* (1984).
16. A. S. Byatt, *Portraits in Fiction* (London: Chatto and Windus, 2001), p. 1.
17. TM, p. 140.
18. Ibid.
19. Ibid., p. 113.
20. Friedrich Nietzsche, *The Will to Power*, trans. Walter Kaufman and Roger Hollingdale (London: Weidenfeld and Nicolson, 1968), Section 617.
21. TM, p. 112.
22. Ibid., pp. 447–8.
23. Ibid., p. 114.
24. Paul S. Fiddes, *The Promised End: Eschatology in Theology and Literature* (Oxford: Blackwell, 2000), p. 42.
25. TM, pp. 110–21.
26. Ibid., p. 112.
27. Ibid., p. 114.
28. Gerard von Honthorst, *Elizabeth of Bohemia* (1642), National Gallery, London.
29. Hans-Georg Gadamer, 'The Art Work in Word and Image', in *The Gadamer Reader*, p. 207.
30. Ibid., p. 209.
31. Ibid., p. 209.
32. Hans-Georg Gadamer, *The Relevance of the Beautiful* (London: Cambridge University Press, 1986), p. 116 (emphasis added).
33. Friedrich Nietzsche, 'Meine Philosophie umgedrehter Platonismus. . .', in *Sämtliche Werke* (Stuttgart: Kröner, 1978), p. 38.
34. Nietzsche, *The Will to Power*, Section 567.
35. Ibid.
36. For Paul Ricoeur's stance on mimesis and the creative imitation of reality, see Fiddes, *The Promised End*, p. 42.
37. Gadamer, 'The Art Work in Truth and Image', p. 215.
38. Gadamer, *The Relevance of the Beautiful*, p. 117.

39. Ibid., p. 64.
40. Ibid., p. 35.
41. Ibid., p. 216.
42. Hans Peter Duerr, *Dreamtime: Concerning the Boundary Between Wilderness and Civilisation* (London: Blackwell, 1985), p. 129.
43. James Risser offers some poignant remarks upon the status of possibility within philosophical hermeneutics. See his *Hermeneutics and the Voice of the Other: Re-Reading Gadamer's* Philosophical Hermeneutics (Albany: State University of New York Press, 1997), pp. 123–38.
44. Martin Heidegger cited by Jürgen Moltmann, *Science and Wisdom* (London: SCM Press, 2003), p. 66. The reference is Martin Heidegger, *Being and Time*, trans. John Macquarrie (Oxford: Blackwell, 1960), p. 63.
45. Ibid.
46. See note 31.
47. Risser, *Hermeneutics and the Voice of the Other*, p. 148.
48. Ibid.
49. Ernst Bloch, *The Principle of Hope*, Vol. 1, trans. N. Plaice (Oxford: Blackwell, 1986), pp. 235–49.
50. Gadamer, 'The Artwork in Word and Image', p. 211.
51. TM, p. 100.
52. Gadamer, 'Autobiographical Reflections', p. 8.
53. Gadamer, 'The Artwork in Word and Image', p. 219.
54. Ibid., p. 219.
55. Ibid., pp. 210–11.
56. Ibid., p. 215.
57. TM, pp. 112–13.
58. Fiddes, *The Promised End*, p. 42.
59. 'To understand an art work is to understand its truth, which necessarily implies understanding its untruth, both in itself and in relation to the untruth of the external world.' Theodor Adorno, *Aesthetic Theory* (London: Routledge and Kegan Paul, 1984), p. 371.
60. Risser offers some poignant remarks upon the status of possibility within philosophical hermeneutics. See his *Hermeneutics and the Voice of the Other*, pp. 123–38.

6. Art and the Art of Language[1]

What does Gadamer mean by his claim that 'art addresses us'? It is a signature claim of philosophical hermeneutics and follows directly upon Gadamer's assertion of the phenomenological priority of meaning in the experience of art. Not only does this emphasise Gadamer's dialogical approach to art but it is the culmination of his critique of aesthetic subjectivism. By asserting the primacy of meaning, philosophical hermeneutics affirms the ontic priority of those cultural horizons which shape a spectator's consciousness and in which he or she must partake as a precondition of achieving transformed understanding. However, a central question remains unavoidable: what type of language does art speak? An answer depends on expanding the conventional meaning of language, as it is usually tied to just the spoken and written. We shall argue that Gadamer's conception of linguisticality extends the notion of language to include any set of communicative relations, including bodily and musical. Our argument parallels a hermeneutic conception of the artwork as a body or 'measure' of relations. The broader conception of linguisticality allows art to be considered as language insofar as, like all sets of communicative relations, the communicative relations that constitute art also have the speculative capacity to refer beyond themselves. This capacity is central to what Gadamer means by 'art addresses us'. The speculative dimension central to the experience of that address clarifies how to fathom the 'truth' of the cognitive content of art's address. A consideration of the relationship between art and language allows Gadamer's aesthetics to revitalise a hermeneutical conception of truth based upon plausibility rather than demonstration.

What is art saying? The idiom Ernst Cassirer uses is almost commonplace: it is not enough that we have the artwork before us as raw material, since 'it is necessary that we penetrate its significance; we must understand what it has to *say* to us'.[2] The mode of expression is even more characteristic of Hans-Georg Gadamer's *Truth and Method*, which stands on the pivotal claim that 'art addresses us'. It is on this claim that Gadamer's rebuttal of sensualist aesthetics rests. And, yet, what does this claim mean? Gadamer's dialogical approach to art is an uncontroversial part of the language turn in twentieth-century European thought but its basis is, we shall suggest, not well understood. It has important implications for how we (if we do) understand both art and language. If humans make art, and if Giambattista Vico's hermeneutic axiom is correct that we can truly fathom only what we ourselves have produced, then do we understand art because it has the mark of language upon it?[3] If the claim that art addresses us is something more than a commonplace anthropomorphism, what does it mean?

On an everyday level, we understand precisely what Gadamer means when he claims that art speaks to us. A painting addresses its viewer just as an evening sky can 'speak' to the passing of a well occupied day. In the face of such eloquence, nature seems, as Oscar Wilde quipped, fated to imitate art. That art speaks to us individually is clear. The truth of what is initially communicated is immediately granted. The respective musical reactions of Bohuslav Martinu and Sergei Rachmaninov to Piero della Francesco's frescoes *History of the True Cross* (1452–56) and Arnold Böcklin's painting *Isle of the Dead* (1880) attest to visual art's direct communicative impact.[4] Yet, for those of a more analytical persuasion, talk of art's language is loose metaphorical talk. If artworks literally spoke they would, no doubt, not have their noisiness excused but be ejected from the gallery for public disorder by intolerant museum attendants. Art, as Gadamer's detractors often insist, does not actually 'speak to us'. Where are its words, its syntax, its propositional assertions? Gadamer admits this much is obvious: art has nothing to do with the statement.[5] If so, why is the pivotal claim that art addresses us repeated throughout Gadamer's corpus? The clue, ironically, lies in precisely the assertion that the experience of art has little to do with statements.

This negative assertion takes little away from the claim that art addresses us, since part of Gadamer's central argument is that language is not exclusively reducible to propositional form. How, then, does a visual language 'speak'? To unravel these questions we need to get away from a commonplace association of Gadamer's dialogism with similar positions in the writings of Bakhtin and Wittgenstein, and appreciate how his approach to art and its power of address is informed by a speculative conception of language that has its roots in medieval thought. And so, if not a commonplace metaphor, what exactly is entailed in the claim that art addresses us?

6.2 THE ARTICULATE LIFE-WORLD

Intelligible utterance in language is dependent upon silent acquaintance with horizons of meaning and association which are ontologically prior to propositional levels of communication. The latter belong, according to Heidegger, to the apophantic domain. Assertions are derivative in that they depend on pre-established understandings:

> When an assertion is made, some fore-conception is always implied; but it remains for the most part inconspicuous, because the language already hides in itself a developed way of conceiving. . . . Assertion necessarily has as its existential foundations a fore-having, a fore-sight and a fore-conception.[6]

An object hypostasised within an assertion undergoes a narrowing of content compared with the complexities of how it is given within immediate experience. Heidegger's division of *aletheic* (disclosive) language and *apophantic* (propositional) language plays a vital role in Gadamer's hermeneutics of art. The aesthetic realm in which art speaks is not a sensualist reduction of the discursive realm but a realm of immediate phenomenological experience, heavily mediated by language and tradition but prior, nevertheless, to the propositional. When he says of art 'So ist es', Gadamer is not arguing that art puts the world into a propositional template which, like a Wittgensteinian picture, can be verified against an original. To the contrary, 'So ist es' speaks to the experience of something being disclosed, of something having *become* the case through art and not of things in the world being 'captured' by art. Art is presentational in that it is

> not an imitation in which to approach an original by copying it as nearly as possible. On the contrary, it is a kind of showing. Here showing does not mean setting out something like a proof.[7]

As we have seen, Gadamer's argument commences with the experience of art (the moment of its address) and not with aesthetics as traditionally conceived, which, because it attends to sensual qualities alone, strips pictorial capture of any cognitive reference. It is precisely the phenomenological apprehension of objects as cognitively significant (as intending something meaningful) which serves as the ground of Gadamer's *recovery* of a phenomenological aesthetics. He states in the essay 'Collected Works and Their Effective History' that his aesthetics is 'anything but aestheticizing'.[8] The aim is not to bring aesthetics back to the 'life-world' (did it ever leave it?) but to prevent the epistemological prejudices associated with the realm of statements from muffling its eloquence.

The life-world is ontologically prior to the world of analysis and reflection and in it we 'know', as Wittgenstein says, 'how to go on'. We laugh and chat with an immediate sense of what is meaningful, appropriate or jarring. For Gadamer, art's address is grounded in the interrogative dimensions of the life-world: our concern with it is exhibited by the sense that art speaks to us. A certain sequence of chords, an unexpected turn of phrase or rays of light glinting on a sculpted surface can turn the head and we find ourselves 'ambushed', having to surrender to the unexpected. Gadamer's defence of art's significant content is exactly the opposite of Clive Bell's.[9] The justification of the cognitive element of art's address stands on the conviction that the life-world is a world of cognitively significant structures preceding any hypostasisation of that world in statements. Bell's subsequent move – the stripping away of any layer of cultural signification from a visual object so that we can (allegedly) perceive its sensual aesthetic qualities alone – is one for which Gadamer has no sympathy. Bell subjectivises the art object by reducing it to a matter of private hedonistic concerns without shareable (and, hence, dialogically transformative) elements of cognitive significance.

The evidentiary nature of art's address emphasises that the artwork itself is a communicative agency. It is not the artist's agency which is emphasised, but the artwork's own presentational power. When art addresses us, it is not that we are offered a representation or reproduction of the empirical world, which we are invited to confirm. Rather, it is the *presented* (*darstellen*) world that speaks or that, in Gadamer's phrase, comes to language. As the previous discussion of likeness argued, the life-world is not depicted in the image but comes forth in a new and transformed way. This mirrors Heidegger's argument that understanding precedes interpretation.[10] Art's address – its declarative 'So ist es' – does not demand verification of the truth of a correspondence between a representation and its object but affirms that, within a presentation, something has indeed come about. Gadamer is utterly persuaded of the evidentiary force of art's disclosures. The problem is how to justify a cognitive claim which cannot be rendered in propositional terms. The thrust of Gadamer's argument is that art's address does indeed have an impelling cognitive force, but in what does the cognitive compellingness of art's speaking reside? What does it mean to say that art has a language, even if we grant that its 'speaking' resides in eloquent silent images? To address these questions, let us consider the signature claim of Gadamer's philosophy, 'All Being that can be understood is language'.

6.3 THE 'TONGUES' OF BEING

Truth and Method proclaims famously,

> *Being that can be understood is language.* The hermeneutical phenomenon here projects its own universality back onto the ontological constitution of what is understood, determining it in a universal sense as language and determining its own relation to beings as interpretation. Thus we speak not only of a language of art but also of a language of nature – in short, of any language that things have.[11]

Note the fourfold conjunction: (1) Being that can be understood is *language*, (2) the *language* of art, (3) the *language* of nature and (4) any *language* that things have. We will connect these four themes by means of arguments that are to follow. The proclamation reflects Gadamer's admiration for Goethe's conviction that every natural particular has a language that addresses us in terms of symbol and, as such, can express the whole nexus of meaning that informs its being.[12] The expressivity of the symbol is central to Gadamer's view of the speculative capacity of language upon which much of his account of art and its relation to language turns.

Gadamer argues that every proposition is conditioned by the totality of language and that every proposition has presuppositions it does not express. That they are unexpressed neither means that they are inexpressible nor that they are unrecoverable. To the contrary, clear expression and effective poetic juxtaposition can illuminate the wider horizons of meaning from which propositions spring.

> Every word breaks forth as if from a centre and is related to a whole, through which alone it is word. Every word causes the whole of the language to which it belongs to resonate and the whole world view that underlies it to appear. Thus, every word, as the event of a moment, carries with it the unsaid, to which it is related by responding and summoning.[13]

The living virtuality of speech is such that it brings a totality of meaning into play without being able to express it.[14] All speaking invokes an infinity of meaning which will never be fully articulated, though the use of each word implies its being. The capacity of words to light up the horizons of meaning which inform their use, Gadamer describes as the speculative:

> The speculative means the opposite of the dogmatism of everyday experience. A speculative person is one who does not abandon himself directly

to the tangibility of appearances (take what is said literally) but is able to discern in what is said the informing horizons of meaning that reach beyond what is immediately stated.[15]

The speculative capacity of a word mirrors or reflects the horizon of meaning that its sense depends on. This is a feature not just of poetic language but also of diplomatic communiqués: the meaning is not stated but inferred. When Gadamer speaks of an artwork or poem 'bringing forth' a world, what is brought forth is not a world *ex nihilo* but that unexpressed world which prefigures the possibility of all speaking. This speculatively intuited world is prior to everything that is recognised and addressed as existing.[16] In effect, the speculative dimensions of language make expressive content possible. What is meant (or silently inferred) can be considered against what is actually said. Neither is a sentence meaningful in itself. Its meaningfulness depends upon the context it lights up. The speculatively revealed world can never be totally objectified but, as the ground of speaking, it is present (co-inheres) within all utterances – an infinity of meaning to be explicated and laid out.[17] Nevertheless, Gadamer contends that the meaningfulness of an image depends significantly upon its speculatively revealed context.

His usage of the speculative casts a double reflection. Not only does it confirm the word's Latin provenance, in that it 'mirrors' what lies beyond what is immediately stated or seen, but its conceptual history also reflects the speculative grammar of the medieval *Modistae*.[18] Intuiting from a belief in God's word that the structures of language 'reflect' an essential reality underlying the physical world, the speculative grammarians pursued a universal grammar – that is, one they claimed was in all languages, irrespective of their individual differences.[19] Nineteenth-century speculative philosophy mirrored this aspiration by seeking to bring the world, experienced as a plurality of parts, under a single unifying cognitive principle. This raises an issue which has some resonance in Gadamer's thought: how does each part residing in an unseen whole or totality reflect that whole and how does what is unseen (the whole) become discernible in the seen? Gadamer may adopt the imagery of the *speculum* but, unlike his predecessors, he is far from assuming that language reflects a fixed order of *logoi* or unchanging forms beyond appearances. What statements and propositions speculatively reflect is not a metaphysical order of Being but the living, moving realm of *Sprachlichkeit* itself. Here and only here does Gadamer invoke anything like a *logos* of the word.

In support of the claim that what statements speculatively reflect is the moving being of *Sprachlichkeit*, the following can be argued. First, the objects about which we speak and reflect are linguistically constituted *Sachen* or subject-matters, which acquire their histori-cally effective being and constitution precisely through their verbal, written and visual transmission (tradition). The linguistic being of such subject-matters means that their constitution is speculatively open, always subject to cultural and historical moderation. Second, the nexus of language and the totalities of meaning it contains does not consti-tute a fixed being but an ever-fluid, transforming and self-presenting realm of linguistic meaning. Linguisticality, then, has a speculative mode of being which reveals itself as it moves and guides, and yet it exceeds all thought. This is Gadamer's thinly veiled invocation of an all-encompassing *logos*. The argument that when thought reflects upon its objects it meets with linguistically constituted subject-matters that antedate reflection is indebted to Franz Rosenzweig, whose concept of speech-thinking is discussed below.

Gadamer's conception of the speculative emphasises a key aspect of language. The speculative dimensions of language are both annuncia-tive and eventual: there is that which is shown (the subject-matter) and there is the process of showing, from out of which the subject-matter emerges. The communicative power of language is performative. It brings things (*Sachen*) into being and in so doing transforms its own self-established horizons. If the speculative is a feature of spoken and written language, it is also a feature of non-verbal language. As we have noted, Gadamer makes an explicit reference to 'the language that things have', 'whatever kind of things they may be'.[20] What is meant by 'language' in such remarks?

There are obvious non-verbal languages, for instance musical, architectural and sculptural. If so, what does it mean to say that Mozart's music 'speaks' to us? It clearly spoke to Max Reger and Alfred Schnittke, as their transcriptions of his music indicate. But if Bach spoke to Respighi in like fashion, is it because his musical language is somehow translated into spoken language? It is plain that musical languages work in a similar way to mathematical or logical languages: they have an autonomy whose operations are not reducible to linguistic relations. Artists are notoriously ambivalent about the reduction of their work to verbal terms. Artworks, it is said, should 'speak' for them-selves. Indeed, Gadamer takes the side of the word-shy artists.

> Language often seems ill-suited to express what we feel. In the face of the overwhelming presence of works of art, the task of expressing in words what they say to us seems like an infinite and hopeless undertaking. . . . One says this, and then one hesitates.[21]

On the other side of the equation, if the language of art is non-reducible, how do we communicate its importance? Whilst I cannot tell you how to play a particular line from Schubert or how to compose a photographic image, I can show you how. However, the significance of a particular style of phrasing – how it enables other composers to achieve different results – will depend upon me giving a linguistic explanation. That explanation may certainly use non-linguistic examples but their coherence will depend on an overarching linguistic interpretive framework. A similar argument is made by Habermas with regard to the cultural assimilation of scientific research. Ordinary language does not translate scientific language into everyday idioms. The challenge is to see the importance of one set of activities in relation to a wider set of cultural operations.[22] This can be achieved by ordinary language. Cross-relationality and not reductive subsumption is critical.[23]

On the relationship of spoken language to non-verbal language, Gadamer remains somewhat obscure. In an interview with Jean Grondin, Gadamer denies that his thesis 'Being that can be understood is language' is equivalent to saying that the universe of language is boundless.[24] 'No, I have never thought and never ever said that everything is language.'[25] Gadamer grants the existence of non-linguistic understanding and emphasises that verbal language is only a special case of linguisticality.[26] When asked about the thesis that 'Being that can be understood is language', he specifically remarks that Being can be experienced and understood only because Being *speaks*, yet this speaking should not necessarily be understood as verbal. To understand something is to 'see it as a sign of something else',[27] to see that the thing concerned stands in a speculative relation to a wider horizon of meanings, for, as he argues in *Truth and Method*, meaning is, above all, a matter of relations: 'meanings, too, are like a space in which things are related to one another'.[28] If expressive content is contextualised, the interpretation of utterances is speculative, in that it must light up the surrounding horizons which inform the image. Meaning is relational: 'all interpretation sees through the dogmatism of a meaning-in-itself'.[29] Indeed, the power of the aphorism or poetic fragment resides in its ability to activate the network of associations attached to the single utterance. Meaningfulness is related, by Gadamer's argument, to speculative capacity, and the capacity of a sign or symbol to refer beyond itself, to other networks of association, is by no means limited to verbal language. Visual signs 'speak' because they both reveal and, in the case of the symbol, somehow contain the horizon of meanings that reach beyond themselves

Two things can be drawn from the argument so far. First, linguisticality is not limited to either the spoken or the written. It includes bodily and visual language. Second, speculative capacity (the power to invoke semantic horizons) is characteristic of all languages. Thus, when an artwork 'speaks', it does so not because its address is verbal but because its images, figuration and mode of composition acquire meaning from their capacity to light up and be lit up by the horizons of meaning from out of which they emerge. To deny the speculative ground of art's intelligible address is also to deny the very ground upon which the meaningfulness of propositions depend. Art is not a spoken or written language but it shares with verbal equivalents a speculative capacity to reveal the contextual relationality upon which its meaningfulness depends.

In other respects, visual culture is indeed language-like. The practice of a visual discipline requires the adoption of inherited conventions and transmitted skills which bear not just on the production of a work but also on where that work is displayed. No matter how radical Dadaist conceptions of artworks may have been, they still required conventional sites for their exhibition. In addition, images function in certain respects like poetic word clusters: their meaningfulness is not intrinsic but lies in the speculatively discernible set of relations in which they are set. The profundity of visual symbols equally relies upon an ability to light up the nexus of unspoken meanings upon which their sense of depth depends. Indeed, Heidegger recognises this quality of the speculative in his notion of the withheld. As well as a visual image bringing aspects of its speculative ground to the fore, it also reveals the presence of the promise of that which has yet to be disclosed. This is the basis of Gadamer's remark that,

> The experience of art acknowledges that it cannot present the full truth of what it experiences in terms of definitive knowledge. There is no absolute progress and no final exhaustion of what lies in a work of art. The experience of art knows this of itself.[30]

Let us briefly summarise.

Visual art entails a language not because it is spoken (which it patently is not) but because, as is the case with other forms of language, the expressive power of its semantic units depends upon their ontological relationality. It is this relationality which comes to light when art 'says' something. This amounts to the thesis that for anything to count as a language it must communicate by virtue of the speculative relations which ground its signs. How is this thesis to be understood in practical terms? What does it enable in the understanding of artworks?

The value of the notion of constitutional relationality is that it enables us to move away from essentialist conceptions of the artwork. Arguments drawn from Heraclitus and Franz Rosenzweig help in this respect. Important to our position is a conception of a thing or work as a measure (Heraclitus) and the suggestion that that measure is a fluid arrangement of relations (Rosenzweig). Let us first invoke Heraclitus, whose doctrine of flux anticipates Gadamer's Aristotelian conception of Being as motion. We shall concern ourselves first with his appraisal of the 'measure in all things'.

For Heraclitus, 'people of no experience ... [are] uncomprehending of the rhythm in things', for rhythm is a type of measure. *Logos* is not so much *word* as a type of constitutional relational arrangement according to a common measure in all things. This suggests that all things are as one, in that, like a text, each thing has its own feel, its own measure or rhythm.[31] Usually, this is understood to imply a universal measure in all particular things rather than the quite different proposal that all singular things (families, groups, species) have their singular measure or rhythm. Thinkers such as Luigi Pareyson follow the latter line of argument; interpretation seeks the singular 'measure' of its text. 'Reading' a text or artwork is a matter of understanding the interaction of its part–whole relationships. A work's measure, its *logos*, is the ratio of its different elements. That there is no final interpretation of a work strengthens the notion of hermeneutic profundity. As a body of relationships, 'it [the work] has a differing aspect from every point'.[32] Because of its speculative vulnerabilities, the relational constitution of a work, its measure, is never closed but always open. This, as we shall see, facilitates the transmission of a work from one reception community to another. The openness of a work reminds us that *passio* is as much a part of communicating as is performance. To have a communicative competence within a visual or spoken language is to confess vulnerability to what the speculative edges of that language draws us into.

Franz Rosenzweig argues that a thing is not so much placed in a horizon with its own 'measure' as gains its effective being from the totality of its horizonal interactions. The being of that thing is not a fixed essence but a measure of unfolding relations in time. Rosenzweig states what Heraclitus implies, namely, that one does not attain truth by stepping out of the river of time, but rather that the truth of a thing (its measure) is that which unfolds in its temporal relations. Beings are not to be grasped *sub-specie aeternitatis* but in the nexus of temporal relations in which we experience them.[33] In similar vein, Gadamer is keenly aware of Husserl's contention that the thing-in-itself is nothing other than the continuity with which various perceptual perspectives on an object shade into one another.[34] Heraclitus and Rosenzweig offer precedents for thinking of things and persons not as fixed essences but as living measures (complexities) which do not exist apart from the totality of their actual and possible horizontal interactions. These conceptions have an important bearing on Gadamer's notion of an artwork and how it speaks.

6.4 SPECULATIVE INTERFACES

Nietzsche believed philology undermines appeals to essentialist meaning: words always point beyond themselves, to other networks of meaning. Language and essentialism exclude one another. The notion that texts and works of art have speculative edges also ties philosophical hermeneutics to anti-essentialism and constructively so, since the speculative openness of works accounts for their capacity for cultural transmission and, hence, historical effectiveness. In the light of these remarks, Gadamer's description of a text is telling:

> A genuine text . . . is exactly what the word literally says: a woven texture that holds together. Such language, if it really is a proper text, holds together in such a way that it 'stands' in its own right and no longer refers back to an original, more authentic saying, nor points beyond itself to a more authentic experience of reality. . . .[35]

This passage invites further observations. First, the text is not a single entity but a composition: a composite of part–whole relations which constitutes its measure. Second, Gadamer never conceives of a text or an artwork as a fixed entity but as a constantly changing unity. Not only is it different from every point viewed but new readings anticipate different modes of completion (*Vollzug*). Third, the analogy of a woven texture appropriately invokes the relationality of part and whole but if it equates a text with a singular piece of cloth, it is misleading. A text is not so much particular but a singular multiplicity, a com-positioning of parts which do not have to be configured in any one way other than that dictated by the work itself. This conception allows us to draw the various strands of our argument together.

The notion of an artwork as a singular multiplicity links the question of art as a language, the notion of a work as a measure of its relations, with the conception of a work's communicative speculative capacity. We have suggested that the address of an artwork is language-like not because it actually speaks but because it is constituted by a body of cognitively significant relations, or what we have termed its measure. Understanding a work and what it says involves, as Pareyson argues, getting a sense of its measure, its patterns and ratios. However, Gadamer's conception of the speculative dimension of images and words reminds us that we should not really talk of artworks in isolation but more in terms of the patterns of cognitive relation they open on to. We are therefore reminded that patterns of significant part–whole relationships do not exist in isolation but cross over in pertinent ways. Words, artworks and texts all entail different densities of part–whole relations and we, as language speakers, inhabit those relations. The hermeneutic cross-over of words indicates why part–whole relations affect and interfere with each other. The standard meaning of a word or image is, in terms of its hermeneutical associations, perhaps less important than its peripheral meanings. Often as not, the peripheral associations bring a formal term or image to life in the mind of the reader or spectator. It is not the transmission of a technical term that transforms my understanding but the way a poet uses a word in such a way as to allow its transmitted meanings to bind into the open edges of my understanding. When this happens, the hermeneutic 'fit' of a word or image is altered, a new circuitry of associations lights up. In hermeneutic terms, the peripheral areas of a word's or image's meaning are precisely the areas which facilitate cognitive movement between reader and work. The looseness of meaning, its very *suggestiveness*, enhances its capacity for transmission and an effective historical life. That same looseness effectively allows one determination of meaning to come into transformative play with others. It enables that recursive looping that characterises Gadamer's doubled hermeneutics. Gadamer's thesis that 'art addresses us' can be defended not because it claims that art literally speaks but because works of art, like texts, have open compositional structures: images, like words, require a hermeneutical background of association to function, and images, as with words, have a speculative capacity which facilitates both the transformation of a spectator's understanding of a given subject-matter and the successful historical transmission of that subject-matter.

What is always a challenge to Gadamer's hermeneutical aesthetics is the commonplace observation that visual art does not verbally communicate. However, visual art does communicate and does so within elaborate hermeneutic frameworks. Indeed, spoken language, like art, requires the same unspoken frameworks to communicate. If the silent evocation of meaningful horizons is what the meaningful address of both word and image depend on, to deny that visual art is a language, because it does not literally speak, suggests that our concept of language is too narrow. To deny that art is a language because it depends on frameworks of meaning that cannot be rendered in propositional form denies the intelligibility of the self-same hermeneutic frameworks upon which the meaningfulness of spoken propositions also depends.

6.5 RELATIONALITY, ESSENCE AND TRUTH

There are considerable hermeneutical advantages to arguing that the language of art (visual composition) is the language of relationality. The prominence of significant relations with a hermeneutical aesthetics constitutes a powerful rejection of *laissez-faire* hermeneutics. The notion of a work as having a relational constitution (having its own measure) does not deny that a work is related to other cultural horizons. To the contrary, such extrinsic relations form part of a work's hermeneutical periphery. It does not follow that because one cannot survey the whole set of networks to which that work is linked, that everything said about the work is, because inconclusive, mere interpretation: anything can be said about anything. For an external relation to inform a work, a demonstrable connection – philological, visual or conceptual – between the work and what informs it has to be made. Caricature would be impossible unless it invoked traces of an original set of proportions. In short, the notion of a work as a measure of interconnecting relations constitutes a major objection to the claim that anything can be said about anything. Cartoons, parodies, variations on a theme, interpretive reconstructions all extend an initial set of relations but none of them will have anything to say unless it achieves an appropriate fit with the original set. The question of fit has relevance to the consequence of Gadamer's suppressed supposition that when an artwork speaks it does so truthfully.

The utility of the relationality argument extends to debates concerning the supposedly 'essential' characteristics of a national school of painting. Discussions about what is a quintessentially French or German style of painting easily become mired in arguments about defining properties and these can be usefully sidestepped by the relationality argument. What becomes important is a characterisable (but variable) set of relations which allows an affinity of styles to be developed. Johann Herder's observation that climate (*Klima*), air and water, food and drink will have an influence on the linguistic organs and naturally also on language and culture is accepted.[36] The clear, moist air of northern Europe facilitates the voice of such as Emma Kirkby, whilst the harsh, dry air of Arabia leads to a much more guttural style of vocal projection. A causal connection between voice and environment is, however, not our concern. What is significant is the affinity between bandings of tone and colour in regional landscapes and the palette of a composer or painter. The spacings and points of emphasis within the diction of a language are often echoed in national compositions, deliberately so in the case of Thomas Tallis's sung settings of *Archbishop Parker's Prayer*

Book (1567) and in Leoš Janáček's operatic reconstruction of Czech conversation patterns. In other words, it is analogous sets of relationships, many coincidental, that characterise discernible affinities and not any appeal to notions of fixed essence.

If an artwork speaks because its language is the language of open structures of relation, Gadamer's conception of the language of art is prescient. There is no demonstrable influence of Gadamer's aesthetics upon the arguments of the French aesthetician Nicolas Bourriaud but his analogous argumentation is supportive. The analysis of the relational nature of art's communicative and speculative capacities indicates that Gadamer's implicit arguments explicitly accord with Bourriaud's discussion of relational art.

> The possibility of a *relational* art (an art taking as its theoretical horizon the realm of human interactions and its social context, rather than the assertion of an independent and private symbolic space), points to a radical upheaval of the aesthetic, cultural and political goals introduced by modern art.[37]

The speculative operations of the artwork which characterise Gadamer's position provide a philosophical underpinning for Bourriaud's claims concerning linkage.

> One of the virtual properties of the image is its power of *linkage* (Fr. *reliance*), to borrow Michel Maffesoli's term: flags, logos, icon, signs, all produce empathy and sharing, and all generate *bond*. Art . . . *tightens the space of relations.*[38]

For Bourriaud, the work of art represents a social *interstice*, a notion derived from Karl Marx to describe trading communities that elude capitalist contexts by removing themselves from profit-led markets. It is in the nature of exhibited contemporary artworks to create free interactive spaces and novel time spans, whose rhythms contrast with those structuring everyday life. The exhibition becomes an 'arena of exchange';[39] the artwork becomes a space for participatory and potentially transformative encounter.[40]

> Each particular artwork is a proposal to live in a shared world, and the work of every artist is a bundle of relations with the world, giving rise to other relations, and so on and so forth, ad infinitum.[41]

In arguments analogous to Gadamer's, Bourriaud argues that relational transitivity

> introduces into the aesthetic arena that formal disorder which is inherent to dialogue. It denies the existence of any specific 'place of art', in favour of a forever unfinished discursiveness, and a never recaptured desire for dissemination.[42]

An artwork thus defined is a *system of differential positions* through which it can be read. It offers the possibility of transformative relations which stimulate interactions far beyond the artist's original imaginings.

Bourriaud's position overtly shares with Gadamer an admiration of art's free transformative capacities. Whereas the relational ontology which is implicit in Gadamer's argumentation about aesthetics finds an explicit endorsement in Bourriaud's reasoning, Gadamer's language ontology, specifically its subtle account of the speculative, gives a persuasive description of both how an artwork addresses us and how such transformative experiences are effected by art's operational language.

There remains one sense in which it might be argued that without verbal and written language the artwork might not, after all, speak for itself. We have put the case that the concept of language can be treated in an elastic manner so as to include any set of meaningful relationships. It is evident that the life-world includes just such a diversity of languages. However, Habermas's claim that the specialist insights of scientific language gain purchase within a sustaining culture only if they can be communicated in a form that can be generally understood, has a relevance here.[43] The same challenge traditionally faces the public acceptance of modernism in music, art and literature.[44] Habermas's point relates to a broader claim of Gadamer, that humanity has its world by virtue of its linguistic capacity: 'language is not just one of man's possessions in the world, rather on it depends the fact that man has a world at all'.[45] The key statement is:

> Language has no independent life apart from the world that comes to language within it. Not only is the world world only insofar as it comes into language, but language, too, has its real being only in the fact that the world is presented in it.[46]

This remark could imply what many art practitioners reject, namely, that an artwork has significance in the life-world only if it can be reduced to a discursive object. Here, Gadamer's thesis that 'Being that can be understood is language' appears to take on a proscriptive nature, namely, only that which can be communicated in written and spoken language has being. Against this, however, are Gadamer's emphatic remarks that language in words is only a special concretion of linguisticality,[47] that 'No, no! I have never thought and never said that everything is language',[48] and, finally, a work of art stands firm against every transforming of it into some other form of statement.[49] Gadamer also comments that 'Being that can be understood [insofar as it can be understood] is language'. This places the languages of art and nature on a similar footing. If grasped in the broadest sense of language understood as a body of significant relations charged with speculative reference, this remark poses no objection for our thesis.

What is referred to as language in this passage is the language of significant relations. However, a problem arises when Gadamer goes on to state that 'What cannot be understood can pose an endless task of at least finding a word that comes a little closer to the matter at issue'.[50] This suggests that that which we cannot find a word for, we cannot understand. On one level, it can be argued that everything that has a place in the life-world has its place inasmuch as it is a discursive object. However, and here we go beyond the literalness of Gadamer's statements, what is identified as a discursive object does not mean either that it has a verbal constitution or that, lacking a verbal constitution, it cannot be understood. To relate this to our thesis that art has a language, we suggest that art clearly is a discursive object (i.e. has a verbally communicable place in the life-world), that being a discursive object does not mean that art has a verbal constitution (i.e. that its language is reducible to spoken or written forms) and, finally, that because it has its own language, albeit a non-verbal language, art is indeed understandable precisely because it expresses itself as a set of speculative relations. Consider the case of music and musical notation.

'Classical' music is clearly a discursive object and, as such, has a hugely significant place in the life-world of occidental culture. Books such as Alex Ross's *The Rest Is Noise* have rendered twentieth-century music more accessible to those whose ears it normally affronts.[51] Similarly, Schubert's *Winterreise* has acquired an almost iconic status in the history of German romanticism. However, though I may be directed to that piece by the literature, this does not turn the object of my interest into an item of verbal discourse. Schubert's *Winterreise* may be identifiable as a discursive object in the discourse but that does not mean it has a verbal constitution. What interests composers such as Hans Zender is that the *Winterreise* is built on a series of discernible note clusters and on sets of germinal ideas which sustain subsequent development in the works of Anton Bruckner and Gustav Mahler. To understand Schubert's compositional language is to *hear* it in the works of subsequent composers such as Luciano Berio and Zender himself. That hearing is certainly no translation into the verbal but it is a hearing of a measure, a hearing of tonal relations and their speculative capacity. It is to hear how those note clusters appear in and guide the thinking of other composers. We can speak no end of Schubert's compositions as discursive objects but unless we acquire a feel for how his language works musically, we will not understand the 'language' they speak. Exactly the same argument can be made about pictorial language.

In the written history of modern European painting, the works of Vincent van Gogh are associated with a fateful shift from the manipulation of paint as a medium of representation to a concern with its tactile properties. There are germinal gestures in van Gogh's later brushwork which bear the seeds of both expression and abstract expressionism. Other nineteenth-century painters struggled with the paradox that the finer the brushwork used to render the detail of a figure more lifelike, the deader its representation becomes. When painters from the social realist group the Glasgow Boys first saw *Le Mendiant* (1880) by Jules Bastien-Lepage, they realised that the quality of pictorial vivacity depended not on finely brushed detail but upon broad and free brush strokes. This formal change in painterly language impacted on their realist intentions. The broader and freer application of paint by brush and knife rendered images more two dimensional and opened the door to, for example, van Gogh's concern with paint's material properties and, hence, to a concern with expression. As with the example of Schubert, we can speak of the history of painting as a discursive object but unless we can grasp the material language of painterly effects that each canvas speaks, we will not understand *their* language. The existence of that language does not depend on me speaking about it. Though the wider significance of what has been achieved within that language may indeed depend upon it being spoken and written about, describing what that language can do is not the same as 'speaking' it and nor is it the same as understanding it. Understanding what happens within the (painterly) language requires that I have a sense of what it can and cannot do but to gain that sense does not demand that I can translate the language of visual composition into the verbal.

Though talking about something (an intense experience of love or the trauma of abuse) is not putting the experience into words, talking about a visual subject-matter is a means of directing someone towards important non-verbal experience. Looking closely at the paintings of van Gogh reveals the beginnings of a concern with paint's materiality and, similarly, listening to the later symphonies of Sibelius will reveal his increasing preoccupation with a rawness of sound which threatens to dissolve all tunefulness. Such descriptions are not linguistic reductions but invitations to enter further into non-verbal sets of significant relations.

Language and the written may point to significant non-verbal relations but they do not reduce them to words. It is precisely in the ability to assemble, compile and map significant non-linguistic experiences that Gadamer is perhaps right about the relationship between verbal language and art. Art may be non-verbal but the cultural significance of what is possible in its languages can be charted only in relation to the verbally constituted world. Such charting does not involve reducing one language to another. When an experienced friend recommends an exhibition or a restaurant, he is not translating his experiences of either into words but is using a verbal form to communicate orders of experience which enable me to say, if I become acquainted with their measure, 'Now I see what you are getting at'. Ordinary language maps non-verbal spaces and cross-relates them in the life-world. Ordinary language may guide us to such portals but, once we pass through them, we must speak the language of the non-verbal territories they open. This is a transition which every practitioner must make, whether dancer or sculptor.

I have no doubt that Gadamer is correct to argue that art does indeed address us and transform our sense of what is meaningful. In this sense, art certainly 'speaks', if not always clearly, then often forcefully. We, too, may speak about what it communicates, though this does not mean that we translate what it 'says' into words. We have argued that an artwork 'speaks' because it communicates in a language of relations and, as such, belongs to the dimension of what Gadamer broadly terms 'linguisticality'. Communicating by means of a language within the realm of linguisticality does not mean that one is communicating in a spoken language. Art's languages may be spoken of, but this does not reduce them to the verbal. What makes art's visual languages *language* (i.e. an instance of linguisticality) is that their signs and conventions have an open, speculative capacity, allowing what is communicated to become woven into other expressive idioms in those languages. There can be, as our previous sections on art practice have suggested, a genuine complementarity between the 'language' of art practice and the 'language' of art theory. However, although it is important to clarify what is an obscure differentiation between verbal and non-verbal language in Gadamer's thinking, we should not become ensnared in a misleading opposition.

On the one hand, the claim that all understanding relies on verbal language culminates in the dominance of discourse theory: only that which can be translated into spoken and written discourse has significant cultural being. On the other hand, the claim that visual, spoken and bodily languages are distinct leads to a radical perspectivism which undermines comparison and exchange. The latter questions Gadamer's faith in the universal dimension of linguisticality. How, then, to keep faith with the latter and (1) avoid the reduction of all modes of language to a universal language and (2) grant the plurality of communicative languages without suggesting a common grammar? Two of Gadamer's statements suggest another way of thinking of the relation between the verbal and the visual:

> A. What cannot be understood can pose an endless task of at least finding a word that comes a little closer to the matter at issue (*die Sache*).[52]

> B. . . . how it is possible to find a pointing word that does not just express thoughts prompted by a picture, but rather leads to a *better seeing* of the work itself.[53]

Statement A suggests that, insofar as one seeks a word to move closer to a subject-matter, the presence of that subject-matter can be sensed independent of a *verbal* understanding of it. A mood, a feeling, a qualitative sense of lovingness or threat makes itself present within one's intuitive awareness and one tries to find the right word for it. Statement B suggests, correctly I think, that the sensitive use of words allows us to become aware of a dimension of a subject-matter we had not previously been alert to. If saying what something is (allowing it to come forth) is not the same as laying claim to what it is (statement), an understanding of a subject-matter can be extended by virtue of its being realisable in a number of complementary media or languages. The interplay between a picture's visual content and a subversive title is a device common amongst artists who wish to disrupt the habitual role of a title and to draw the spectator into an altogether different way of seeing and thinking about a subject-matter. By juxtaposing a photographic image of a dish of fruit with a painting of a monk reading under a tree, hanging with the title *Trappist Cloister* (1928), André Kertész evokes something of the essentially silent pleasures and temptations of reading.[54] Word and image are brought to play off one another. A finer example of the complementarity of the written and the visual is provided by Anglo-Saxon scholarship.

Catherine Karkov contends that in the Junius II manuscript, the visual imagery is not purely illustrative, secondary to the text.[55] The 'illustrative' content illumines the written by offering an independent visual commentary upon it. The visual and written narratives moderate each other in different ways. It is not that the visual imagery translates the poetic material into a new form (thereby rendering the original redundant) but that each new reading/viewing activates the interplay between the written and the visual in different and unpredictable ways. In Gadamer's terminology, the interplay between media allow complementary realisations of a subject-matter to emerge. It is mutual participation and interplay that are key, not the translation of one medium into another. The open, speculative edges of verbal and visual images facilitate interaction, participation and continuous hermeneutic transformation. Such speculative interaction indicates that the visual and the written are both are instances of a broad linguisticality. This reasoning rightly undermines a prejudice against illustration as a secondary form of art. The speculative capacity of communicable relations to cross over and inseminate one another undoes this bias. The philosophical postulation of subject-matters as transcending capture by any one language allows visual and verbal language to complement their different realisations of a shared content. And so, we return once more to Gadamer's pivotal claim that art 'speaks' to us.

That art can communicate so directly that we are impelled to talk about it testifies to Gadamer's claim that art does indeed 'speak'. It speaks because its non-verbal communicative structure functions as an instance of linguisticality (i.e. an open set of speculative relations). That spoken language functions speculatively does not reduce non-verbal language to the spoken. It does indicate, however, how significant associations in verbal and visual communication continually complement and influence one another. The complementarity between seeing and thinking speculatively is at the core of Gadamer's notion of *theoria*, which we considered above. However, the final issue requiring comment concerns the implications the relational conception of an artwork has for how the relation between art's speaking, the cognitive content of that speaking, and truth might be configured.

A. J. Ayer's magnum opus, *Language, Truth and Logic* (1936), offers, paradoxically, a title resonant with one of Gadamer's own but alludes to very different concerns with language, truth and method. Ayer's conjunction of titular nouns would evoke in Gadamer's mind a resonance of two philosophical prejudices the historical afterlife of which worries him. These are that the truth of an assertion resides in its reflecting the nature of the object thought and that the truth of an assertion lies in its propositional form. The argument to be drawn from Gadamer's position is hostile to both prejudices. It demands that the relationship between language, cognitive content and truth in his aesthetics be more fully articulated. Had Gadamer attended to this relationship more directly, he need not have defended the cognitive content of art's address against models of propositional truth, since the 'truth' (plausibility) of both can be shown to depend upon hidden presuppositions and a tacit acceptance of hidden hermeneutic operators. A regrettable aspect of Gadamer's thought is that by being overconcerned with propositional truth models, he gives them greater credence than they merit. What is at issue is not a perpetuation of needless divisions between the arts and sciences but the articulation of a more convincing concept of hermeneutic truth. The issue of art's address, its language, mode and cognitive content, inevitably brings the question of truth to the fore.

The argument that art's address has an impelling cognitive force raises the question of what that compellingness resides in. Gadamer's unquestioning acceptance of art's evidentiary force shifts the question of truth from verification to hermeneutical plausibility. This requires explanation, the form of which already lies within our argument as presented so far. The broader conception of language (linguisticality) reveals what the persuasiveness of art's address depends on. That 'art speaks' and can do so forcefully reveals the (ontological) 'truth' (i.e. the effective presence) of structures of pre-understanding which dispose us to accept the cognitive force of art's address.

The cognitive impact of art's address phenomenologically precedes the realm of propositional discourse. Positioning the question of truth prior to propositional discourse does not pose a problem for Gadamer, as he never supposes that truth lies exclusively in the realm of statements. The relational conception of an artwork and its speculative participation in horizons of meaning which transcend it suggests that, for an experience of art to be persuasive, it has to be congruent with those that constitute the work. The appropriateness of an interpretation can be appraised in terms of fit. If successful, the interpretation will simultaneously initiate a centrifugal and a centripetal impetus. It will allow the work to be graspable as a particular instantiation of the set of relations it is connected to, and make whole elements which, prior to the interpretation, were grasped only as separate. The point is arguably this.

There is no doubt in Gadamer's mind that a work operates 'truly' when it discloses to the spectator the fusion between its constitutive relations and those which inform it. The persuasiveness of that disclosure – its ability to immediately speak – depends upon the hermeneutic 'fit' between the work (what it discloses) and what that disclosure itself discloses, that is, the horizons of meaning that inform it. Gadamer never questions the supposition that when an artwork addresses us, it truly addresses us. 'Truly' operates here in the sense of a proper fulfilment of an inherent function: the disclosure of a (wider) world.

There remains, however, a distinction between the truth of art's disclosure as event (that it occurs) and the truth of what that event discloses (its cognitive content). The latter concerns, as we have suggested, hermeneutical plausibility and not propositional verification. The evidential force of art's address resides not in the fact that it makes a verifiable statement but rather that what is disclosed is recognised as transforming what was previously known in another way. The truth of

the address concerns the plausibility of the hermeneutical fit between
what the artwork displays as a singular piece of art and the informing horizons of meaning surrounding both it and the spectator. As
Gadamer observes, 'not everything is provable. What must be accepted
as true here aims at what is believable'.[56] In a suggestive passage he
comments:

> One would really honour the realm of the *Geisteswissenschaften* much more
> adequately, I think, if we brought them back under the older concept of
> rhetoric, where one deals with believable statements and not scientifically
> compelling proofs. This also applies for historical research, as well as for the
> sciences of law and theology, and as a matter of fact *it also applies to the
> experience of art*. In it there may be ever so much knowledge and science,
> but that has nothing to do with an artwork as a statement (proposition).[57]

The truth of art's address is, then, a matter of convincing rhetorical
relations between the stated and the disclosed, on the one hand, and
the wider hermeneutical horizons from out of which the work appears
and into which the work is received. In short, the truth of art's address
is a matter of experience, which is refuted not by analysis but only
by further experience.[58] This once again emphasises the importance
of aesthetic attentiveness, of acquiring the eye and the ear necessary
to discern the consistency of relations within a work. Thus, both the
ability of art to address us and its ability to do so truthfully depends
on wider horizons of pre-understanding which grant art its cognitive
warrant. The plausibility of art's address (the persuasiveness of its
cognitive content) rests upon the same hermeneutical grounding as
propositional discourse. Both require the tacit acceptance of unstated
presuppositions which influence the persuasiveness of the shown or
stated. These presuppositions are what Gadamer refers to when he
argues that artworks speak because of what speaks through them. The
'truth' of what is said depends on the viewer's sense of how plausible
the fusion of declarative foreground and hermeneutic background is
within the artistic disclosure. That plausibility can never be a matter of
proof but is a matter of how convincing the artwork is in fusing its own
disclosure with the horizons of meaning that inform it. On this basis,
the artwork can be said to truly *speak* and to speak *truly*. With this
suggestion our argument comes full circle.

   Our argument has attempted a response to the question, what does
Gadamer mean by the claim that 'art addresses us'? This requires
expanding the conventional meaning of language as spoken and written
to include any set of communicative relations, for example bodily or
musical, under the general term 'linguisticality'. This notion parallels
the hermeneutic conception of the artwork as a body or 'measure' of

relations. Art can be considered as having a language insofar as its constitutive relations point, like all sets of communicative relations, beyond themselves. Such speculative capacity is central to what Gadamer means by the assertion that 'art addresses us'. The hermeneutical structure of this address explains not just its cognitive component but also how its truthfulness is experienced in the form of an overwhelming convincingness or plausibility.

NOTES

1. This is a reworked and extended version of the article 'Philosophical Hermeneutics, Art and the Language of Art', *Aesthetic Pathways*, Vol. 1, No. 1, Dec. 2010, pp. 4–29.
2. Ernst Cassirer, *The Logic of the Humanities* (Clinton: Yale University Press, 1974), p. 173.
3. Vico's axiom, *verum factum*, is first developed in his work of 1710, *De antiquissima Italorum sapientia*.
4. Bohuslav Martinu, *The Frescoes of Piero della Francesca* (Nice, 1955) and Sergei Rachmaninov, *The Isle of the Dead* (Dresden, 1908).
5. Hans-Georg Gadamer, 'Collected Works and Their Effective History', in *The Gadamer Reader*, ed. R. E. Palmer (Evanston: Northwestern University Press, 2007), p. 415.
6. Martin Heidegger, *Being and Time*, trans. John Macquarrie (London: Blackwell, 1960), Sections 31–4.
7. Hans-Georg Gadamer, 'The Play of Art', in *The Relevance of the Beautiful* (London: Cambridge University Press, 1986), p. 126.
8. Hans-Georg Gadamer, 'Collected Works and Their Effective History', in *The Gadamer Reader*, pp. 409–27.
9. In his key work *Art* (1914), Clive Bell argued for an aesthetic appreciation which would see paintings solely as patterns of two-dimensional forms and celebrate them independent of cultural expectancy and habit. For a discussion of Bell's position, see Anne Sheppard, *Aesthetics* (Oxford: Oxford University Press, 1987), pp. 46–7.
10. Heidegger, *Being and Time*, Section 32.
11. TM, pp. 474–5.
12. 'In the last analysis, Goethe's statement "Everything is symbol" is the most comprehensive formulation of the hermeneutic idea. It means that everything points to another thing.' Hans-Georg Gadamer, *Philosophical Hermeneutics*, trans. D. Linge (Berkeley: University of California Press, 1976), p. 103.
13. TM, p. 458.
14. Ibid., p. 459.
15. Ibid., p. 466.
16. Ibid., pp. 474–5.

17. Ibid., p. 458.
18. See E. J. Ashworth, 'Language and Logic', in *The Cambridge Companion to Medieval Philosophy*, ed. A. S. McGrade (London: Cambridge University Press, 2003), pp. 73–120.
19. See Jeffrey Bardzell, *Speculative Grammar and Stoic Language Theory in Medieval Allegorical Narrative* (London: Routledge, 2008).
20. TM, p. 476.
21. Ibid., p. 401.
22. See Paul Ricoeur, *Hermeneutics and the Social Sciences*, trans. John Thompson (London: Cambridge University Press, 1981), p. 81.
23. The critical essays on art and photography by John Berger are brilliant in this respect. John Berger, *The Sense of Sight* (New York: Vintage International, 1985).
24. Gadamer, 'Collected Works and Their Effective History', p. 417.
25. Ibid., p. 417.
26. Ibid., p. 420.
27. Ibid., p. 417.
28. TM, p. 433.
29. Ibid., p. 473.
30. Ibid., p. 100.
31. G. S. Kirk and J. E. Raven, *The Pre-Socratics* (Cambridge: Cambridge University Press, 1975), p. 188.
32. Friedrich Nietzsche, *The Will to Power*, trans. Walter Kaufman and Roger Hollingdale (London: Weidenfeld and Nicolson, 1968), Section 568.
33. Benjamin Pollock, 'Franz Rosenzweig': http://plato.stanford.edu/entries/rosenzweig. It can be argued that the power of the image relies on its ability to bring that nexus to a summation.
34. TM, p. 448.
35. Hans-Georg Gadamer, 'Aesthetics and Religious Experience', in *The Relevance of the Beautiful*, p. 143. Gadamer may have derived the image of language as woven threads from Wilhelm von Humboldt, who commented: 'Man lives principally, or even exclusively with objects, since his feelings and actions depend upon his concepts as language presents them to his attention. By the same act through which he spins out the thread of language he weaves himself into its tissues.' Wilhelm von Humboldt, 'The Nature and Conformation of Language', in *The Hermeneutics Reader*, ed. Kurt Mueller-Vollmer (London: Blackwell, 1985), p. 105.
36. Johann Gottfried Herder, *Philosophical Writings*, trans. and ed. Michael N. Forster (Cambridge: Cambridge University Press, 2002), p. 148.
37. Nicolas Bourriaud, *Relational Aesthetics*, trans. Simon Pleasance and Fronza Wood (Paris: Les presses du réel, 2002), p. 14.
38. Ibid., p. 15 (original emphasis).
39. Ibid., pp. 15–17.
40. Ibid., p. 18.
41. Ibid., p. 22.

42. Ibid., p. 26.
43. Jürgen Habermas, *Postmetaphysical Thinking* (London: Polity, 1995), pp. 38–9.
44. The art criticism of such authors as Herbert Read and John Berger have played a major role within Britain in allowing the British art public to warmly embrace the modernist tradition.
45. TM, p. 443.
46. Ibid.
47. Gadamer, 'Collected Works and Their Effective History', p. 420.
48. Ibid., p. 417.
49. Ibid., p. 414.
50. Ibid., p. 417.
51. Alex Ross, *The Rest Is Noise: Listening to the Twentieth Century* (London: Fourth Estate, 2007).
52. Gadamer, 'Collected Works and Their Effective History', p. 417.
53. Hans-Georg Gadamer, 'The Artwork in Word and Image', in *The Gadamer Reader*, p. 195 (emphasis added).
54. André Kertész, *On Reading* (London: Norton and Company, 2008), p. 54.
55. Catherine Karkov, *Text and Picture in Anglo-Saxon England* (Cambridge: Cambridge University Press, 2001).
56. Gadamer, 'Collected Works and Their Effective History', p. 415.
57. Ibid. (emphasis added).
58. 'The same thing cannot become again a new experience for us; only some other unexpected thing can provide someone who has experience with a new one.' TM, p. 316.

7. *The Redemptive Image*

7.1 VARIATIONS ON AN ORIGINAL THEME

In the essay 'Creation as an Open System', Jürgen Moltmann proposes that 'redemption is ... nothing but the restitution of the original – restoration of the beginning'.[1] His remark offers three concluding routes of reflection for this study of Gadamer, hermeneutics and aesthetics: first, Gadamer's endeavour to redeem aesthetics by absorbing it within hermeneutics; second, Gadamer's development of a mode of aesthetic attentiveness that returns us not to an original way of seeing but to a way of seeing which facilitates origination within and amongst aesthetic ideas and subject-matters; and third, the ability of the aesthetic image to serve a twofold redemptive function in relation to the complexities of human experience. The doubled hermeneutics operating within Gadamer's account of our experience of art is both summative and projective in character: the poignant image can bring to resolution strands of meaning already at play in our environment and anticipate how our current understanding of the world might be transformed through its medium.

Moltmann's remark may seem an odd one to bring this study to a close: if there is no final word in hermeneutics (which Gadamer grants), there is no first word and, hence, no original word. This implies that, in verbal and visual language, there is no original covenant assuring arrival at a last meaning. Yet a Heideggerian undertone to his remark suggests that the original be equated with the authentic; that is, returning to an original is to be understood as re-engaging with an on-going attentiveness which allows for the continual origination (coming forth) of meaning without end and its endless transformative capacity.[2] The practice of aesthetic attentiveness emerges as that mode of being that is ever open to the transformative possibilities within actuality. Such transformation requires the full participation of the spectator and not the disinterested detachment of the Kantian subject.

7.2 A PHENOMENOLOGICAL RE-DESCRIPTION OF AESTHETICS

Gadamer shares von Balthasar's conviction that aesthetics needs to be re-articulated within a new set of categories. Both thinkers are uncomfortable about the way classical aesthetics has been dominated, for the most part, by the static, if not still-born, images of the beautiful and the eternal. Whereas von Balthasar strives for an aesthetics that expresses the movement of divine creation, Gadamer seeks, in his later writings especially, an aesthetic framework that tactfully acknowledges his Aristotelian notion of the being-in-motion that is life.[3] To this end, he strives to free aesthetics from those aspects of Kantian and romantic thought that ground aesthetic response in subjective consciousness. The philosophical justification for this effort resides in the claim that unless the experience of art can be anchored in something other than personal preference, art's claim to truth will never be redeemed.

As we have argued, the question of subjectivity confronts traditional aesthetics with three hindrances: the marginalisation of aesthetics, the devaluation of aesthetic appearance and the forfeiture of any rational status. To overcome these challenges, Gadamer initiates a strategic move. He insists that aesthetics must be absorbed within hermeneutics. The justification for this strategic claim is that the experience of art is primarily an experience of meaning, an experience of art addressing us. The consequences of this claim are extensive.

1. Asserting the primacy of meaning in the experience of art immediately establishes that aesthetic response is communal: it presupposes that the spectator must belong to a language world which extends beyond his or her immediate consciousness. If the experience of meaning is primary, differences between the vehicles of meaning become secondary. It is what word and image bring us to see that is critical.

2. The assertion of meaning's primacy allows Gadamer both to articulate the intentional nature of linguisticality (that word, image and symbol point to subject-matters of significant cognitive content) and to emphasise its speculative character (verbal and visual meaning demand participation in horizons of semantic significance that extend beyond the range of a spectator's usual consciousness). Pointing-to presupposes a pointing-from. Participation in horizons

of meaning situates the spectator, providing the orientation of both context and tradition.

3. The phenomenological primacy of meaning reveals the deep species interests guiding aesthetic responses. No longer is the aesthetic subject a detached aesthete, content to dwell within the momentary idiosyncrasies of feeling, but a situated participant, not only formed by but also capable of informing the key life-interests that define his or her mode of being.

4. The assertion of meaning as primary concomitantly affirms linguisticality's speculative dimensions. Without the spectator's participation (knowing or unknowing) in the wider horizons of those meanings associated with a practice, discipline or tradition, an artwork's ability to change transformatively the configurations of meaning in a spectator's horizon would be impossible.

5. The assertion of meaning as primary proclaims the actuality of interacting part–whole relationships. The assertion is consistent with philosophical hermeneutics entailing a non-essentialist stance. What a spectator knows of a subject-matter and what a historical subject-matter allows a spectator to know of it is a consequence of changing positions and adopting new perspectives within fluid part–whole relationships. The identity of a work, subject-matter or spectator is accumulative and, because accumulative, open and, because open, always subject to change.

6. The primacy of the experience of meaning emphasises its cumulative, perspectival and collective nature. Such accretions are visual and literary, confirming that theoretician and practitioner may share the same subject-matter despite approaching it from very different perspectives. The participatory and collective dimensions of the experience of meaning in the arts dissolves the unconstructive opposition between theorist and practitioner. It does not deny the specificity of either stance but permits and encourages a dialogical mutuality that allows both parties to see the perspective of the other as offering an additional insight to his or her own. This is the formal basis on which a hermeneutically reconstructed aesthetics promises a distinct and informative integration of both theory and practice in the arts and humanities. It suggests, furthermore, that the distinctiveness of a discipline's approach to a subject-matter in the humanities resides not in being hived off from others but in becoming, to the contrary, open to other orientations. Not only does interdisciplinary mediation allow the subject-matter to 'become more' but such openness permits each discipline to acquire a consciousness of its distinctiveness – to become more itself – in

and through its relation to other and different approaches to a shared concern. This is consistent with the hermeneutic axiom $x = x+$, that is, x acquires an awareness of its nature because of and in its relation to $x+$. The argumentation is attractive. It avoids vague appeals to openness. Gadamer's account of meaning and the transmission and reception of subject-matters offers a robust philosophical grounding for interdisciplinarity within the humanities. Operating within and between hermeneutical cross-currents upholds the transformative motions in and through which the humanities renew their being.

7. The primacy of meaning in the experience of art clearly individuates Gadamer's aesthetics from Kant's. Kant holds that aesthetic experience is indifferent to whether its object is real: a work's aesthetic success depends upon its artistic merit and not upon whether it offers an acceptable likeness. Should the work be damaged or destroyed, its objective co-relative is unaffected. Gadamer's presentational aesthetics is notably anti-Platonic in its claim that a work's disappearance diminishes the reality of that which presents itself through it: any diminishment of art diminishes the historical effectiveness of a given subject-matter. Aesthetic experience is no longer antithetical to the actual but contributes to the realisation of the possibilities held within it.

8. The assertion of meaning as primary allows philosophical hermeneutics to develop aesthetics from a science of sensibility into a poetics of the arts. Establishing the philosophical preconditions of the experience of meaning is synonymous with developing an account of how art generates and communicates meaning, or, to put it in other terms, with how artworks work. Philosophical hermeneutics presents visual or verbal images as significant placeholders in a spectator's life horizon, in those of his or her cultural tradition as well as in other, broad, historical horizons associated with the image. The artwork may be said to work when, in the experience of art and by means of its significant placeholders, the aforementioned horizons interlock and affect one another transformatively. A reader or spectator arrives at a new understanding of an image not by dint of will or effort but by participating in and attending to the movement of subject-matters across the related hermeneutical fields it stimulates. This 'poetics' is relevant not only to the understanding of art but also to revealing, explaining and defending the cognitive content of the humanities. Philosophical hermeneutics transforms aesthetic reflection into a poignant attentive practice, open to and welcoming of the unexpected's challenge to received experience.

In consequence, the status of aesthetic education is potentially radicalised. The poetics of aesthetic experience which derives from it emerges as a paradigm for rethinking the transmission and reception of meaning across the humanities.

The consequences of Gadamer's claim that aesthetics must be absorbed within hermeneutics are plainly extensive. The claim does not dissolve aesthetics but initiates a phenomenological re-description of aesthetic experience so that the discipline can be established as a cognitively significant mode of a subject's being-in-the-world. Aesthetic experience is redeemed as a form of hermeneutical engagement with the world, that is, it gives expression to not a subject's feeling but a subject's being. The dialogical framework of this phenomenological re-description demonstrates that though the intensity of aesthetic experience is not reducible to words (it is always a question of finding better or more appropriate words), the consequence is not solipsism. The content or about-ness of our experience of art is expressible in public terms. If so, further questions become possible. Are the presentational aspects of a work appropriate to its content? Once liberated from the enclosure of private feeling, engagement with such questions can generate an aesthetic collegiality. This re-description redeems an artwork's truth claim. The truth of a work becomes equivalent to the power of its effective historical legacy, that is, its truth relates to the transformative power it exercises in spectorial reception (application). Truth content has little to do with the verisimilitude of an image in relation to an external objective co-relative but much more with the degree to which a singular set of multiple relations constituting a work achieves an effective transformation of the pre-understood of a subject-matter and how that transformation in turn realigns our understanding of the relationship between ourselves and the world. In short, as well as challenging key claims of Platonic and neo-Kantian aesthetics, Gadamer's phenomenological re-description of aesthetic experience displaces world-estranged aestheticism with a participatory epistemology that repositions the spectator within a world of meanings, demonstrates that artistic and poetic images are primary instruments for navigating such a world, and attributes to both word and image powers of formative and transformative agency.

Grounding his phenomenological re-description of aesthetic experience in linguisticality allows Gadamer to radicalise the importance of aesthetic education. The resultant poetics of aesthetic experience becomes foundational for understanding the transmission and reception of meaning across the humanities. The move is instrumental in redeeming the applicative dimension of hermeneutics.

Gadamer's poetics invites a revaluation of the social and economic value of the humanities, a value all too often hidden by the obvious. The poetics identifies aesthetic experience as the occasion of colliding horizons of meaning, in which the concerns of artist and spectator meet and differentiate themselves. Transformative experience does not involve the emergence of novel meaning but rather, as Gadamer suggests, the joy of recognising a subject-matter 'as if' anew, perhaps even 'to arrive', in Eliot's words, at 'where we started and know the place for the first time'.[4] Transformative experience is necessarily transitive, involving moving from what we thought we knew to the realisation that we never knew it that well at all. As we have argued, movement is central to the practice of aesthetic attentiveness. The practice of attending follows movement in subject-matters; the painting leads the eye, the text draws its reader.[5] Such movement is not in itself important. It is what it initiates or brings into play that is key, what emerges from the cross-currents of meaning as the subject-matter and expectations of the spectator meet. Exposure to aesthetic experience induces movement in the horizons of the spectator so that he or she begins to think of a subject-matter differently.

The well-being of a tradition, as well as of the horizons and concerns of a spectator, require that they remain in motion. Movement, as Gadamer insists, is the life of the spirit. Intellectual and creative renewal depends upon a degree of disruption. The vitality of social and economic endeavour, let alone that of higher education, demands adaptability and the skills of thinking beyond the restraints of the customary and the expected. Exposure to the strange and unexpected can be unsettling but, as Gadamer suggests, no one can be protected from experience.[6] In an environment of change, a creature formed by dint of experience survives, it might be argued, only by constantly questioning and testing of its expectancies. Here, the social and economic significance of the humanities can be effectively and emphatically asserted. The practice of aesthetic attentiveness across the humanities requires controlled environments within which participants can safely expose their cultural expectancies to the unexpected and test their capability for transformative response. This re-affirms the importance of aesthetic education. It is impossible to predict the nature and extent of the challenges that the future holds but the quality and depth of response will be key. If transformative experience arises when the horizons of meaning attached to an artwork collide serendipitously with those of the spectator, the extent and creativity of the spectator's response will be informed by the width of the cultural horizons he or she can draw on. The value of discipline canons is not that they perpetrate exemplary practice but that they lay down in the spectator or reader the foundations of response repertoires that only the future will test. Not to invest in the attentive practices of the humanities, not to nurture the ability to dwell within spaces of hermeneutical challenge and not to teach how to be patient in developing as yet unknown but wished for responses to such provocations is to disinvest in our collective ability to respond creatively to the inevitable challenges of the future.

7.3 THE REDEMPTIVE SPACE

Another consequence of asserting the experience of meaning as primary is the affirmation of presentation and appearance as the dominant mode of an artwork's effective being. As we argued, meaning asserts or presents itself: it comes forth. It is not a copy of something else, nor does anything hide behind it: it is what it shows itself to be, an epiphany, an appearing and a showing. With these terms Gadamer openly extends Heidegger's ontological revaluation of the artwork as event: *appearing* is of the essence. With this assertion, Gadamer puts to one side the reality/appearance distinction of much European aesthetics. Plato's doctrine of *mimesis* is inverted in favour of a reworking of Aristotle's developmental account. Appearance is, therefore, not alien to the being of a subject-matter. Its multiplication magnifies the actuality of the thing constituted by a set of perspectives. The more perspectives we have of it, the more it becomes. However, this raises a question about the process of appearing itself.

Following Heidegger, Gadamer insists that the fundamental characteristic of Being is its self-presentational nature. Being is self-presentation and is not different from itself in presenting itself:[7] *appearing* is the very essence of the process. Heidegger's essay 'The Origin of the Work of Art' does not imply that, with regard Being, there is an original *x* which is the *fons et origo* of all appearing. As that which is, the process of appearing has never begun to become, nor has it ever ceased from becoming. It is that endless process of origination which maintains itself in constant disclosure and withholding. The argument allows philosophical hermeneutics to make a strong ontological claim on the part of aesthetics. That which shows itself in aesthetic experience is not secondary to reality (a copy of an objective correlative) but is the very process of showing and withholding that is a subject-matter. In Gadamer's understanding, then, art no longer veils or hides the real but shows it (gives expression to it) in its own disclosures and withholdings. Gadamer's hermeneutical aesthetics stands, then, on the claim that art's processural character neither copies nor distorts the real but manifests (and hence returns us to) the presentational process of origination which is Being itself. This allows philosophical hermeneutics to offer a telling twist on Moltmann's notion of the redemptive as a restoration of the beginning.

For philosophical hermeneutics there is, of course, no original to return to, since if from the beginning was the word, there has also been ambiguity, confusion, lack of transparency, but never a single original meaning. Rather, it is the constant play of disclosure and withholding that *is* original. The play is the play of possibilities within the speculative horizons which circumscribe word and image. The question is how to discern, be open to and develop such possibilities. Philosophical hermeneutics insists that transformative understanding is possible only so long as movement in and between its enabling horizons is maintained. Gadamer is thus openly opposed to those bureaucratic, institutional and ideological factors which, by intention or default, attempt to stifle the natural slippage of linguistic meaning or regularise the productive ambiguity essential to creative engagement. Instrumentalist thinking is managerial in nature: it disciplines and controls its social and cultural environment according to the norms of its technical ambition. Gadamer shares Heidegger's anxiety concerning the displacement of aletheic language by apophantic language, a simplified language of such force that, when used by ideologues, can persuade us that its schemas of description present actuality as it is. They do no such thing; they re-describe the world in such a way as to suit business, technical or commercial intervention. Heidegger looked specifically to aletheic poetry to recall us to an awareness of the mystery of Being and to participate (once more) in the immanent origination of Being in its self-disclosing and withdrawing. Gadamer follows a similar but more combative route, which, though imbued with a sense of the speculative, both eschews Heidegger's more overt language mysticism and provides a practical setting for his own advocacy of aesthetic attentiveness.

The question of origination prompts a question of original purpose: what does a hermeneutical aesthetics emphasise? The capacity of art to expressively disclose the real (the self-presenting processes of origination) or, as we suggest, the achievement of transformational understanding achieved by participating in those processes of origination? Slight but discernible strands of mysticism and quietism inflect Gadamer's articulation of the speculative but the account of aesthetic attentiveness makes clear that the *summum bonum* of philosophical hermeneutics is not just contemplation for its own sake of the self-presenting play (origination) of actuality. If it were, Gadamer's critique of subjective aesthetic consciousness would collapse into self-contradiction. Apart from the paradox that contemplating actuality as whole would promote blindness (one cannot stand outside it to view it whole), reducing actuality to sheer contemplative spectacle demands precisely what Gadamer's aesthetic strives to overcome, namely, that negative episte-mological distanciation which allows a subject to reduce the world to a visually objectifiable and, hence, manipulable field. However, within an actuality of self-presenting part–whole relations, seeing can only be seeing from within and seeing is more a matter of achieving different perspectives within a given field. Indeed, the intensification of visual experience hints at the *summum bonum* of philosophical hermeneutics, that is, the transformation of understanding.

The value of expanding the visual perspectives available to a specta-tor lies not in their numerical multiplication *per se* but in increasing the likelihood of that spectator's exposure to sets of part–whole rela-tions capable of transforming the horizons of understanding he or she *already* inhabits. Informing the spectator of the history of different painterly or poetic genres is not an end in itself but a necessary means. Its value is extrinsic, not intrinsic; it lies in the potential increased visual perspectives have for achieving subsequent transformative effects. Articulated within the framework of philosophical hermeneutics, the function of aesthetic education must be to acquaint the spectator with those frameworks of seeing that have been (or promise to be) recog-nised for their transformative powers relative to an established cultural horizon. Let us turn to a remark of Gadamer's that brings several lines of argument together:

> We should have no illusions. Bureaucratized teaching and learning systems dominate the scene, but nevertheless it is everyone's task to find his free space. The task of our human life in general is to find free spaces and learn to move therein.[8]

Participating contemplatively in the movement of aesthetic ideas and subject-matters is to participate in processes of origination in which *things happen*. Participation in such processes is not just passive. Engaging with different horizons of understanding *makes things happen*, that is, it can draw out and actualise possibilities held within one's immediate horizon. The argument endorses Gadamer's commit-ment to the priority of the possible over the actual. Each actualisation of the possible brings back to mind a range of existential possibilities held within a spectator's horizon, possibilities which are invariably uncovered only when an alien horizon comes into contact with the spectator's own, forcing a rethink of what was thought to be known.

The emphasis upon actualisation and transformation strengthens the Aristotelian argument within Gadamer's position that life maintains, enhances and intensifies itself in movement. Commending contemplation of the originating movement of aesthetic ideas and subject-matters is, then, not an end in itself but a means to creating those circumstances whereby the bringing together of different horizons can transform insight. The commendation of aesthetic attentiveness and contemplation is a challenge to those bureaucratic and ideological powers that endeavour to limit or control serendipitous creativity.

Gadamer's advocacy of contemplating aesthetic origination does not venerate the ontic origination and self-presentation of Being *per se*. What it bids us recognise and participate in are Being's transformative powers, as occasioned in the meeting of different horizons of meaning. In the case of philosophical hermeneutics, Moltmann's argument that 'redemption is ... nothing but the restitution of the original – restoration of the beginning'⁹ cannot imply a return to any first word. In philosophical hermeneutics, the phrase 'In the beginning was the word' has another connotation. At the logical beginning of what is understood as human culture and society – or of what Hegel calls objective spirit – stands the word, which is to say, that human culture is inconceivable without linguisticality. It is because of language that humanity, as Gadamer famously claims, has a world at all.¹⁰ Philosophical hermeneutics does not formally deny an evolutionary account of language but holds that, within a phenomenological framework that prioritises meaning, human existence and linguisticality cannot be thought of apart from one another. *Dasein* implies that, phenomenologically speaking, we cannot stand outside the changing totality of part–whole relations that constitute linguisticality: the being of human culture and the being of the word (*onto-logos*) are inseparable. The beginning at issue is that of immanence.

Onto-logos, phenomenologically conceived, is incommensurable with any talk of a first word. This suggests that if all talk of an original first word is disallowed, the being of linguisticality and the perspectival worlds it sustains maintain themselves only by constantly coming into being and passing out of being. To borrow Nietzsche's phrase, the world of linguisticality exists:

> it is not something that becomes, not something that passes away, or rather: it becomes, it passes away, but it has never begun to become nor ceased from passing away – it maintains itself in both.¹¹

The notion of *onto-logos* returns us to a key conception in philosophical hermeneutics, the Aristotelean notion of *poesis*, which simultaneously

links the term 'poetry' with that for 'making'. Within a phenomenological framework in which meaning is primary, linguistic and visual
making implies an indissoluble connection between the act of expressing (the saying or the showing which brings forth), the expression itself
(what is stated verbally or visually) and what comes into expression
(the speculative networks of meaning which ground an expression and
provide its sense and direction). Making, conceived as the simultane-
ous bringing forth and occlusion of meaning, is primary. Through the
expressive act, the immanence of linguisticality's onto-genesis is upheld,
each emergent expression resonating and renewing the speculative horizons out of which it arises and, subsequently, effects. *Onto-logos*, the
living being of the word (i.e. linguisticality), is maintained in the ever-
present play of meaning. The doctrine of aesthetic attentiveness attends
to the movement within aesthetic ideas and subject-matters. Being open
to such movement is, in Moltmann's terms, a restoration of the beginning, that is, a becoming-aware-of and an engaging-in the immanent
renewal of linguisticality and its speculative horizons.

Aesthetic attentiveness is not concerned with such movement as
sheer spectacle. It requires that the movement of aesthetic ideas and
subject-matters be discerned, but not for their own sake. The issue is
not becoming aware of the subject-matters *per se* but of how exposure
to their movement might induce change and transformation within the
spectator's horizons. Establishing the free space of aesthetic attentiveness is not without hermeneutical function. First, the contemplation of
original and originating movement within aesthetic ideas and subject-
matters seeks to displace the rigidity of institutionalised ways of seeing.
Second, dismantling hindrances to seeing and participating in such
movement endeavour to create circumstances which might expose the
spectator to new and unexpected horizons of meaning and, hence, to
the possibility of a transformation in his or her own perspective. The
redemption that a hermeneutically orientated aesthetic attentiveness
seeks is to restore openness to the immanence of that constant creativity
which is the movement of Being. Once again, participation and engagement are key.

7.4 THE REDEMPTIVE IMAGE AND THE FIGURING OF TRANSFORMATION

To assert the primacy of meaning in the experience of art is to imply
the primary need for hermeneutics. To argue for the primacy of the
word, irrespective of whether it is the spoken word, the written word
or, indeed, the silent word of the image, is to suggest that obscurity

and opaqueness of meaning have also always been present. The inability to fix the meaning of a word or image definitively has promoted much scepticism as to whether any clarity of meaning is possible. Philosophical hermeneutics concurs with such doubts, in that its commitment to the historicity of all meaning denies that the meaning of an aesthetic idea or subject-matter can ever be fully determined. However, whereas philosophical hermeneutics denies the possibility of experiencing a fully objectified meaning, it does not deny the possibility of an experience of meaning. To accept that obscurity of meaning always accompanies the word or the image is to accept that there are indeed experiences of meaning which subsequently become opaque. Participation and engagement with horizons of meaning are key once again.

The primacy of meaning which Gadamer asserts with regard to the experience of art concerns a relational experience of meaningfulness. Philosophical hermeneutics does not seek as its principal ambition to decipher or decode the intrinsic meaning of a poetic utterance or painterly image. That would be to objectify the artwork as a challenging scholarly puzzle. A hermeneutically orientated aesthetics seeks engagement with a work. Analysis and scholarly endeavour may lead to such engagement but remain a means to an end. As we previously suggested in our discussion of Gadamer's doubled hermeneutics, to experience a work as meaningful is to experience its framework of meaningful relations permeating and transforming one's own horizon of concerns. An experience of meaning is, then, not the experience of an essential, incontestable meaning but of what is, essentially, a transformative experience of meaningfulness, a fusion of horizons whereby the horizons of a spectator are significantly altered. Such epiphanies of meaning are, of course, transient and finite. Their importance has nothing to do with creating one-off novel episodic meanings but lies in their relational ability to initiate change across frameworks of meaning, transforming the nature and direction of personal and cultural narratives. This brings us to the redemptive power of the image as the fulfilment of hermeneutical hope.

Gadamer acknowledges that human life always stands in a horizon of desired or feared, or, at any rate, still undecided future possibilities.[12] Lines of meaning remain open, ambiguities remain. Living amongst fragments of meaning makes us curious about the circumstances that might complete them. Literary and visual images in which sets of part–whole relations are brought to completion intimate, aesthetically, what such completeness within actuality might be like. These observations reflect for Wolfgang Iser a more fundamental condition. Reflecting on

the arguments of Dieter Henrich and Helmut Plessner, he remarks in
this respect that two major issues pose themselves: 'first, the ground
from which human beings have sprung is unfathomable and thus
appears to be withheld from them. Second, human beings have also
become unavailable to themselves; we are but do not know what it is to
be'.[13] Philosophical hermeneutics concurs with such anti-essentialism.
Iser argues that perhaps the 'unending activity of interpretation . . . [is]
a response to these basic unavailabilities'[14] or, to put it in Gadamer's
terms, the hermeneutical quest for an anticipated completeness is an
attempt to complete and close an open framework of meaning such
that no lines of meaning scatter in the void.[15] Even philosophical hermeneutics admits that this is to pursue the unattainable. The axiom x
always equals $x+$ denies the possibility of such closure. The experience
of meaningfulness is, as we have argued, not an experience of a singular framework of meaning as closed and complete but an experience
of relational meaning, whereby exposure to one set of meaningful
relations transforms another in an on-going and open manner. Why,
then, the pursuit of the unreachable and the unattainable? As we have
argued, the pursuit of the final word is not the end of but a means to
hermeneutical transformation. It is what the interpretive quest brings
to pass that matters. It builds access to ranges of other and different
interpretations. Exposure to them triggers the ever immanent end of
philosophical hermeneutics, not the emergence of a final word but the
epiphany of a word or image capable of transforming the spectator's
initial horizon. The artistic image or the poetic word redeems the hope
wagered in any hermeneutical openness to experience. It does so neither
by disclosing the last word, nor by revealing *the* meaning of existence,
but by achieving a transformative experience of meaning between
personal and collective horizons that renders participation and involvement in existence meaningful. Such redemption is not available to the
disinterested by-stander but only to those who engage with and participate attentively in the play of meanings an image can transform. In
relation to its hermeneutical context, the image facilitates an experience
of meaning transformed, not of meaning completed. This redeems the
hopes of those who tarry awhile amidst the open movement of aesthetic
ideas and their subject-matters, waiting for that chance disclosure of
meaning that is neither final nor complete but transformative. It is the
power of words and images to transform meanings across horizons that
renders Gadamer's double hermeneutics effective and justifies the case
for absorbing aesthetics within hermeneutics. In an unfinished world,
the experience of art redeems what can always be hoped for in hermeneutic practice: a transformation of meaning.

NOTES

1. Jürgen Moltmann, *Science and Wisdom* (London: SCM Press, 2003), p. 34.
2. The artwork opens up in its own way the Being of beings. See Martin Heidegger, 'The Origin of the Work of Art', in *Poetry, Language and Thought*, trans. Albert Hofstadter (New York: Harper, 1971), pp. 39, 17–20.
3. For an informative account of Gadamer's Aristotelian conception of Being, see James Risser, *Hermeneutics and the Voice of the Other: Re-reading Gadamer's* Philosophical Hermeneutics (Albany: State University of New York Press, 1997), pp. 123–9.
4. T. S. Eliot, 'Little Gidding', Canto V, *The Four Quartets* (London: Folio Society, 1968), p. 55.
5. TM, p. 474.
6. Ibid., p. 356.
7. Ibid., p. 487.
8. Hans-Georg Gadamer, *On Education, Poetry and History: Applied Hermeneutics*, ed. D. Misgeld and G. Nicholson (Albany: State University of New York Press, 1992), p. 79.
9. Moltmann, *Science and Wisdom*, p. 34.
10. TM, p. 443.
11. Friedrich Nietzsche, *The Will to Power*, trans. Walter Kaufmann and Roger Hollingdale (London: Weidenfeld and Nicolson, 1968), Section 1066.
12. TM, p. 112.
13. Wolfgang Iser, *The Range of Interpretation* (New York: Columbia University Press, 2000), pp. 155–6.
14. Ibid.
15. TM, pp. 112–13.

Bibliography

PRIMARY SOURCES

German

Gadamer, Hans-Georg, *Gedicht und Gespräche* (Hamburg: Insel Verlag, 1990).

Gadamer, Hans-George, *Gesammelte Werke* (Tübingen: Mohr Siebeck, Uni-Taschenbücher, 1987).

Gadamer, Hans-Georg, *Hermeneutik-Ästhetik-Praktische Philosophie: Hans-Georg Gadamer im Gespräche* (Heidedelberg: C. Wiener Universitäts Verlag, 1993, rev. 1994).

Gadamer, Hans-Georg, *Hermeneutische Entwürfe, Vorträge und Aufsätze* (Tübingen: Mohr Siebeck, 2000).

Gadamer, Hans-Georg, *Kunst als Aussage, Gesammelte Werke*, Band 8 (Tübingen: Mohr Siebeck, 1993).

Gadamer, Hans-Georg, *Wahrheit und Methode* (Tübingen: J. C. B. Mohr, 1960).

English

Two Gadamer bibliographies are of importance. Lewis Edwin Hahn's *The Philosophy of Hans-Georg Gadamer* (Chicago: Open Court, 1993) contains a 'Selected Gadamer Bibliography' with sections on: Gadamer's books and monographs in German with their English translations; books in English that are collections of Gadamer's articles; published articles and their English translations; interviews and videos (published interviews and archival tapes); and secondary sources – bibliographical resources, book-length studies and essay collections. A second bibliography is the extended edition of Etsuro Makita's *Gadamer Bibliographie* (Frankfurt: Lang, 1995).

Gadamer, Hans-Georg, *Literature and Philosophy in Dialogue: Essays in German Literary Theory*, trans. R. H. Paslick (Albany: State University of New York Press, 1994).

Gadamer, Hans-Georg, *On Education, Poetry and History: Applied*

Hermeneutics, ed. D. Misgeld and G. Nicholson (Albany: State University of New York Press, 1992).

Gadamer, Hans-Georg, *Philosophical Hermeneutics*, trans. David E. Linge (Berkeley: University of California Press, 1976).

Gadamer, Hans-Georg, *The Gadamer Reader*, ed. R. E. Palmer (Evanston: Northwestern University Press, 2007).

Gadamer, Hans-Georg, *The Relevance of the Beautiful* (London: Cambridge University Press, 1986).

Gadamer, Hans-Georg, *Truth and Method*, ed. and trans. Joel Weinsheimer (London: Sheed and Ward, 1989).

SECONDARY SOURCES

Adorno, Theodor, *Aesthetic Theory* (London: Routledge and Kegan Paul, 1984).

Adorno, Theodor, *Hegel: Three Studies* (Cambridge, MA: MIT Press, 1993).

Adorno, Theodor, *Negative Dialectics*, trans. E. B. Ashton (London: Routledge and Kegan Paul, 1973).

Aristotle, *Ethics*, ed. J. A. K. Thomson (London: Penguin, 1975).

Arthos, John, *The Inner Word in Gadamer's Hermeneutics* (Notre Dame: University of Indiana Press, 2009).

Ashworth, E. J., 'Language and Logic', in *The Cambridge Companion to Medieval Philosophy*, ed. A. S. McGrade (London: Cambridge University Press, 2003).

Ayer, A. J., *Language, Truth and Logic* (London: Penguin, 2001).

Balthasar, Hans Urs von, *Theo-Drama: Theological Dramatic Theory, Vol. 1: Prolegomena*, trans. Graham Harrison (San Francisco: Ignatius Press, 1998).

Bardzell, Jeffrey, *Speculative Grammar and Stoic Language Theory in Medieval Allegorical Narrative* (London: Routledge, 2008).

Baumgarten, A. G., *Texte zur Grundlegung der Ästhetik* (Hamburg: Felix Meiner, 1983).

Berger, John, *The Sense of Sight* (New York: Vintage International, 1985).

Berlin, Isaiah, *The Magus of the North: J. G. Hamann and the Origins of Modern Irrationalism* (London: John Murray, 1993).

Bernstein, J. M., *The Fate of Art: Aesthetic Alienation from Kant to Derrida and Adorno* (London: Polity Press, 1992).

Bloch, Ernst, *The Principle of Hope*, Vol. 1, trans. N. Plaice (Oxford: Blackwell, 1986).

Bloch, Ernst, *The Spirit of Utopia* (Stanford: Stanford University Press, 2000).

Bourgeois, Jason Paul, *The Aesthetic Hermeneutics of Hans-Georg Gadamer and Hans von Balthasar* (New York: Peter Lang, 2007).

Bourriaud, Nicolas, *Relational Aesthetics*, trans. Simon Pleasance and Fronza Wood (Paris: Les presses du réel, 2002).

Bruns, Gerald, 'The Hermeneutical Anarchist: Phronesis, Rhetoric and the Experience of Art', in *Gadamer's Century: Essays in Honor of Hans-Georg*

Gadamer, ed. Jeff Malpas, Ulrich Arnswald and Jens Kertscher (Cambridge, MA: MIT Press, 2002), pp. 44–76.

Byatt, A. S., *Portraits in Fiction* (London: Chatto and Windus, 2001).

Caputo, John (ed.), *The Religious* (London: Blackwell, 2002).

Carroll, David, *The States of Theory: History, Art, and Critical Discourse* (Stanford: Stanford University Press, 1990).

Cassirer, Ernst, *The Logic of the Humanities* (Clinton: Yale University Press, 1974).

Cixous, Hélène and Mireille Calle-Gruber, *Rootprints: Memory and Life Writing*, trans. Eric Prenowitz (London: Routledge, 1997).

Clark, Timothy, *The Poetics of Singularity* (Edinburgh: Edinburgh University Press, 2005).

Collingwood, R. J., *The Idea of History* (London: Oxford University Press, 1961).

Cooper, David, *A Companion to Aesthetics* (Oxford: Blackwell, 1992).

Danto, Arthur, *The Transfiguration of the Commonplace* (Cambridge, MA: Harvard University Press, 1981).

Davey, Nicholas, 'Baumgarten's Aesthetics: A Post-Gadamerian Reflection', *British Journal of Aesthetics*, Vol. 29, No. 2, 1989, pp. 101–15.

Davey, Nicholas, 'Gadamer's Aesthetics', in *The Stanford Enclopedia of Philosophy* (2007): http://plato.stanford.edu./entries/gadamer-aesthetics/

Davey, Nicholas, 'Lest We Forget: The Question of Being in Philosophical Hermeneutics', *Journal of the British Society for Phenomenology*, Vol. 40, No. 3, Oct. 2009, pp. 234–8.

Davey, Nicholas, 'Philosophical Hermeneutics: An Education for All Seasons', in *Education, Dialogue and Hermeneutics*, ed. Paul Fairfield (London: Continuum, 2011), pp. 39–60.

Davey, Nicholas, 'Philosophical Hermeneutics, Art and the Language of Art', *Aesthetic Pathways*, Vol. 1, No. 1, Dec. 2010, pp. 4–29.

Nicholas Davey, 'Review of Colin Davis, *Critical Excess; Overreading in Derrida, Deleuze, Levinas, Zizek and Cavell*', *Screen*, Vol. 53, No. 2, summer 2012, pp. 180–2

Davey, Nicholas, 'Sitting Uncomfortably: A Hermeneutic Reflection on Portraiture', *Journal of the British Society for Phenomenology*, Vol. 34, No. 3, Oct. 2003, pp. 231–46.

Davey, Nicholas, 'The Hermeneutics of Seeing', in *Interpreting Visual Culture: Explorations in the Hermeneutics of the Visual*, ed. Ian Heywood and Barry Sandywell (London: Routledge, 1999), pp. 3–30.

Davey, Nicholas, 'Truth, Method and Transcendence', in *Consequences of Hermeneutics: Fifty Years After Gadamer's* Truth and Method, ed. J. Malpas and S. Zabala (Evanston: Northwestern University Press, 2010), pp. 25–54.

Davey, Nicholas, *Unquiet Understanding* (Albany: State University of New York Press, 2006).

Davies, Oliver, 'The Theological Aesthetics', in *The Cambridge Companion to*

Hans Urs von Balthasar, ed. Edward T. Oakes and David Moss (Cambridge: Cambridge University Press, 2004), pp. 131–42.

Davis, Colin, *Critical Excess: Overreading in Derrida, Deleuze, Levinas, Žižek and Cavell* (Stanford: Stanford University Press, 2011).

Dilthey, Wilhelm, *Selected Writings*, ed. H. P. Rickman (London: Cambridge University Press, 1976).

Dostal, Robert, *The Cambridge Companion to Gadamer* (Cambridge: Cambridge University Press, 2002).

Duerr, Peter, *Dreamtime: Concerning the Boundary Between Wilderness and Civilisation* (London: Blackwell, 1985).

Dufrenne, Mikel, *The Phenomenology of Aesthetic Experience* (Evanston: Northwestern University Press, 1973).

Eagleton, Terry, *Holy Terror* (Oxford: Oxford University Press, 2005).

Eliot, T. S., *The Four Quartets* (London: Folio Society, 1968).

Faye, Jan, *After Postmodernism: A Naturalistic Reconstruction of the Humanities* (London: Palgrave Macmillan, 2012).

Fiddes, Paul S., *The Promised End: Eschatology in Theology and Literature* (Oxford: Blackwell, 2000).

Figal, Günter, *Erscheinungsdinge* (Tübingen: Mohr Siebeck, 2010).

Fiumari, Gemma Corradi, *The Other Side of Language: A Philosophy of Listening* (London: Routledge and Kegan Paul, 1990).

Forbes, Peter, *Dazzled and Deceived: Mimicry and Camouflage* (London: Yale University Press, 2009).

Giddens, Anthony, *Modernity and Self-Identity* (London: Polity Press, 1995).

Giddens, Anthony, *New Rules of Sociological Method* (London: Hutchinson, 1987).

Gjesdal, Kristin, *Gadamer and the Legacy of German Idealism* (Cambridge: Cambridge University Press, 2009).

Goethe, Johann, *Maximen und Reflexionen* (Munich: Deutscher Taschenbuch Verlag, 1968).

Gombrich, Ernst, *Art and Illusion: Studies in the Psychology of Pictorial Representation* (Oxford: Oxford University Press, 1983).

Gombrich, E. H., *The Sense of Order* (Oxford: Phaidon, 1984).

Grondin, J., *Introduction to Philosophical Hermeneutics* (Albany: State University of New York Press, 1994).

Habermas, Jürgen, *Knowledge and Human Interests* (London: Heinemann, 1972).

Habermas, Jürgen, *Postmetaphysical Thinking* (London: Polity, 1995).

Habermas, Jürgen, *The Liberating Power of Symbols: Philosophical Essays* (London: Polity, 2001).

Hahn, Lewis Edwin, ed., *The Philosophy of Hans-Georg Gadamer* (Chicago: Open Court, 1997).

Hampshire, Stuart, *Thought and Action* (London: Chatto and Windus, 1959).

Hampson, Daphne, *After Christianity* (London: SCM Press, 2002).

Harries, Karsten, *The Meaning of Modern Art* (Evanston: Northwestern University Press, 1968).

Harrington, Austin, *Art and Social Theory* (London: Polity, 2004).

Hegel, G. F. W., *Hegel's Introduction to Aesthetics: The Berlin Lectures*, trans. T. M. Knox, ed. Charles Karelis (Oxford: Oxford University Press, 1979).

Heidegger, Martin, *Being and Time*, trans. John Macquarrie (London: Blackwell, 1960).

Heidegger, Martin, *Poetry, Language and Thought*, trans. Albert Hofstadter (New York: Harper, 1971).

Herder, Johann Gottfried, *Philosophical Writings*, trans. and ed. Michael N. Forster (Cambridge: Cambridge University Press, 2002).

Heywood, Ian, *Social Theories of Art: A Critique* (Basingstoke: Macmillan, 1998).

Iser, Wolfgang, *The Range of Interpretation* (New York: Columbia University Press, 2000).

Jenkins, David Fraser, *John Piper: The Forties* (London: Imperial War Museum, 2000), plate 71.

Kant, Immanuel, *Critique of Pure Reason*, trans. Norman Kemp Smith (London: Macmillan, 1970).

Kant, Immanuel, *Kritik der reinen Vernunft* (Hamburg: Felix Meiner, 1956).

Kant, Immanuel, *The Critique of Judgement*, trans. J. C. Meredith (Oxford: Oxford University Press, 1978).

Karkov, Catherine, *Text and Picture in Anglo-Saxon England* (Cambridge: Cambridge University Press, 2001).

Kelly, Michael, 'A Critique of Gadamer's Aesthetics', in Bruce Krajewski, *Gadamer's Repercussions: Reconsidering Philosophical Hermeneutics* (Berkeley: University of California Press, 2003), pp. 103–22.

Kelly, Michael, *Encyclopaedia of Aesthetics*, Vol. 2 (Oxford: Oxford University Press, 1998).

Kertesz, Andre, *On Reading* (London: Norton and Company, 2008).

Kirk, G. S., and J. E. Raven, *The Pre-Socratics* (Cambridge: Cambridge University Press, 1975).

Kögler, Hans Herbert, *The Power of Dialogue* (Cambridge, MA: MIT Press, 1996).

Kolokowski, Leszek, *Positivist Philosophy: From Hume to the Vienna Circle* (London: Penguin, 1972).

Krajewski, Bruce, *Gadamer's Repercussions: Reconsidering Philosophical Hermeneutics* (Berkeley: University of California Press, 2005).

Lang, Christian, *Hermeneutik, Ideologiekritik, Ästhetik* (Hanstein: Forum Academicum, 1981).

Lawn, Christopher, *Gadamer: A Guide for the Perplexed* (London: Continuum, 2006).

MacGregor, Neil, *A History of the World in 100 Objects* (London: Allen Lane, Penguin, 2010).

MacIntyre, Alasdair, *After Virtue* (London: Duckworth, 1993).

MacIntyre, Alasdair, *Whose Justice? Which Rationality?* (London: Duckworth, 1988).

Makkreel, Rudolf A., *Imagination and Interpretation in Kant: The Hermeneutical Import of the Critique of Judgement* (London: University of Chicago Press, 1990).

Margolis, Joseph, *The Arts and the Definition of the Human: Towards a Philosophical Anthropology* (Stanford: Stanford University Press, 2009).

Marino, Stefano, *Gadamer and the Limits of the Modern Techno-Scientific Civilization* (Basel: Peter Lang, 2011).

McGregor, Joanna, 'On the Pleasures of Harrison Birtwistle's "Difficult Music"', *Guardian*, 22 May 2009.

McIntosh, Mark, *Mystical Theology* (Oxford: Blackwell, 2006).

Menke, Christoph, *The Sovereignty of Art: Aesthetic Negativity in Adorno and Derrida* (Cambridge, MA: MIT Press, 1999).

Midgley, Mary, *Science and Poetry* (London: Routledge, 2001).

Milbank, John, *The Word Made Strange: Theology, Language, Culture* (Oxford: Blackwell, 1998).

Moltmann, Jürgen, *Science and Wisdom* (London: SCM Press, 2003).

Mueller-Vollmer, Kurt, ed., *The Hermeneutics Reader* (London: Blackwell, 1985).

Murdoch, Iris, *Existentialists and Mystics* (London: Chatto and Windus, 1997).

Murphy, Sinéad, *Effective History: On Critical Practice Under Historical Conditions* (Evanston: Northwestern University Press, 2010).

Nancy, Jean-Luc, *The Ground of the Image*, trans. Jeff Fort (New York: Fordham University Press, 2008).

Newark, Tim, *Camouflage* (London: Thames and Hudson, 2007).

Nietzsche, Friedrich, *Human, All Too Human*, trans. R. J. Hollingdale (Cambridge: Cambridge University Press, 1986).

Nietzsche, Friedrich, *The Gay Science*, trans. Walter Kaufmann (New York: Vintage, 1974).

Nietzsche, Friedrich, *The Will to Power*, trans. Walter Kaufman and Roger Hollingdale (London: Weidenfeld and Nicolson, 1968).

Nightingale, Andrea Wilson, *Spectacles of Truth in Classical Greek Philosophy: Theoria in Its Cultural Context* (Cambridge: Cambridge University Press, 2005).

Pannenberg, Wolfhart, *Theology and the Philosophy of Science* (London: Darton, Longman and Todd, 1976).

Pareyson, Luigi, *Verità e interpretazionei* (Milan: Mursia, 1971).

Paterson, Don, *Orpheus: A Vision of Rainer Maria Rilke* (London: Faber and Faber, 2006).

Pieper, Josef, *In Tune with the World: A Theory of Festivity* (South Bend: St Augustine's Press, 1999).

Pippin, Robert, *Hollywood Westerns and American Myth* (New Haven: Yale University Press, 2010).

Pippin, Robert B., *The Persistence of Subjectivity: On the Kantian Aftermath* (Cambridge: Cambridge University Press, 2005).

Pollock, Benjamin, 'Franz Rosenzweig': http://plato.stanford.edu/entries/rosenzweig

Polyani, Michael, *The Tacit Dimension* (Chicago: Chicago University Press, 2009).

Redding, Paul, *Hegel's Hermeneutics* (Ithaca: Cornell University Press, 1996).

Ricoeur, Paul, *Hermeneutics*, trans. David Pellauer (London: Polity, 2013).

Ricoeur, Paul, *Hermeneutics and the Human Sciences*, trans. John Thompson (London: Cambridge University Press, 1981).

Rilke, Rainer Maria, *Letters to a Young Poet*, trans. M. Norton (New York: Norton, 1954).

Risser, James, *Hermeneutics and the Voice of the Other: Re-reading Gadamer's Philosophical Hermeneutics* (Albany: State University of New York Press, 1997).

Risser, James, *The Life of Understanding: A Contemporary Hermeneutics* (Bloomington: Indiana University Press, 2012).

Rosenzweig, Franz, *Understanding the Sick and the Healthy: A View of World, Man and God* (Cambridge, MA: Harvard University Press, 1999).

Ross, Alex, *The Rest Is Noise: Listening to the Twentieth Century* (London: Fourth Estate, 2007).

Rossi, Osvaldo, *Gadamer e le arti* (Ancona: Transeuropa, 2002).

Scheiffele, Eberhard, 'Questioning One's "Own" from the Perspective of the Foreign', in *Nietzsche and Asian Thought*, ed. Graham Parkes (Chicago: University of Chicago Press, 1991), pp. 31–50.

Schiller, Friedrich, *On the Aesthetic Education of Man*, ed. and trans. E. M. Wilkinson and L. A. Willoughby (Oxford: Clarendon Press, 1982).

Schleiermacher, Friedrich, *Schleiermacher: Hermeneutics and Criticism and Other Writings*, ed. A. Bowie (Cambridge: Cambridge University Press, 1998).

Schmidt, Dennis J., *Between Word and Image: Heidegger, Klee, and Gadamer on Gesture and Genesis* (Bloomington: Indiana University Press, 2013).

Sennett, Richard, *The Craftsman* (London: Penguin, 2008).

Sennett, Richard, *Together: The Rituals, Pleasures and Politics of Cooperation* (London: Allen Lane, 2012).

Sheppard, Anne, *Aesthetics* (Oxford: Oxford University Press, 1987).

Smith, Christopher, 'Plato as Impulse and Obstacle in Gadamer's Development of a Hermeneutical Theory', in *Gadamer and Hermeneutics*, ed. Hugh Silverman (London: Routledge, 1991), pp. 23–41.

Steiner, George, *Real Presences* (London: Faber and Faber, 1989).

Strawson, Galen, 'Against Narrativity', *Ratio*, Vol. 17, No. 4, Dec. 2004, pp. 428–52.

Tate, Dan, 'Art as Cognitio Imaginativa: Gadamer on Intuition and Imagination in Kant's Aesthetic Theory', *Journal of the British Society for Phenomenology*, Vol. 40, No. 3, Oct. 2009, pp. 279–99.

Tate, Dan, 'Transforming Mimesis: Gadamer's Retrieval of Aristotle's Poetics', *Epoché*, Vol. 13, No. 1, 2008, pp. 185–208.

Taylor, Charles, *Modern Social Imaginaries* (Durham, NC: Duke University Press, 2004).

Todes, Samuel, *Body and World* (London: MIT Press, 2002).

Vlacos, Sophie, *Paul Ricouer and the Theoretical Imagination*, PhD Thesis, Cardiff University, September 2011.

Warnock, Mary, *Imagination* (London: Faber and Faber, 1976).

Weil, Simone, *Gravity and Grace* (London: Routledge and Kegan Paul, 1972).

Weinsheimer, Joel, *Gadamer's Hermeneutics: A Reading of Truth and Method* (New Haven: Yale University Press, 1985).

Weinsheimer, Joel, *Philosophical Hermeneutics and Literary Theory* (New Haven: Yale University Press, 1991).

Williams, Rowan, *Grace and Necessity: Reflections on Art and Love* (London: Morehouse, 2006).

Williams, Rowan, *Lost Icons: Reflections on Cultural Bereavement* (Edinburgh: T. and T. Clark, 2000).

Wittgenstein, Ludwig, *Philosophical Investigations* (London: Blackwell, 1953).

Wolff, Janet, *Hermeneutic Philosophy and the Sociology of Art* (London: Routledge and Kegan Paul, 1975).

Wright, Dale S., *Philosophical Meditations on Zen Buddhism* (London: Cambridge University Press, 1998).

Index